C000243104

About the

Craig Stone was a bit homeless, then a bit more homeless, then a bit rich, then a bit poor again – but has always been a bit of a writer. He has 100k Twitter followers, a beard that ruins his face, and a wife who reminds him that his face is ruined by his beard. His second novel, *Life Knocks*, was shortlisted for The Dundee International Book Prize.

Other books by Craig Stone

Life Knocks
Deep in the Bin of Bob
How to Hide from Humans

The Squirrel that Dreamt of Madness

Craig Stone

Matador
9 Priory Business Park,
Wistow Road, Kibworth Beauchamp,
Leicestershire. LE8 0RX
Tel: 0116 279 2299
Email: books@troubador.co.uk
Web: www.troubador.co.uk/matador
Twitter: @matadorbooks

ISBN 978 1785890 666

British Library Cataloguing in Publication Data.
A catalogue record for this book is available from the British Library.

Printed and bound by CPI Group (UK) Ltd, Croydon, CR0 4YY
Typeset in 11pt Bembo by Troubador Publishing Ltd, Leicester, UK

Matador is an imprint of Troubador Publishing Ltd

Author Details

Twitter: @craigstone_
Website: thoughtscratchings.com
Facebook: Craig.Stone.1272

Illustration by

alexpatrickillustration.myportfolio.com
edseasyalex@gmail.com

"Poverty is the worst form of violence."

Mahatma Gandhi

Prologue

Better To Live Dreaming, Than Dream Of Living

We dream of the world we could have made, and wake up in the world that we did.

As children we're asked *what* we want to be when we grow up. The question should be *who* do we want to be. We are asked what do we *dream* for our lives. Our answers when young are full of achieving the impossible: spacemen, writers, actors, time travellers, superheroes, ninjas, artists, explorers, stuntmen. And then, eventually, someone older with no idea of the possible says, "impossible" and the children who wanted to become spacemen, writers, actors, time travellers, superheroes, ninjas, artists, explorers, and stuntmen all shuffle into an office and become members of *staff*: a name which turns employers into wizards and people into sticks.

People too weak to follow their own dreams will always disparage your own.

How can you follow a dream that you cannot see? You believe.

We are told to grow up and stop dreaming. Our twenties are spent putting our dreams so far to the back of our minds that the only way the human race can cope is by having them at night, when we aren't around to switch them off.

In the office I worked in until yesterday, the staff sit back rotting, chubby-fingered on creaking chairs, waiting for the chance to pinprick the thought bubbles of any person who might be caught dreaming. The pins used are sharp words, and the staff hunt in packs. When one speaks, the others sit nodding into screens like drinking-bird perpetual motion machines, biscuits in hand, crumbs falling into their coffee: slurping and silently farting themselves through the morning.

"I wanted to be a lot of things when I was your age too, Colossus. I dreamt of being an actor, but we have to live in the real world. Growing up is about accepting you can't become what you dreamt about when you were young."

The ginger crumbs fall from nodding heads.

The air smells of children being told by elders Father Christmas doesn't exist.

I listened to the dream poppers reaffirm life choices as their health deteriorated, their children drifted, and they grew to be never more at home than when they were at work, sitting in creaking chairs, eating ginger biscuits. Until, one day, a ginger biscuit snapped, along with my patience, and I walked into a park to pursue my dream of becoming a writer.

My name is Colossus Sosloss, and I didn't know it then, but quitting my job was the first step on my journey to awesome. *This* is the story of what happened when I left my home and office job, and lived in a park to write what became this very book. *These words*, every word you have already read, and are about to read, were all written while in real life I was homeless, and living under a tree.

Day One

free at last

I enter Gladstone Park as the sun is setting. I wander around looking for the safest place to settle down for the night. I'm not looking for armed guards and bulletproof limousines, but I am trying to avoid needles and people with dead teeth and ghosts for eyes. Tomorrow I'll find where I want to sleep permanently, but tonight I just want to get into my sleeping bag and be away from any people before it turns too cold. The main concern lurking persistently in my mind, a fat man wearing oven gloves trying to open a packet of Skittles, is I'm going to need somewhere to leave my bags, or I'll be forever chained to them, like an ageing rodeo star to horses.

No retired rodeo star leaves his house without apples in both his pockets in case he sees a horse.

I've been to this park before, and from previous visits I know there's an old abandoned house at the top of the park in the corner. Standing tall and proud, yet waiting to be pulled down, an old king watching time and power slip between his fingers, as those closest to him whisper about his Alzheimer's.

I slowly walk up to the house, as my mind runs away from me.

What have you done?

This is insane.

The old house is surrounded by a corrugated iron fence, and one of the iron shutters is bent back, allowing access to the inside grounds. I could place my bags inside the broken shutter, and I don't think they would be found by anyone wandering around the park. I avoid the abandoned house for now because it's late, and I'm not sure who else occupies this park at night.

I'm probably not the only homeless person here.

Beyond the abandoned house I find a small wood, which could provide protection for the night.

I walk inside, alone, following the path as the trail darkens. In the middle of this small wood, I find an ideal clearing to settle down for the night because it's spacious and hidden. The floor is littered in cans of beer and rubbish. This area, like the abandoned house, is too ideal. Any gangs or homeless people also living in the park would congregate here. I don't want to be the unwanted intruder. When people have nothing, they claim nothing is theirs. I don't want to be stabbed for sitting on the wrong tree stump. I'm not a tough tramp, so I continue looking for a safer bedroom. I walk out of the small wood and onto the path, and head back down toward the main park entrance.

A tramp is a person who moves from place to place with his life possessions on him, like a turtle. The definition of a bum is a person without a home or job, who stays in one place. I have no job, no home, and my life is in three bags, including my sleeping bag: I am a bum.

At the age of thirty I'm finally defined by indefinableness.

The setting sun disappears fast and sly, a ninja slipping into the shadows as he's caught short needing the toilet.

I have no experience with sleeping in parks. I'm convincing myself moving to a park is the right thing to do, and by the end of this experience I will prove there's nothing to fear, we don't need security keeping us safe at the price of our happiness, and if you're not happy, it's possible to wield the universe to your dreams if you only allow it to.

This is real and there's no turning back.

I am a complete idiot.

I've never seen such a devastating moon so close to earth. I feel like an ant in the shadow of an orange. I imagine what psychological damage an ant would sustain if it was staring up at what the ant thought was its moon, yet it was just an orange, and I picked the orange up and ate it. The ant would wake from nightmares, screaming about how the moon was eaten by giants, before eventually being committed to a mental home for insects whose minds cannot cope with their size, or the true scale of their existence. As I look up into tonight's giant moon, the moon reminds me I'm just an ant, yet the surreal nature of perspective, also makes me thankful I'm not just an ant.

I walk back down the hill, sit on a park bench, place my bags at my feet and take in my surroundings. Ahead of me green park stretches up and over a hill toward the abandoned house I've just returned from. The old house dominates the skyline, a pensioner refusing to get off the bouncy castle at a kid's birthday party.

To my left, and over a bridge, is the rest of the park, split in two by old railway tracks.

Now the sun has gone, and the moon is out, it's cold: a lot colder than I expected.

The universe stretches above me for ever. They say higher ground is an advantage in battle. If aliens ever attacked, we wouldn't stand a chance. The stars and the galaxy look beautiful, but then, everything looks beautiful from a distance.

I look at the ground around the bench I'm sitting on, and it's covered in dog shit.

I'm having doubts. I'm nervous about living in a park on my own.

I need to hear a friendly voice, so I call Grace before the battery dies on my phone, and I lose all contact with the outside world.

Grace is twenty-four: just old enough to know better, just young enough to do it anyway and get away with it. She's a long-distance runner, a heart of gold, patience so short she makes short fuses seem like marathons. She has a small head, nose and a tiny mouth. When she gets angry her small nose grows large, like a puffer fish, and her mouth disappears like an ostrich hiding in the sand. Her ears, regardless of the depth of anger being felt by her nose and head, remain steadfast, unmoving, and are always attached to the side of her small head regardless. Her chin gives nothing away, a marvellous poker player in its own right. On occasion I have found Grace's company as calming as the hum of fridges at night, and her hello as peaceful as the sound of newly formed ice dropping into place for use in the day. Her actual voice sounds clashing, irritable, and subtly pensive: two happily married French knights fighting in heavy armour for an ugly princess neither wants to win.

Hearing Grace's voice, even if she sounds like weary swords clashing into shields, is a good thing.

I dial her number, and listen as she answers her phone, in tears.

I see ping-pong balls float down waterfalls.

My thoughts switch to a lost washing machine playing jump rope with two girls on an empty cobbled street. The girls hang on to each end of the skipping rope. They move it up in the air and around toward the base of the washing machine. The rope hits the washing machine because white goods can't jump.

The girls don't want to play with the household appliance again.

I find this thought calming.

I wonder how long she can cry for. I shouldn't have told her I was going to live in a park.

I go to assure Grace I'll be okay, but she talks over me and explains she's sorry for being so upset, but she ran a marathon earlier and is in tears because she can't believe how happy she is. Grace warbles on about her race and I try to assure her

I'm fine, or let her know I have done what I said I would and moved into a park, but she talks over me again.

Anyway Colossus, I'm so fucking tired, and I need my beauty sleep, so goodbye.

And so I say okay, the first word I've spoken, but by the time the word has left my mouth, I'm talking to myself. Grace hung up, ungracefully.

I feel more alone than before I called her.

These days, instead of saying 'hang' up the phone, we should say 'push the button' because hanging up the phone is quite 1984.

The bench I'm sitting on has two missing slats and is mostly holes. Somehow, it's failed at being a plank of wood. The sun has now gone, and in the darkness the park feels larger, like space, and I'm losing my mind to it.

I sense some movement by my feet. My mind whispers to me that the holes in the bench have been caused by a caterpillar the size of a dog, which lazily crawls out from the bushes at night looking for its favourite meal of homeless peoples' feet. I look down at my feet, they're nothing special, but I'm not prepared to lose them to a dog-sized caterpillar.

Not on the first night.

I stand and walk up the hill, stopping halfway, by the biggest tree in the park.

Defeated by darkness, tonight, I have no choice but to sleep where I am, wherever that is.

I remove my Argos sleeping back from the packaging and lay it across the dark floor. One minute ago I was standing on grass. Now I'm floating in space, and the night feels lonely and alienating.

This is the side of the moon Pink Floyd sang about.

How can you be a lonely soul when shoes come in pairs?

The Argos in Cricklewood is not famed for its range of high-quality sleeping bags, or their diligent staff, and I'm pensive as I pull out my sleeping bag: will it be an iron, or a set of Reindeer colouring books they failed to shift at Christmas?

I pull exactly what I ordered from the packaging, and roll out a green, well-padded, sleeping bag. The Argos catalogue proudly states my sleeping back is 450GSM. Other bags have a GSM range of between 200 and 400. The cost of the bag directly relates to the quantity of GSMisminiminisms. I don't know what GSMS are, but as I have 450 of them. I hope they're helpful in some way. I don't want them to be Garbling Saxophone Microphones: tiny microphones built in to the lining of my sleeping bag, immediately converting every thought and word I have, and say, into a debate chaired by Gerry Rafferty about the science of saxophonic noise.

I stare at my puffy sleeping bag and accept I'm doing this. It has happened. I've left everything, and I'm now in a park on my own, embarking on my first night of homelessness. My family and friends all said this is a crazy idea and so I've had to learn how to ignore fear by putting it in a box and wrapping the box in duct tape, placing it in a bin liner, and burying it behind the Mona Lisa in the Louvre, Paris.

The cold wind slices my face and pushes invisible weight into my skin. The wind moves my cheeks and leaves damp traces on the surface of my face, a ghost's tears splashing in slow motion onto a bright green leaf.

My daily routine has completely changed, the focus now is not submissive servitude, but self-serving attitude. I no longer have to live in a small studio flat, and work all hours to only just about pay my rent. I no longer have to live with Mohammad, my former landlord, who was half friend, half bastard.

I've turned doom upside down into woop. I'm free at last.

I stand over my sleeping bag with the cold wind whipping invisible scars into my skin, and feel a single pound coin in my pocket. I take the coin out of my pocket, and throw it into the darkness.

This is freedom.

This is what Martin Luther King was banging on about, excluding the obvious racial tension in America during the 1960s.

Martin Luther King's speech would have been odd if he'd said, "I have a dream, there's this figure waiting at the end of my bed, and he doesn't say anything but I'm so scared, and all I want to do is wake up, but it's the last thing any of us have any control over."

I get into my sleeping bag fully clothed, still wearing my shoes. I search for the zip to fasten the side to become snug, but as I pull the zip toward my face from my feet, it gets caught immediately, and breaks. I stretch to reach down by my toes to the area where the zip is stuck to pull it toward my face. I could get out and do it, but I'm on my back now, and like a son who refuses to use the instruction manual, I persevere, fixing the zip my way. Moments before my back snaps in half, propelling my mouth over my shoes, the zip releases itself. I pull it up toward my freezing cold face. The zip gets caught again leaving a two-foot gap between my head and the rest of me. Icy air pours in, making me a man winding down the window in the front seat of a drowning car.

The sleeping bag has a hood attached, so I'm able to lift this over my head. Once in the hood, regardless of the two-foot gap, I'm really warm.

Four minutes later, and I'm sweating.

I lay back warm and comfortable. I think about not having to go to work in the morning, and the thought makes me smile. This morning, when I woke, I had keys for the office, keys to rooms in the office, keys for my studio flat and keys for a bike never used. I left my flat this morning the owner of eight keys, now I have none.

If I dream of a silent black screen, would I wake up tomorrow thinking I hadn't dreamt at all?

I hope in the night I don't get set on fire by prawn-skinned drunks. I also hope I'm awake before they mow the lawns on those industrial mowers, because they wouldn't be expecting me, and my sleeping bag is green. Being cut into small red squares of flesh and scattered across green grass would be a terrible alarm clock.

I close my eyes.

I wait for sleep to run me over, put me in the boot of its black car and drive me into tomorrow.

I see Martin Luther King punching the air on a podium as I fall asleep, his words ring through my subconscious:

Free at last, free at last, thank God Almighty I'm free at last.

Day Two

big bees sound like
small power lines

I didn't sleep because my ears tuned to the sounds of the night. My mind pictured the origin of those sounds. Sleep doesn't come easy when a broken twig conjures images of a hulking mental patient snapping the arms off children, over by the park bin.

The Sounds of Parks at Night, original or panpipe, is an album currently unavailable.

I poke my nose out of my sleeping bag. The world is freezing cold and smells of dog faeces.

If mankind ever sends a dossier to an alien race asking for investment into our planet, we might need to spin that last sentence a bit.

The theme music from *Space Odyssey* loops in my head as I lower the zip on my sleeping bag so I can see, in the light of day, my brave new world.

A gaggle of mute humans runs, chased by talking monkeys on horseback.

My eyes are surprised, two normal-looking runners, no signs of crazy monkeys from the future. A green truck is parked on the nearest path to me. Two park staff bounce from the truck and head energetically toward random points, dropped marbles spilling from a safer existence.

One walks up to the bins, the other heads in my direction.

I want to go back to sleep but feel ashamed. I don't want the park guy to stumble on a homeless guy, and have a moment where he feels awkward, and I don't want to feel awkward for putting him in an awkward position. I don't want him to think of me as homeless, or a lost cause. I want to avoid people, because there's only one thing worse than being homeless, and that's people who are not, knowing you are. I don't need to explain my life, or my actions, and I'm not asking for help. As the guy slowly ambles toward me, wearing bowling balls for shoes, I pack up my bags. All I need to do is get rid of my sleeping bag and put it back in its pack, because without the sleeping bag I'm just somebody up early in the morning, sitting under a tree. With the sleeping bag I'm nobody up early, sitting under a tree: a slight, but important difference in how I'll be perceived.

I get out of my sleeping bag and move to put it back in its original packaging. My sleeping bag doesn't fit back inside. I fold the sleeping bag, and then roll it up. It doesn't fit. I pull the zip up to flatten it slightly, it doesn't fit. I fold the sleeping bag in half, it doesn't fit.

Instead of folding the sleeping bag lengthways I fold it widthways, it doesn't fit.

I roll the sleeping bag tightly from the feet to the head in the smallest ball imaginable, it doesn't fit.

Not only does it not fit, it's not fitting by the entire width and length of the sleeping bag.

I'm getting practically *nothing* in.

How the fuck did my massive sleeping bag ever fit inside this stupid little green bag? The stupid little green bag has become the size of those clear plastic bags parents put sandwiches in before shipping their kids off to school!

If most of the sleeping bag was getting in except the hood I would have hope, if *any* of the sleeping bag was getting in I could blame myself, but all I'm getting in is the start of the hood.

I'm annoyed.

I roll my sleeping bag from the head to the feet, it doesn't fit.

I fold my sleeping bag by rolling the head to the middle, then the feet to the middle, then halving it and rolling that, it doesn't fit.

Getting my sleeping bag back into the original packaging is like trying to fit a claustrophobic elephant into a telephone box using the arcade-machine claw blindfolded, directed by a war criminal using a walkie-talkie, who's recently taken a vow of silence. Argos has deliberately sold a product designed to make every family camping holiday difficult, and the word Argos is Greek for easy.

My face is cold. I've only just woken up.

I look to the heavens in frustration and discover three pink circles surrounded by black feathers staring down at me. As I blink, one of the pink circles expands, then contracts. From its centre, a white splurge exits and drops, landing directly on my sleeping bag.

That would not have happened if my sleeping bag had gone back into the original packaging.

My hands are cold, my nose is running, and giant flies keep landing on me. These flies are fat, hairy, living the good life. I watch the flies dart onto my bag, then onto my legs, then back onto my bag, then onto my forehead. My coat is crawling with yellow bugs about one millimetre in length. Dark orange bodies and yellow heads. My sleeping bag is too big for its bag. I'm cold, tired, my bed has bird poo on it, my skin itches, fat flies sporadically land on my forehead, and a park keeper is walking in my direction.

A butterfly flutters by and lands on the corner of my notepad. I watch it, silence falls, and I forget for a second. The butterfly takes off and flutters by, the sound of the park comes back into focus, and I remember I'm fucked.

There is a small, green spider on my arm that, in turn, notices there's a colossus living thing underneath its eight legs. I blow it off gently, but my breath is so cold I freeze the spider, encompassing it in ice.

The spider falls to the floor and shatters into sixteen pieces.

There are an awful lot of bugs in nature.

I focus on my sleeping bag, ignore my crawling coat. The bugs don't have teeth, so for now at least, my life is not in immediate danger.

I grudgingly accept my flotsam pug-legged, lulling lummox of a sleeping bag isn't going to fit back into its original packaging, which is now an additional bag to carry.

So is the sleeping bag.

This leaves me with a problem. I have my two original bags, a bag too small for a sleeping bag and a sleeping bag.

My original problem of where to hide two bags has doubled.

I jump on the sleeping bag, grab its head and punch it. I punch it again. I grip it around the collar and pull it toward my face, talking to it, a mafia boss speaking the last words to a bloodied enemy.

I put on an Italian accent, because that's how much fun I am.

"You better let me know how to put you back in your bag. You hear me, Puffy? I want to know what Argos knows, I want to know what they don't want me to know, so you better start talking, pal, you better start unzipping, you better start spilling your Garbling Saxophone Microphones all over this park or..."

The crushing of aluminium can.

A plastic bag flexing in and with the morning wind.

I look up. The park keeper stands above me, his mouth open slightly. The litter picker in his left hand grips a can: in his right hand he holds a clear rubbish sack. This is embarrassing for me, but the poor bloke must be thinking he's stumbled upon a complete lunatic.

A look in his eye wants to ask what a Garbling Saxophone Microphone is.

The silence highlights the awkwardness.

I search to find the words explaining the problem with my sleeping bag, but feel weird. He's looking at a homeless person who threatens sleeping bags in Italian accents, and searching for his words too. All the words in the world have left both of our minds at the same time. He looks straight at me, too afraid to look anywhere else in case I attack. He brings the can from his left hand into the clear plastic bin bag in his right.

I've made better first impressions.

He is a man who works hard and takes pride in his job. A man who takes his can collecting seriously, refuses to let random events, or homeless people, come between him and his rubbish. The type of person who likes getting drunk so they can walk up to a stranger, get right in their face, and shout into one of their eyeballs, "I'VE SEEN THINGS!"

He's a short man, the size of an acorn. His head is large, heavy too. His head weighs him down, forces him to walk a little bit sideways every time he takes a step forward. He ends up further away from where he plans to walk by the time he arrives. He looks like two pillows tied together with old rope, then stuffed in a bag. His worried face has been drawn on by a rhino with arthritis. He has dark skin and dreadlocks which tie behind his large head.

His facial expression is full of bewilderment, surprise and anger: he's a spider with arachnophobia. His smooth forehead is his main feature, so large it makes the rest of his face crumpled. Too many features fit into too small a space. His skin is lumpish, a school child stuffing an apple into their face and refusing to swallow. His lips don't open to reveal his wonderful smile.

He's wearing a wedding ring. I suspect he's a dad.

His face is flabbergasted because his internal monologue is screaming, "What if my children saw this man?"

When we're young nothing offends us, except adults telling us what should. Then when we become adults, nothing offends us, except we are offended on behalf of our young. There's nothing to get offended by, yet we are always being offended, which I find offensive.

Without taking his eyes off me, he backs away one step at a time, turns and heads to the green truck, no longer wearing bowling balls for shoes. His small shoes are shiny, too shiny I think, for his type of work. I watch him shake his large head and waddle sideways and forwards as he walks. The other park keeper waits for him.

I pinch my beard and a squirrel darts nervously down the stump of a tree: a crow lands and patrols the foreground.

If I pinch my beard again, will one more squirrel climb down the tree and another crow land?

The crow walks with its head held high, chest out, looking for intruders. The squirrel moves fast, head and body low, intruding. Yet the park belongs to neither.

The sun warms up the park. My fingers return to the ends of my hands.

The only bag my sleeping bag is going to fit in is my main bag, my biggest bag holding numerous t-shirts and jumpers. My sleeping bag is going to be warmer than my jumpers and t-shirts, so I empty my main bag, and stuff my sleeping bag inside. My sleeping bag fits. My main bag now swells to capacity, a snake digesting a piano stool.

On the floor at my feet are my clothes, now homeless too. I have a lot in common with them. I have no choice but to throw the rest of my clothes into the homeless charity bin situated in the car park. I throw my clothes into the park's charity bin for homeless people who live in parks and need clothes, leaving me, too, short of clothes. My clothing options reduced to what I'm wearing, an extra pair of trousers and two pairs of fresh underwear.

The irony of not having enough space, while living outside of confinement, is not lost on me.

I'm happier as I stare at my bags. The large bag containing my sleeping bag I'll hide, along with my other bag containing my extra trousers, underwear and some washing essentials like soap, toothpaste and toothbrush. My third bag, my smallest, I'll have on me at all times, it's a smaller record bag, and contains books and food.

Now I have my bags sorted, I need to hide the two bags I don't need.

I climb a small tree and place them on the lowest branches. To me, they look well hidden. I move to the path nearest the tree and sit on a bench, so I can keep an eye on my bags to get an idea of how safe they would be if I left the park. If my bags can stay in the tree, strange fruit, I can head out in search of food and toilets without looking too homeless. I can fit in, while fitting out. I can go to a pub and order a coke, and use the toilets, without being asked to leave.

Perception is how we're treated and, at least for now, I would like the inevitable decline in the perception of me to be as graceful as possible, so the harsh treatment phases in, rather than it being an immediate and harsh transition.

Babies ease from no face to beautiful child with thoughtless ease.

I hope the transition is as smooth when an adult decides to descend into ugly.

Behind its owner a sagging dog lags along the path, tail wagging, nose smelling last night's kebab-filled bins, tongue dripping, brain wondering what its mouth and belly are missing. The dog reminds me this morning I could smell an undercurrent of dog faeces. Nothing overbearing, but somewhere there's a lot of it.

I sit with just my small record bag. With my larger bags hidden up the tree, I am removed from the shamed *homeless* demographic, and placed in the acceptable *friend of park* group.

A big bee lands on me and takes off again, there's no rest time when saving the planet.

Big bees sound like small power lines.

A lady walks by with her dog and says good morning to me. I smile and say good morning back.

I'm just a guy sitting on a park bench, with one eye on his bags up a tree.

I see another tramp wobbling along with his hands over his ears. He's been placed under a large bell and whacked with a massive spoon, leaving him to judder along the path toward me dazed and confused. He has a beard. His hair is long and messy. His eyes are glassy, two-way mirrors, but instead of him looking out and being protected from those looking in, he looks at them from the outside, leaving him no idea of what's going on inside his own head: a stranger to himself. He wears a black suit jacket too small, covered in stains. Straw sticks out of his sleeves. He carries a blue bag I'm certain contains strong alcohol. He was buried weeks ago, but has since eaten his way out of his coffin and taken a part-time job as a scarecrow who drinks on the job.

Worzel Bummidge.

Worzel walks toward me. I worry because I have no idea what the etiquette is between tramps. I look down and stare at the ground: the same course of action I would take on public transport.

The rule of public transport is to pretend you're travelling in private. When talking shatters the illusion, people wind up their invisible window in silence. Homeless people don't often get on public transport, but when they do, it's to break the silence.

Worzel ambles nearer and stops at the bin next to me. He stands, looks down at me like the god of the discarded. I don't move my eyes from the floor.

He smells like he never watched cartoons as a kid.

He mutters a conglomerate of inebriated obscenities at me,

but they're laden with so much alcohol the words are heavy and fall from his mouth to the floor, dying from liver failure before they have a chance of reaching my ears. The word 'fuckity' did not die, and lays isolated on the concrete path uncontrollably shaking: a violent jelly causing concern to wobbly old ladies enjoying cake at a church function. Worzel turns, falls against the bin and spits a bird-sized piece of phlegm to the ground, into his wobbling swear word. His phlegm is red, and lands like a blob of wax found on the back of a medieval letter, his swear word his only possession.

He walks away, juddering back up the path.

If he had bounced away instead of juddered, I could have called him trampoline.

A man throws his dog a stick. The stick lands directly beneath the tree hiding my bags. The dog may look like Lassie, but refuses to move toward the stick. Lassie has chosen this moment to be a selfish cunt, so the owner moves toward the stick to retrieve it himself.

The guy walks to the stick, picks it up, looks up and stares into the tree.

He squints, places his hands over his eyes, as if his hands help him see.

The man looks concerned. Lassie barks impatiently. He turns and runs back with the stick and a big smile on his face. His tongue lolls from side to side as he runs.

In Superman III, *Superman turned bad. In* Spiderman 3, *Spiderman turned bad. In* Lassie Three, *Lassie will grow a beard, smoke cigarettes, push kids down wells and lock them in abandoned mines.*

I hear the sound of a truck, and watch as the park vehicle drives in my general direction.

This is it, they're going to pull up beside me and tell me to leave or they'll call the police.

The park vehicle drives over the railway bridge at the bottom of the path, up the hill, over another path and up to where I'm sitting. I look down at my shoes.

The vehicle drives past me, to my relief, turns left, and stops directly under the tree my bags are in.

My relief turns to stress.

Two men get out, one of normal height, and both stare up at the tree.

I walk toward the men with my hands held high above my head, palms facing them, displaying the internationally recognised symbol for *please don't burn down my village, we'll get the gold, we just need a few more days.* The midget park keeper has an expression on his face like a frustrated professional jigsaw putter-togetherer who has spent two years on a 200,000-piece jigsaw puzzle from 1926, only to find out the last piece is missing. He shouts as I make the walk of shame and retrieve my bags. My head is down. He comes close to my face and shouts into my ear, *don't leave your bags up trees!* He tells me I've got to keep my bags with me or he'll enjoy throwing them away. He tells me he would smile as he watches them burn from the match that he lights. His forehead pushes up against the side of my face. I stare at my shoes. The other guy, a bald guy, places my bags at my feet. I pick them up and walk away.

I walk away with my eyes shut, half expecting a blow to land on the back of my head. The angry guy has long since buried his capacity for fun. His voice is hollow and a betrayal to who he could have been, an empty carousel still spinning in the wind on a derelict promenade. I was expecting his voice to sound smooth and chilled, West Indies, but he reminds me of an old headmaster at the end of a long day walking into the supply cupboard, to discover the school has completely run out of red pens. The old part of me wants to shake hands, get to know his name, but all he sees is a homeless guy making his park a mess, the usual *hellos* and *what's the weather likes* do not apply.

I'm Yogi Bear and he's the Park Ranger, only he thinks I'm

on heroin and used to beat my wife, and I think he's a violent wally suffering from severe short-man syndrome.

Why say burn all my belongings? That's so specific, so aggressive. I understand because I'm homeless I don't get the usual greetings, the foundation of civilisation, but no eye contact? Immediate threats of violence? His first words were about burning everything I own. That's just not how people meet.

That's how fear says hello.

I walk away with my bags and onto the path, by the bin and Worzel's phlegm. I follow the path up and over the hill, along a black fence and to the highest point of the park. This new area is away from the path and can't be accessed by large vehicles, so I hope the park keepers visit it less.

I'm up in the area near the old house, which is a short walk away, to the right, opposite me. This is also the area Worzel walked toward. He is mostly likely living in the old house. Three large trees and several bushes provide cover in this area. The largest tree has the black fence running behind it, and leaves which hang all the way to the floor.

I place all my bags under this tree and lean back against the black fence. Sitting behind the leaves I feel a sense of exclusion, sent upstairs to my room as a naughty child, but instead of going to my room, I sit on the stairs and listen to conversations I shouldn't.

From here, I can see the world, but the world cannot see me. Perhaps that's partly to do with the leaves, and partly to do with *the world does not see what the world does not want to.*

A black poodle with a wet nose, and a prizewinning smile that could sell pedigree chum and hold down your average greeting job in a shop, waggles up to me, but as the dog is about to lick my hand his owner bellows his name, like he's looked up to see his son in the middle of a motorway attempting to cross the lanes on a pogo stick. The dog turns and runs back, leaving me to ponder the phonetic similarities between poodle and Judas.

There's no *good morning* from the dog owner. No eye contact. I have my bags with me, so I'm now beneath basic pleasantries.

I'm deemed so unsafe not even Tim the poodle can lick my hand or smell the air around me. I consider closing my eyes and licking myself, but I doubt I can do it well enough to fool my memory into recalling the events differently.

The only true leap of faith is the leap of faith between people.

Looking around, I'm surprised how few places there are in a park to hide my bags. I can't leave them where I'm sitting, a good place to sit and not be disturbed, but the tree is still in the easily accessible part of the park. Through the gap in the leaves I study a bush opposite. I get up to take a closer look.

This bush is at the bottom of a small slope, and looks like a tree that had a breakdown sometime near puberty. At some time the bush stopped growing, fearing the sun. The branches and leaves point back to the earth, where they hit grass and crawl around in a large circle on the floor. Nobody can see into the centre. I can't imagine anybody would necessarily want to look closely into the bush.

The bush is not ideal, because the bush is in the middle of an open space. I leave my bag of clothes and sleeping bag inside the bush, keeping my third bag on me at all times.

I step back, it's not perfect. Should someone be looking for my bags in every bush, they would find them, but for anyone taking a stroll across the park, they're invisible.

This hiding place will have to do, until I find a better one.

An anagram of 'bush' and 'tree' is 'bees hurt', and they do.

I leave my bags under the bush and return to the tree the black fence runs behind, with only one bag over my shoulder, just like other people, just like everyone else.

I lean against the trunk and sit to watch the obvious world in secret.

A bald guy with a blonde comb-over, an indication to all sorts of mental deficiencies, wanders up to a nearby tree in the field of my vision. He wears a rainbow-coloured t-shirt and normal jeans, several sizes too big for his frame. His coat is white, unwashed. He looks like an American bad guy from an eighties film, rebelling against his hippie upbringing, while still living at home with his parents until his plans for world domination take hold. His mum walks downstairs to her basement, where he's lived since he was sixteen, asks for the hundredth time if he wants his coat washed, the guy shouts at his mum to get out, and throws his teddy bear at her. He screams about her not respecting his need for privacy, before whispering, *because I'm trying to take over the world.*

He's in his late thirties. I watch him walk to the tree opposite me. He lifts his hands above his head, moves his arms out to the side and waves them around like a child, in slow motion, attempting to fly an imaginary plane. He makes a noise, a humming, vibrating sound. He shifts his weight quickly from side to side.

He brings his arms above his head. He holds his hands together, like a human torpedo.

He hums louder. He moves from side to side faster. He stops. He shakes his head.

He puts his hands on his waist, and looks annoyed.

He slaps the tree.

"Don't you say *that* to me!"

The man sounds hurt, but if the tree spoke I didn't hear it.

I've never seen a person slap a tree before. I would have missed this if I was in still the office.

His voice is a fat rabbit with a pointy nose being eaten alive by a blind cannibal chicken, mistaking the rabbit for his usual meal. An expensive voice, a schooled voice, he may have been out of place during his schooling, leading to all manner of complications, like a close relationship with trees.

The man storms away from the tree.

I'm witnessing lovers having a regular tiff in public, only one is a tree. I'm a homeless guy they don't know, peering through the leaves of another tree, writing down what's happening in real time.

He walks by another tree, stops and smiles.

"You didn't have to say that."

His voice is sultry now. The tree has just told him what lovely thick hair he has. He raises his hands above his head and resumes the torpedo position. He hums again. He moves from side to side. This time he's distracted. As he builds up momentum he looks longingly back to the tree he slapped. He stops vibrating. He brings his hands down to his side. He tells the tree he's rubbing up against he's really sorry, but he's just realised he's making a mistake.

The man walks back to the tree he slapped. He laughs, as if he's been told he looks sexy when he's mad. I don't think he does, but I don't know him as well as the tree seems to.

"Do you mind if I cut in?"

The man refers to the invisible tree dancing with his tree girlfriend.

The crazy tree ball, happening in his mind.

He puts his hands above his head and resumes his torpedo stance.

He moves from side to side. He breathes deeply.

His breath quickens. He shudders. He falls against the tree. He gives the tree a long hug.

He thanks the tree. He calls the tree baby and breathes into the bark. The tree appears to be an old lover, or a new lover. He gently brushes the bark with the side of his face, rubs the bark up and down and groans deeply. He calls the tree baby one more time.

I don't wish to judge, but this is exactly what's happening.

I guess he has difficulty sustaining relationships with adults but then, for all I know, maybe he's happily married with children because of his relationship with trees. The man walks away whistling without a care in the world, but if I was him I'd have a lot on my mind all of the time. I consider walking out from beneath my tree, slapping the man and telling him that's the last time I trust him with my wife.

I turn to the tree I'm sitting under and think about making the vibrating noise, but without an indication my tree is fine with it, I would be violating the tree.

Madness, I realise, not beauty, is in the eye of the beholder.

I turn my phone on and my dad has left a worried answerphone message.

I don't like causing concern among friends and family, but it's a sad consequence beyond my control.

Life is a constant struggle between doing what you want, doing what others want you to do, and not wanting to do anything.

So, at some point, you have to stop playing to the crowd to get off the stage.

And people think *that's* crazy.

People think because I want to get off the stage, and search the bins behind the theatre something is wrong in my head.

Yet to not look for the strings, to cut them from your shoulders, to me, is madness.

To speak your mind, first silence your thoughts.

I'm living Martin Luther King's dream of freedom, but as a white guy in a park in a multiracial society.

I don't know what I'm doing.

Madness

It was 1998 and Oleg Stukonlove, or Stuck-on-love as his friends knew him, was twenty-one years old and canoeing a stretch of the river Nile for charity. He would eventually raise £14,016 and fifty-six pence for a children's orphanage, and they would use £43 of that money to buy a plaque to properly commemorate the group suicide of twenty-seven budgies, and the disappearance of a dog with no nose.

Oleg wasn't canoeing up the Nile just for charity. At the top of the river, where his journey ended, the reason his nickname was Stuck-on-love waited. There were many other things at the end of the Nile too: villages, crocodiles, forests, waterfalls, wildebeest and African grey parrots. But mainly, there was Bridgette. A twenty-one-year-old, hair dyed purple, child of the earth who had flown to a village in Africa to help with an unusual disease nobody could quite understand.

She was a nurse first, but a philosopher before.

The people from the tribe she was trying to help had a problem. Their ears kept falling off. When the reports first fell onto her desk back in England she had laughed. Then she looked at the photographs and felt bad. Oleg saw the photographs and felt bad at first, and then read the report and laughed. He didn't laugh at the reports because he found them funny, he laughed at the reports because he didn't know how else to react. And when

Oleg didn't know how to react, he laughed. Some people, when confused, or in strange waters, react with violence, or they run: Oleg laughs. That was one of the reasons Bridgette loved him, he was built on building blocks of colour.

Oleg was proud of his capacity to reduce the household budget, and he lived by purchasing food at reasonable rates, and he thought he would die by purchasing food at reasonable rates. He and Bridgette liked to joke he spent so much time looking for food bargains he was bound to die with a mouldy baguette in one hand, and a past-its-sell-by-date Eastern European sausage in the other.

Bridgette knew she was going and Oleg knew when Bridgette said she was going he had to let her go and meet up with her later.

She was on a plane the next day, while Oleg searched for cheaper travel arrangements.

"*It turns out,*" Bridgette said in her first letter to him, "*the people of the tribe are becoming infected by the tools they use to pierce their ears, causing an infection which, if untreated, eats away at the flesh causing ears to detach from heads within a two-week period.*"

"*But the real problem,*" Bridgette wrote, "*is not the ears falling off, but the hungry lions the dead ears attract.*

"*The ears, my darling, change colour and smell while still on the side of the face. By the time they drop, they have spent a good few days practically screaming at the animals of the jungle to come closer and see what has died. Some nights we hear screaming, and by the morning there are less people in the village. The poor tribespeople actually think this is a stage of the disease process. They think first the ear falls from the head and then the whole body explodes, leaving behind only an arm or a head. This surprises me because they live in a jungle, so I thought they would be perfectly aware they attract lions. They think it's down to magic and not praying and all sorts of curiously wonderful non-scientific reasons that you will no doubt first laugh at then apologise for. When they told me I was most stern faced, but as I write this I must confess to having a small private giggle of my own. Anyway, darling, if you want to see me alive again, and uneaten by a lion, please paddle fast. I should not need to remind you of your great love for me, so if a lion eats me before your arrival you will only have yourself to blame for an eternity. Is that cruel, my love?*

"P.S. Should I be eaten, a short grieving stage of one to three years will be sufficient. For this period I must insist you do not shave any of your body hair. This is not just to mock you publicly, though I cannot deny that is why I originally came up with this plan, it is also so I know that no other woman will be interested in you for a sufficient time so that you do not disgrace our memory.

"Promise you will do this for me? I would do the same for you. Oh, and bring shotguns!"

And so Oleg paddled up the Nile as fast as he could in his canoe with a map, a fishing rod, a compass, a big pack of water, a sleeping bag, a potato sack full of rolls and a plastic bag full of potatoes. He didn't think he would have much use for the potatoes, but when he left he was carrying them. He thought they might come in handy if he could trade them. Down by his feet sat the three shotguns he had managed to buy with his remaining money and bartering skills. Unfortunately he could only obtain three cartridges, and he had doubts whether the third cartridge was even a cartridge at all. It looked more like five coins glued together. He knew little about shotguns or their ammunition, and even less about bartering, so he thought there was little point in complaining. Oleg had bought the guns from a skinny man with more weight in his beard than in his whole body. The beard was so heavy the tradesman was hunched over and unable to make eye contact. The tradesman had a wizard-like quality. He wore a hood covering the top of his head, and somehow cooked bacon in a land without pigs.

Oleg didn't trust him, but still sat for a while to enjoy a sandwich.

As Oleg paddled down the river, staring at the shotguns, he felt like he had purchased all he could – it was not as if sitting behind the old wizard, on the edge of the Nile, had been an old Russian tank. He was paddling down the Nile, and felt quite fortunate to find any weapons at all.

Bridgette and Oleg met five years earlier on a windy night in a skate park.

Neither skated, in fact they both hated skaters and skateboards and all those activities associated with skating; the graffiti, the lack of safety equipment, the smoking youths, the long hair, the lack of interest in the greater world and that desire to be thought of as cool.

They thought the concept of keeping it real made everything fake.

Mutual hatred over skateboarding first brought them together, yet their love was born from a young boy's broken testicle.

Oleg and Bridgette stood at opposite sides of a skate park watching the skaters – both quietly judging the other for being the type of idiot who stood and watched teenagers act cool in skate parks. A young skater leapt from the top of a large column of steps. As he and the board landed, a snap and a twang echoed around the skate park matched only by the silence of the young boy.

Oleg and Bridgette were the only observers who laughed.

The young boy hopped, jumped, and after thirty seconds of hopping and jumping screamed out loud in pain, tears of panic flushing his face. Even the kids knew this was serious, that's why most of them had left, and the few who remained filmed the video on their phones to later post all over the Internet.

"Call my mum! Call my mum! I've broken my nuts!"

Oleg and Bridgette independently weighed up that a broken nut on a young boy was quite serious and both felt bad at the same time. They helped the young boy into an ambulance while his few remaining friends sang a song about how he only had one ball, because his other had been ripped out in a skateboard fall.

Oleg asked Bridgette out for a coffee so she didn't think he drank too much alcohol and Bridgette accepted, even though she would have preferred to get drunk. She didn't want to suggest a pub in case Oleg thought she might have a drink problem. So they found themselves staring at each other over a coffee, both pretending it was the best drink in the world, when all they wanted was red wine.

Outside the world whipped and howled as Oleg confessed he hated the wind. He said it made him nervous and if he focused on it, he only heard screaming. Bridgette laughed nervously at her brown sugar sachet, and Oleg cleared his throat and tried to change the conversation to anything that made him sound less like a serial killer.

"Okay, Bridgette – write on your napkin the worst place you could ever think of dying and I'll write mine, and then after three we show each other."

They both scribbled, hands guarding napkins, to prevent the other from looking.

"One…"

"Two… "

They turned over their napkins at the same time to read what the other had written.

Oleg read Bridgette's.

"Skate park!"

And Bridgette read Oleg's.

"Skate park!"

And they looked up and smiled at each other and Oleg lost himself in Bridgette's face, just for an eternity.

Bridgette had long blonde hair she didn't need to fix in the mirror because it looked perfect unfixed. Her face was completely symmetrical, no one feature stood out, leaving her whole face as the point of beautiful impact. Like a painting in an art gallery, to truly appreciate her beauty, she was best viewed from a few steps back. She was a well-spoken lady who had some voice training and had spent some of her youth in choirs, so there was a harmonious tone to her voice Oleg found relaxing. She would never spit out her words, never chew the ends off or munch up their beginning. Her words were spoken true from start to finish and sounded like laughter. She smelt faintly of new books and warm bread and would continuously mock her intelligence when she was the smartest person Oleg had met.

Bridgette's eyes, Oleg once thought, confused him because whenever he looked into her eyes he saw himself staring back and whenever he thought of himself staring back he always imagined two discarded traffic cones lying upside down in a shallow river. He said this made him feel uneasy.

Many years later, as he watched a film with his daughter, Oleg realised what he thought was the only feature he couldn't understand about Bridgette was actually the feature that made the most sense.

"True love is the recognition through the eyes of one soul's counterpoint to another."

His daughter had laughed. The film was a comedy. The line was cheesy but Oleg started to cry and couldn't stop. He cried so often he kept an onion in his pocket. When his daughter worried that he was crying, he would pull the onion out of his pocket and say he was having a reaction and leave to cook something in the kitchen.

In the kitchen Oleg stared at the onion with tears (both alive and dying) rolling down his face. He knew it wasn't him crying: his soul was cleaning his eyes to search for Bridgette. Oleg turned his attention from the onion to the window. Every window in his house had one or several wind chimes. He used to, long ago, fear the wind, but Bridgette's voice sounded like laughter, and when she laughed it sounded like wind chimes, and now he welcomed the wind as a courier service that delivered memories of an old friend.

Oleg reached the village of the people with no ears, at the end of the river Nile, and hugged Bridgette. They spoke of their undying love. Before Oleg could think about celebrating becoming the first man to canoe the Nile, someone in the village shouted a word that Bridgette understood but Oleg did not.

"Lion, Oleg, bloody lion!"

Bridgette grabbed Oleg's hand and they ran with the rest of the villagers, taking refuge behind a tree.

A tree the hungry lion strolled menacingly toward.

Oleg had never seen a lion before, but he immediately understood the panic domesticated humans feel when faced with a truly wild being.

For our entire lives we tame ourselves to promote human bonding, but life inevitably boils down to every man for himself.

The lion paced slowly back and forth ten feet from the tree, a hulking wild menace, honed to promote fear in the wild. Eyes that life died in.

"Oleg, the guns."

But Oleg, in all the panic, had completely forgotten the guns.

The lion nuzzled an ear on the floor, before eating it whole and licking its lips.

"Oleg, where are the guns?"

"They're in the canoe."

Bridgette didn't need to tell Oleg her view on that.

"The canoe?"

Oleg hadn't taken his canoe out of the water because he'd been distracted by his reunion with Bridgette and by the shouts of "Lion!"

"There it is!"

Oleg, Bridgette and the villagers watched Oleg's red canoe float away down the river, behind the lion, and out of view, taking the shotguns with it.

Bridgette didn't need to tell Oleg her views on that either.

"At least one of those cartridges was a stack of coins."

Bridgette's silence told Oleg to stop talking, and that's when an idea struck him.

In his left hand he gripped a small white plastic bag. Inside that plastic bag were two potatoes.

"Honey, do you think lions eat potatoes?"

"No. They eat meat. They eat people."

"You and the villagers run. I'll throw these."

"Oleg, a lion is not going to be scared of potatoes."

"But it might be distracted."

The villagers mumbled and muttered among themselves as the lion, having eaten the ear, walked with intent toward the tree.

Bridgette said something to the villagers that Oleg did not understand.

"What we need are more ears."

"Well, I only have two potatoes."

Bridgette sighed. The lion walked closer.

Thirty yards.

Twenty yards.

"Oleg, I love you deeply but you are a bloody fool for forgetting those guns."

"I love you too. I promise to get eaten first."

"As well you bloody should."

But Bridgette squeezed his hand and they both knew if they were going to die, they were going to die together. Though neither had the time to discuss the practicalities of how you get a wild lion to adhere to a promise of love by eating two people at the same time. Bridgette knew Oleg's terrible potato idea was all they had. So she took control of the operation, to optimise its potential.

"Oleg, when I say *throw the first potato at the lion*, you throw the first potato, *at the lion*."

Bridgette spoke to the villagers, then instructed Oleg to throw the first potato.

Oleg looked confused, which confused Bridgette. Bridgette raised her eyebrow, which Oleg knew meant he had permission to speak freely, even if his words were going to make him sound like an idiot.

"What potato is the first potato?"

Bridgette lowered her eyebrow, which gave Oleg his answer. Ten yards.

Oleg searched the bag and removed the big potato. Oleg thought it looked like a fat traffic warden picking flowers.

Bridgette squeezed Oleg's hand, and in that squeeze was all of their years.

"Throw the potato at the lion."

So he did. As the potato left his hand the villagers made a run for it. The lion hunched down looking ready to run and kill, but just before he moved, the potato struck the lion between the eyes.

The lion was unhurt, but confused. The lion looked down, and sniffed the potato.

"Throw the second potato."

"We don't want to piss it off, Bridgette."

"Throw it, *Oleg*."

Oleg reached into the bag and gripped the second potato. This potato was a lot smaller, thinner and oddly shaped at the end like it had been in an accident: it reminded Oleg of the skateboarder's broken nut from the night of their first date.

As the lion sniffed at the first potato, Oleg launched potato number two.

Potato number two failed to hit its target, landing harmlessly next to the other potato.

The lion looked toward the tree, straight at Oleg.

"You idiot, Oleg."

"Shall I throw a shoe?"

"We don't want to piss it off."

"We are one potato too late for that, my love."

The lion sprinted toward the tree, growling and snarling, claws extended, ferocious teeth showing. Wild eyes separated from rational thought: a strange way to describe a lion, because eating food to stay alive is entirely rational.

The lion reached pouncing distance, and crouched into the second before blood.

A moment any child who has lived with a family cat understands.

A bird squawked. A huge African grey parrot swooped down from the tree, then returned to the sky, taking with it one of the lion's eyes.

The parrot was back in the tree before the lion could blink.

The one-eyed lion took two steps backwards, and with his left side blinded the parrot swooped down again, from the lion's blind side, and took its other eye. The blind lion took several paces back and sneezed, then pawed at the holes where its eyes had once been. In the lion's blind fit of panic and rage it became disorientated, and charged headfirst into the river.

The blind lion swam across the river hoping to catch up with its vision, but it found only a crocodile. The crocodile bit the head off the lion first and drowned the rest. The river turned red and the villagers cheered.

"The poor thing."

Remarked Bridgette.

"At least he didn't see it coming."

Quipped Oleg. Bridgette gave her love a squeeze.

He couldn't throw a potato, but he could make up cracking jokes in times of tension.

The villagers cheered the river of blood and gathered around the two potatoes Oleg had thrown. They picked up the larger potato that looked like a traffic warden, and the smaller potato that looked like a young boy's broken testicle, then raised them above their heads in joyful worship.

"The madness of starvation."

Oleg was right.

The lion had moved into the village to hunt for people because it was starving, the parrot was protecting the people who fed the parrot and the crocodile would normally leave a lion, but not when under the possession of an empty stomach.

Bridgette and Oleg made a promise later, after they had bartered a new canoe in exchange for the two heroic potatoes, that when they got home they would buy an African grey parrot so he could always watch over their relationship.

Bridgette made Oleg promise two more promises that night – the first, should one of them ever become mortally wounded, the other would try and get the mortally wounded to the skate park so they could die in the worst place they could imagine. Oleg wasn't sure he got the joke, but it was an easy promise to make because he had no intention of keeping it. The second promise was, whoever died first had to have their ashes eaten by their future parrot. Oleg laughed because he didn't know how to react, and for half a second he thought she might be losing her mind. Bridgette's silence told him she wasn't joking.

She really was the master of silences.

"One or both of us could have died today if it wasn't for the parrot. Parrots live to be over a hundred years old. If I die, or you die, and we are fed to a parrot, then even if there are years between our deaths we will still be together."

"In the stomach of a parrot?"

"Why not?"

"There wouldn't be much room."

"Oleg, it's what I want."

Oleg sighed.

"Well, if I can agree to take my last breaths in a skate park I guess I can agree to being cremated and fed to a parrot."

"Good. And you are so my promise-bitch."

Bridgette teased him and playfully pinched his leg, but they both knew it was true: Oleg was her promise-bitch.

They returned to London from the river Nile and set up home in Willesden Green, and moved into a house just a mile or so from Gladstone Park. In the top room of their house, in a cage by the window, lived their African grey parrot called Madness. They chose the name Madness because it seemed the most apt. The lion, the villagers, the crocodile, the parrot and possibly even the two potatoes, had all been touched by madness.

When they married, Madness was maid of honour.

In the room next to Madness, slept their baby daughter Chloe.

Five years had passed since the lion had almost killed them and a further two would pass as a happy family under the protection of Madness. Then, before Chloe was old enough to remember how wonderful her mother really was, Bridgette was told she had cancer. Weeks turned to months, which turned to a year, and in that time hope in fate being kind was replaced with a realisation fate is no more than Death's hangman: in the end merciful to no one, indiscriminately dropping Death's axe at different times.

Bridgette was dying and Oleg, Chloe and Madness all knew it.

Oleg nursed her through the illness and Madness was

moved into their bedroom at her request. Bridgette called Oleg to her bedside early one evening, before the pain kicked out the painkillers. Oleg arrived from the kitchen in a hurry, too fast to drop the onion he'd been about to chop for dinner.

He knelt down by her bedside, placing his onion in his pocket, and placed his ear near her mouth.

He scooped her cold hands into his.

Bridgette's words sounded like laughter, now with wind chime intent, and she breathed them gently into his ears.

"My promises are going to bite me in my arse."

She smiled, but showed no teeth.

"Forget the promises, Bridge."

"Oleg, I want you to promise me one more thing."

"Anything."

"Keep them."

She wasn't joking.

Bridgette raised her eyebrow, which Oleg knew meant he had permission to speak freely, but this time even though his response was going to make him sound like an idiot, he had no doubt he was being intelligent.

"I promise."

Oleg held her hand, gave it a squeeze and moved his head toward her mouth as she indicated she had one more thing to whisper.

"You are still my promise-bitch."

"Always."

He felt her breath on his ear: weak, brittle and rattling along like a bag of spanners sitting on a New York subway train.

Her lungs worked twice as hard to breathe in half as much.

Oleg saw a vast lake only an inch deep and frozen. The lightest touch on its surface, a bird landing or a child throwing a stone, would send shattering cracks across her entirety, turning what was a lake into a puzzle of shattered memories.

For a second Oleg imagined his wife as an ice cube.

He knew the sun was coming, and it didn't matter where he moved her to, she was melting.

We only borrow the breaths we take in life. Every breath we borrow we give back, including our last. In the end, no matter how we lived, we all die feeling owed.

Bridgette asked Oleg to bring her Chloe.

Bridgette made Oleg promise to take extra special care of the parrot because she would be living inside Madness. She told Chloe to grow up kinder than her environment, and more thoughtful than she could think how to be.

Oleg crushed the onion in his pocket, intended for dinner, with his right hand. He squeezed his daughter's hand with his left.

For the rest of Chloe's life, any time someone squeezed her hand, she smelt onions.

Bridgette whispered four words. The four words Oleg knew to be her last. The four he'd always hated hearing her say. The four words he never wanted to hear from the moment they first laughed at a broken testicle and revealed matching napkins in a coffee shop, to avoid his confession he sometimes heard screaming in the wind.

"I have to go."

Bridgette knew she was going and Oleg knew that when Bridgette said she was going he had to let her go and meet up with her later. He drove his daughter and dying wife to the skate park and placed her body on the most interesting, and therefore, ridiculous ramp.

Bridgette died on the largest stunt ramp in the skate park at 9.06pm on the 6th August 2005. The worst place either of them could imagine dying.

Oleg would later spend a lot of time watching what he hated. And he eventually started to think maybe Bridgette's promise wasn't so crazy. He learnt to love the skate park and it became one of Chloe's favourite places.

He slowly realised nothing is here to be disliked. Everything is for the joy of someone.

Bridgette was cremated and Oleg stuck to his promise.

He fed Bridgette's ashes to Madness.

There was a funeral service and a memorial for people to pay their respects to Bridgette. And, it being Bridgette's funeral, people came from all over the world. Members of the African tribe from the end of the Nile arrived. They wanted to give Bridgette some of the ears they had kept that had fallen from their heads. Due to UK customs laws no separated body limbs are allowed into the UK without prior authorisation. Luckily one of the village elders, a tough woman and a stickler for details, had pre-empted the problem of bringing in human body parts and she ordered three tribesmen to use tape to stick the loose ears onto the sides of their heads. They looked extremely odd coming through customs with the ears of different people taped to the sides of their heads. The customs officer knew something wasn't right about the people, their faces seemed out of balance and disproportionate, but she couldn't place why, so the tribe were allowed into the UK.

To this day Oleg still has sixteen ears in his freezer and no idea what to do with them.

Oleg was certain Madness would outlive him.

When Chloe was old enough he sat her down and told her all about her wonderful mum, making her promise him one promise: when he died, she would feed his ashes to Madness.

Perhaps if they were both dead, but in something living, they would find each other, and Oleg could finally stop his soul from crying through his eyes.

Three days ago, the cage of Madness was being cleaned. Madness hopped out, looked left then right, bobbed her head up and down three times, looked back once, and then jumped out of the window.

Madness thought she was flying. Falling feels like flying, for a moment.

Madness flapped, but her body had grown used to living in a cage and being fed peanuts and bananas. She was overweight. More experienced at acting like a monkey than a parrot. She plummeted toward the ground, wings flapping, eyes wide, chubby belly flopping. She swallowed a fly. Her eyes bulged. She stretched her wings out as far as she could. She managed to control her fall with more style than she deserved to be able to. She stuttered down through the air like a disproportionately folded paper aeroplane in a storm, landing not on concrete, but on a branch of a tree on the other side of the road. Madness wanted to go back to her cage, her favourite mirror, her fiancée with the round golden face and ding dong voice, her nuts and lumps of banana, but the mind of Madness is only small, and comes with a short memory. She knew she had to concentrate but had forgotten what on. She stopped looking for home and wondered why she was staring at houses. She placed her head under her wing, afraid for a moment of everything in the world that wasn't under her armpit.

A tall, dark figure stared up at the parrot in the tree. The figure wore dark trousers, and a dark hood covered his head and face.

Madness concluded she *must* be heading to the park, and in a birdbrain moment, spread her wings and hopped off the branch. She fell, hit a branch, and flapped like a Tennessee bride holding a fan in the summer. She wobbled. She managed to gain a little momentum. The concrete floor and watching dark figure turned to blue sky, and Madness flew like a fridge with a broken door in the direction of Gladstone Park.

The dark figure licked his lips, noted the direction of the parrot, and followed.

Madness flew into the park three days ago.

The dark figure entered the park three days ago.

Tomorrow morning will be my third day in the park.

I never knew any of this at the time, but my decision to leave my job and move into Gladstone Park was about to become part of a greater story, which I would later be forced to write to earn money instead of sucking man tackle. A story I have called The Squirrel that Dreamt of Madness.

Day Three

everyone comes from their own way

I wake up, it's so cold I can't feel my feet and my face is numb. At least if a flesh-eating caterpillar eats me from the ground up I won't feel anything. I feel dirty and need a wash but the sun is already in the sky, so rather than have a tramp shower I opt for the hobo hot tub. I change my socks so I feel a bit fresher. My trousers and boxer shorts have not been changed for three days. On the upside I have toothpaste and mouthwash, so while my body is slowly turning black and attracting obese flies, my teeth are beginning to look American, and when I smile at night ships sailing toward land are safer.

The word begone is a Russian doll. A small, single word, which contains so many others, and when all the smaller words inside line up, they look like a bridge: Be Beg Ego Go On One.

I haven't been eating much.

A sandwich yesterday, an idea the day before, a spider this morning as I slept.

There's a café next to Willesden Green tube station and in the café I can drink a tea, feel less like a tramp, more like a person and get some warmth.

Every man, housed or not, needs a mission.

When I walk into the café the customers will whisper about the bearded man who must have dead sardines in each of his pockets. People will ask me how my sardines came to stop living, and I'll tell them the sardine in my left pocket died of a long-term illness and when people ask about the sardine in my right pocket, my right pocket will move, indicating the fish is still alive.

I'll grab the pocket and scream *he drowned in a boating accident* while running out of the shop.

The café is for later, for now I take all of my bags and sit down on one of the park benches near the main path. It's eight in the morning. The rising sun vaporises the cold air. A creepy mist spreads out before me suffocating the park silently. Jack Frost sits in the shadow of a parked car, waiting for a victim, smiling. The odd runner runs, the odd walker walks, the old couple fulfil their stereotype and shuffle and huddle along in silence. The old man looks angry for no reason, impatient with death: the woman clings on to her compassionate face, explaining he wasn't always like this. I hear the rumbling of a truck and look left. The midget park keeper rides a vehicle, but I'm not sure what kind of vehicle it is. It looks like the type of lawnmower you have to sit in, only lacking any of the equipment to make it a lawnmower.

I make a mental note the park keeper starts his job early. In future, to hide my bags safely, I'll need to be up, and my bags will need to be hidden before he starts his shift.

He drives his odd vehicle that isn't a lawnmower along the same path my toes are touching, and heads toward me. I tuck my feet in, should he want to run them over. The vehicle passes me; I look up from my bench as he looks down from his lawnmower that isn't a lawnmower.

We hold eye contact. I stare at his giant head, to check he's still angry.

He is.

His eyes are on me, checking to see if I still look homeless.

I do.

I nod.

He returns the nod, but his head is so big by the time he's completed his nod, he's gone. It will be good for him to have me around. He's a really angry little man, the kind who when writing with pencils snaps the nibs because he can't grasp weight and pressure control. If you can't control the pressure you put on a pencil, you can't expect to control the pressure you put on yourself.

Now he has a focus, someone to hate.

I'll rationalise and direct his turmoil away from himself.

It won't make my life much fun, but he'll live longer because of it.

He isn't the type of person who should be running a family park. I'd prefer my local park keeper to be chubby, with a soft face and warm broad smile. Someone who looks warmed in an oven by a gran with a large family, who loves nature.

That's the mixed up world we live in, the system created: the biggest criminals wear suits and steal metaphorical watches while shaking hands and smiling to faces.

Those in charge should be charged by those not in charge, and those charged by those in charge should be in charge.

I'm probably not the type of person who should be in a family park either. As far as tramps go he could do worse. I don't drink or take drugs. I'm not sitting on the park bench barking at bins and telling every woman who walks by she's out of this world in the voice of a drunk alien eating a newspaper.

The sun, high in the sky, is both suffocating and sight restricting, like sitting between two fat people and behind one tall person at the cinema.

I'm worrying *again* about my bags. I don't want them taken because I would die from cold in the night without my sleeping bag, but nor do I want to be a slave to my possessions, either physically or mentally. If I'm worried and thinking about my bags all day then no matter where I am, I've not put them down: a CEO going on holiday with his work Blackberry might physically be on a beach, but his brain is still wearing a suit and sitting at a desk consuming too much caffeine.

I need to find the best place possible to hide my bags and forget them.

I leave my bags under the same broken bush I put them under yesterday, the park keeper didn't find them, nor did anyone else: I believe they're safe. I push them in as far as they go, then cover them with branches and leaves. My notorious sleeping bag's bag, not content with being too small for its purpose, acts like a beacon from inside the bush because it has a luminous orange strip around it, so it can't be lost in bushes. I hate this bag more than the moment you think you're being waved at, so you wave back, but there's someone behind you; better looking, more charismatic and *actually* being waved at.

I walk back to the bush and throw my grey coat over both bags, walk back to the fence and turn. I pretend I'm not me, to see if who I'm pretending to be notices the bags.

The best way to get an impartial opinion.

I am legendary bush observer Peter D. Out, whose once-successful career had famously tired and faded to nothing. Peter D. Out was the most eminent bush observer in his field and he travelled from park to park in London inspecting the measurements of London's bushes, specifically their leaves. Anything unusual or out of place inside a London bush, he would spot it immediately.

His bush-observing career was cut short by injury when Peter found a leaf from one bush growing inside another. The bush community's NASA equivalent of discovering life on Mars.

Peter took a step back from the leaf to marvel his discovery, but took one step back too many, and fell down a rocky bank. A day before children played at the bottom of the quarry. Six-year-old Thomas had left his action man behind. Peter landed on Princess Cinderella Mountain, snapping his back in half as he did. He bounced off the mountain, crumpled to the ground, where his left eye fell into action man's gun, blinding him there and then.

Before his accident, nobody in his field could touch him.

After his accident, anyone who wanted to touch him could, because he was in a wheelchair and unable to move. And a lot of people did, because in his able-bodied life he made a lot of enemies by being a bit of a bastard. Peter has large lips, which he needs because his mouth is his striking facial feature. Two rows of narrow, pointy teeth snap under his blotchy dry face. His eyes constantly water, like he's forever treading on a plug while running to the toilet.

A Venus flytrap suffering an allergic reaction after accidentally eating a wasp.

Peter's career, like his sight and ability to stop people touching him, never recovered.

As Peter, I look at the bush. Peter can't see my bags, so he wheels himself out of my mind.

I walk down to the fence. I follow it along to the path, and follow the path toward the park exit. I see another tramp further along the path, so I sit on the nearest bench and bring my notebook to my face. This guy is bald, scruffy, and his bloodshot eyes search, in panic, to find and consume anything that might knock years from his life.

His cheeks are puffy and red, a consequence of his body deciding to push more blood to his brain, in the hope he might wake up and think to participate in anything other than slow suicide. He gets on his hands and knees and crawls around the base of a bin. He picks up something so small I can't see what it is. He smells it with his ears, and tastes it with his eyes. He decides the object isn't what he's expecting, and puts it back on the ground. He circles the bin again, and this time brings something up to his face, something large enough for me to see: half an inch of a cigarette.

The man puts the fag end in his pocket.

Inbin & Hedges.

I feel sorry for Inbin. His days are spent feverishly and desperately searching for consumables designed for two things, addiction and death. Inbin smiles a black smile at finding another cigarette end. A smile reserved for a girlfriend twenty years ago, and ten years before, his mother.

Now his smile is a stranger resting on a haunted face, only coming out for poisons turning him into a ghost.

I'm yet to see a homeless guy without alcohol or looking for alcohol. Inbin and Worzel's lives are not about finding a home. They're not on their hands and knees on the ground outside estate agents trying to find keys: they're on their hands and knees around bins trying to find stale alcohol or nicotine. Homelessness is not their main concern, getting to a place that absolves them of all responsibility as soon as possible is. Worzel and Inbin are not addicts because they're homeless; they're homeless because they're addicts.

That said: to judge is to have the arrogance of thinking you know where someone else is coming from. You can't, everyone comes from their own way. In thirty days it might be me crawling around a bin trying to find a needle or can. Perhaps we're all machines, and if I'm subjected to the same conditions, for long enough, I'll behave in a manner befitting to those conditions, and who I was before will become a shameful memory to block out and never look back at: an honest farmer returning from war forever avoiding his reflection.

Inbin & Hedges finishes searching the bin he's circled twice and gets gingerly to his feet. He looks around self-consciously, hoping nobody has seen him: his former self, surfacing for a moment. He brings the cigarette butt to his mouth and lights up. He breathes in, and coughs: a rattling helicopter with a broken blade crashing into a herd of trombone playing sheep falling off a cliff into a DIY shop with a discount on spanners.

The cough, like Worzel's before, ends up on the ground in the form of spit the size of a baby bird.

Inbin struggles away, up the path, wheezing for air he now wants.

It's impossible not to worry about my bags.

On my way to the café my mind turns to another homeless guy who hangs around near where I'm heading. This 'homeless' guy annoys me because whenever I see him, he shuffles rigidly along and hodgepodges crookedly up to people asking them for a single pound coin.

He's around my age, which I think may be one of the reasons I hate him so much.

He sits under the cashpoint and asks people for coins, unable to ascertain cashpoints give notes.

Once he's received a single pound he shuffles, an old pirate with two wooden legs, into the shop next door and buys a can of Stella, which he drinks while asking for another pound in a voice that sounds like someone punching an old lady in the throat. This is how he spends his day, getting drunk on peoples' goodwill: drinking it down, an out of place, fangless vampire who, despite having no teeth, has somehow managed to sustain his weight problem.

He has no bags, and is always in different clothes.

Four days ago I left Sainsbury's with a steak pie. It was 6.30pm and the steak pie was going to be the first thing I'd eaten that day. I was looking forward to the pie. As I took the pie from its packaging I entered human shark pie frenzy.

A mode full of gnashing teeth, saliva, red mist, pie and memory loss.

The last time I entered human shark pie frenzy mode I was in a darkly lit, damp stairwell with mesh windows and a puddle of urine in the corner. I woke up in the Pacific Ocean with a fridge in my jaws and a car parking ticket stuck through my right eyeball.

The sound of a homeless guy standing by a bin, as they often seem to be, threw me out of my frenzy. He was a black man with a grey beard and dreadlocks so old they could be snapped off and used as sticks to attach birdseed to. He wore shorts ripped at the edges. A buttonless black shirt revealed his bony, grey-haired chest.

Robinsbum Crusoe.

When Robinsbum spoke his voice was creaky and cold, a slow-paced slur made his letters an old lady in a nightdress walking up a broken staircase with a glass of milk in her hand, and a book she'll never read in the other. His words sounded good in the moment, but would go off if ignored for too long.

He called me brother, and asked me if I had any food.

My pie was out of the wrapping and so close to my mouth small bits of pastry sat on my teeth.

The wide-eyed look of Robinsbum seemed full of dreams, and his bony frame and spindly fingers clasped around my consciousness. I gave Robinsbum my steak pie, but rather than thank me, he smelt the stench of opportunity, and without bringing the pie to his mouth, asked me for money.

I told Robinsbum Crusoe I had none, he was so annoyed he threw my pie in the bin without eating it. His actions dropped the glass of milk onto the broken staircase, shattering my opinion of the hungry man with big dreams.

In that moment, to me, he was just another selfish bastard.

People, by the definition of free will, transcend their environment a million times in their life, but they do so in a million selfish ways never recorded.

In this moment, homeless Robinsbum Crusoe had transcended himself to become my Pol Pot.

He never wanted food. I don't think he wanted money either.

What he wanted was something he couldn't ask for publicly without looking morally questionable, and in his eyes, that was my fault.

I walk into the café and don't speak because the girls working know who I am, because I used to be a regular customer. They tell me *green tea* and I nod. They say they'll bring it over.

The two girls give me a double take. They only half believe it's me.

Usually, when I visit this café, I have a suit on and I'm clean shaven. I would visit on my way to work, or on my way home from work. They see me now with a beard and clothes I've been in for three days and a look they can't place: the look of having slept the last two nights in a park.

I sit down and smile as I'm served green tea. Usually they ask how I am, but today they do not.

The girl serving me nods and smiles. I return her gesture in kind. She's attractive with short blonde hair in a side parting. I was going to ask her out once, but instead I surprised both of us by ordering a strawberry tart. It was the first time I had ever ordered one.

I have the same two problems I had on day one, only the second one is becoming more pressing: where to hide my bags and where to take a shower. A leap of faith into people's inherent kindness resolves the first problem. I believe people won't take what isn't theirs if they can see it's a homeless guy's stuff.

I have not yet resolved the issue of where or how to wash.

I take a sip of green tea and stare out at the sunny London day. Perhaps it's because I'm in a café, I'm not sure, but I look out of the window and recall the time I was beaten up for being dressed as a fish-finger sandwich. I take another sip from my tea and consider how time changes the moment.

It wasn't funny then, but it makes me smile now.

I need to seek some kind of routine, even in the park. We're all creatures of routine. Routine gives us the illusion of safety, makes us forget our hearts could explode at any beat or that cancer cells have probably started to form inside our doomed bodies, and I'm no different.

As I leave the café the day is so hot, if heaven is above us then angels had better be fireproof. I panic my bags are gone, a parent suddenly remembering they left the oven on, with their baby inside the house. I hurry back, walking faster the nearer I get to the park.

The first person I see inside the park is the park keeper, sitting on top of his vehicle that isn't a lawnmower. He's driving toward me. This time I don't look up to make eye contact, I keep my head staring at my shoes, as if the only way I can power my feet is if I stare at them. He says nothing as he passes me. I see his shoes from my peripheral vision; they are still ridiculously shiny for someone who works in a park. I walk up the path, over the bridge, and to the clearing not far from the abandoned house. I need to check on my bags, I need to know they're safe.

My bags are still in the middle of the ugly bush.

Seeing my bags untouched makes me feel relief.

I relax.

My bags are within sight, so I take off my shirt and lay in the sun.

From this hill I can see miles of green grass. Trees sway in the distance, people dancing to music I can't hear, houses beyond the trees don't sway at all, they've not been invited to the party. Beyond the houses is the city of London, heavily smoking: if you can make it there, you can make it anywhere.

But you won't.

Sounds wake under heat. Birds refuse to fly in dangerous conditions. Children laugh as they run after ice cream vans, their voices melting together. Pneumatic drills bore into the ground, tearing up peace. Usually on days like this I would be stuck in an office asking colleagues where we all went wrong, and they would all answer they didn't know. That's the sad part, nobody has to do anything wrong to end up living a life that feels like it's not their own, all they have to do is take a step back, and hope for the best.

A crow carrying a piece of bread lands by my side.

These are not big events, but the smallness of them is their point. The crow, the bread, the sky, the trees, the grass, and the breeze: they should be everyday events for everyone, but the city takes them from us, replacing them with plastic plants that can live without sun. Everything around you right now, that's not yours to control or own, is symbolic of who you have become.

Some days I am the flower beneath the machine. And the machine rolls slowly on, blocking the sun, without a care for what it tramples beneath.

I sit in the sun until it fades. The temperature drops, dark rises. The cold begins.

In the dark I stand and follow the path, to see if the park has a public toilet. I walk up by the pond, over to the abandoned house, off the path, through a gated door, and to my literal relief I find one.

The kind of toilet only seen in horror films: an eerie feel, as if the toilet is a secondary function and its main function is to eat children alive, as they use the facilities. The room is small. To close the door I have to squeeze between the sink and the toilet.

There's a light switch.

I flick it. Nothing turns on: a fumbling, scary moment with a faceless girl.

There's no mirror.

A tree breaks through the ceiling and peels away the roof. Five thin branches sprawl from the tree, fall down the back wall and onto the floor. They claw toward the door, the long bony fingers of a witch trying to reach the back of her large oven for the body of the last child she cooked for dinner. The clawing branches wait for someone to walk through the door so they can be grabbed and hurled up high, where the tree above sucks their brains out, drains their bodies, and then spits their heads and skin back into the toilet so the evidence can be flushed away.

I blink, wishing my imagination was weaker than my need to stay in reality.

The new toilet seat is out of place and shimmers against the dark backdrop, which invites people to sit down and drop more than their guard.

I leave the toilet, happy that finding one has resolved one issue. The toilet closes at 8pm, but that's fine with me. The toilet is too small to shower in, and because the toilet is the only one in the park, attempting to shower before 8pm is too risky, with the likely result being police action.

I take my bags from underneath the broken bush, and walk in darkness back to my sleeping place under the large tree, with the black fence running behind me.

I settle down in my sleeping bag for the night. My mind wanders to how I'm going to wash.

The thoughts before sleep, the problems we don't want to face when fully awake.

Some people never sleep, but their problem is really the day.

I'll need a shower tomorrow. The only way I can see it happening is standing naked in the park with a bottle of water over my head.

I fall asleep hoping to get a brainwave that resolves this issue.

I get nothing.

Day Four

find the light

Hide your bags somewhere else, you're an idiot for leaving your bags under a bush so out in the open, the park keeper hates you, you're an idiot. What are you doing? You aren't changing the world, you are running away from it. Get up, get up and hide your bags before the park keeper comes, you can't get out of this, you need to hide your bags, take them to the wood, dog shit, dog shit, you're going to die. You are depressed. This is a breakdown. You need psychological help.

My eyes open after my mind. All eyes always do.

I'm clutching my sleeping bag close to my cold face. I tried to sleep using my small bag as a pillow, but the edges are hard and plastic, so eventually I gave up and tried to rest on my arms.

The cold morning mist rests on my skin, an invisible lady with icy hands stroking me awake.

I slept with my two bags behind me, with my back to them, so I feel less alone, and to reduce the chances of them being stolen.

As my eyes open I'm flooded with alertness. I need to get up and hide my bags in the wood. I need to do it before the park keeper, or anyone else, sees what I'm doing.

So I do.

I get up and out of my sleeping bag. The cold bites my skin

through my jumper, but I try to ignore it. The sun is a white snowball in the sky. I stuff my sleeping bag into the large bag it fits into, pick up my other bag with my remaining clothes in, and walk to the wood. I leave my little bag (the one I carry around with me) where it is, propped up against the black fence under my tree. It's 5am, so nobody else is around, just me: alone in the park. I follow the path to the small wood in the right-hand corner of the park. I leave my two bags under bending sticks, in between long grass, and a few yards away from the twisting path.

The wood is deserted during the day.

This is the part of the day I hate, the most painful. Despite the freezing temperature, I need to take my coat off and cover my bags with it. My coat is grey, so by placing my coat over my bags I hide the bright orange strip, turning them into large rocks. I take my coat off and rest it over my bags. I take a step back to admire my work: nobody will find them in the day.

Other homeless people inhabit the wood at night, so I'll collect my bags before dark.

For now, my bags are in the safest, most discreet place I've found. Content, I follow the path out of the wood. I walk across the wet grass and sit back under my tree. I lean against the cold black fence and hug my small bag close to my chest, my only friend in the world. I sense my bag is male, but I don't know why. He's grey, with a square face and looks like he's spent too many years being serious about everything.

Perhaps we both need this break, my bag and I. Much like Tom Hanks in *Castaway* had Wilson his American football, I decide to name my bag and keep him as my only friend. I prop him up on my shaking knees and stare at the grey leather square. Unlike Wilson, he has no name or label across his face, so naming him is going to be difficult.

I want his name to be true to who he is: he's a record bag, so I know he likes music.

Bongo.

I only have to shake in the cold for two hours, maybe three, then the sun will stop being a snowball and start heating up the planet.

I open my small bag, Bongo, and pull out my toothbrush and toothpaste. I brush my teeth. Once I've brushed, I take a swig of water from the bottle in my bag, swish the water around, and spit the water into the ground next to me.

A homeless guy spitting into the ground.

Bird-sized phlegm.

Time passes, the sun slowly rises.

I sit homeless, ostracised from society, and remember my old work shoes and how they used to cause me a great, yet subtle, indignity. I hated those shoes because with each step I took they squeaked. A squeak nobody else could hear but me, but I was sure everybody could hear it, so I walked either at the back of groups or as far away from people as possible. People thought I was trying to avoid, or didn't like them. My parting from others was compounded when a member of the group tried to consolidate it. With a friendly arm around my shoulder and a warm smile, my colleague asked why I kept my distance. I told him my shoes squeak to me, and I didn't want them squeaking to anyone else. The hand on my shoulder became the cold prodding action of a child pushing around a Brussels sprout. He thought I told him my shoes *speak* to me, and I didn't want them to speak to anyone else.

Once they thought I thought my shoes spoke to me, they left me alone.

The shoes embarrassed me. They were a constant reminder that with every step I took I was so poor I had to put up with shoes slowly driving me mad. Eventually all I could hear was the squeak *squeak* of my shoes, even when I wasn't walking or wearing shoes. Even when my shoes were locked in a cupboard, out of sight, I could hear them: squeak, *squeak*.

I was hypnotised to convince my brain that a squeak was a dolphin talking: one of my favourite noises, but something went wrong, and the hypnotist turned dolphin noises into the sound of shoes squeaking.

I've hated dolphins ever since. At the height of my anger toward dolphins I purchased a tin of tuna that didn't have *dolphin friendly* on the side.

It was a relief to listen to the park, and not squeaking shoes.

I try to picture a dolphin in my mind and see a black leather shoe. My brain has not fully recovered.

The sun wars over my skin, fighting a thousand battles against the retreating army of cold. The sun wins eventually, but any victory is short lived, because it's a battle designed for both sides.

I stand, and walk to the other side of the park. I've not been to the other side yet, and I'm curious to see what's over there. I put Bongo over my shoulder, my only friend and walk down the hill. As I reach the path, his strap snaps and he falls to the ground, broken. I look at Bongo on the ground. His zip is open, both his sides have parted. He screams in pain. I bend down by his side, and place a hand on his leathery face. He's cold. I move to zip him up, the bag equivalent of closing human eyes on death. His zip is stuck, perhaps the cold has halted his mechanism, I don't know, but I can't close him.

I hold his strap in my hands, broken in half, Bongo beyond recovery.

Bongo is dead. He died before he spoke his first word to me, and I, to he. I place my head in my hands. A voice tells me *this is my fault*, and I must confess, Bongo's death isn't entirely an accident. Before I left for the park I poured the coins I had in my flat into Bongo. Ten pounds of small change is a fair weight, Bongo carried that entire weight, until just now, when the weight snapped his neck in half. With Bongo broken I'm forced to pick up my bag and carry it around with me like I'm walking around with a deer I just hit with my car. And, because the bag is laden with coins, it's heavy, and I'm carrying the weight. I'm no longer a casual park dweller carrying a bag, but a poor man who can't afford a bag with a working strap. I walk across the park, holding my bag like a deer with a broken neck.

The coins jangle with each step.

Jangle, jangle, jangle.

The jangling gets louder and louder, disappears when I stop walking, then starts again when I start taking steps. I have an item I have to carry around I cannot afford to replace, which publicly degrades me by making an embarrassing sound.

My new bag is my old shoes.

This is my fate, being embarrassed publicly is part of my historical DNA. Hundreds of years ago my ancestors were locked in stocks, and marched through villages as excited mobs splashed buckets of warm urine over their faces, for entertainment.

Life is going to change for me. One day I'll walk across this park with a new bag that doesn't jangle and in the finest shoes cut from the most expensive leather. Actually, I don't desire expensive decorations. Maybe I'll just have my ambition validated by moderate creative success.

A white square hits me on the head, and it hurts.

I look to the ground. On the floor in front of me is a clock. I look up into the tree to see where this clock could have fallen from. Sitting on one of the branches, is a man.

The man grins, cracking crusty lines across his red face.

"Trains."

He stretches his arms out toward the clock. He said *trains* like he didn't mean to say the word trains. What he's really saying, by his body language, is he wants me to pass the clock back. I know full well it might be a stupid move to give this guy his clock back. He could throw it at me again, but harder. I bend down, and throw the clock back up into the tree. The guy reaches for the clock, grasps air, and leans forward. He looks for a horrific moment like he's going to fall from the tree.

He wobbles, and pushes his weight onto a thin branch. The branch snaps.

He falls from the tree, hits the ground face down with a flat thump, right in front of me.

The man doesn't move.

In the space of a few hours I've killed a bag and a person.

I take a forward step. I stare at the back of his head. He's rounder than a football. I wonder how he hasn't bounced straight back up into the tree. He's so puffy, if I shot him he would bleed feathers. He only moves sideways, like a crab. Thumb-size, disobedient arms lead to massive fists that, together, look like confused worms asked to build a paper-cup phone but instead hold up cabbages. His legs are long and thick but bend at inappropriate points like a trapeze artist with a vitamin D deficiency. From behind, with his fat body, pointy ears and red skin, he resembles a space-hopper. The man has on what I'm certain is a ginger wig, trimmed and side-parted, like his hair belongs to his mother, even if the fairies have long since taken his brain.

I should check for a pulse. If he's dead, am I responsible? The fall doesn't look *that* far, but maybe he has the luck of a person who tries honey for the first time and dies from anaphylactic shock.

His hand twitches. The burp of Death leaves his body from somewhere with an explosive rumble. He's getting out of bed in the morning and has all the time in the world. I gag. I pick up the clock again, with the intention of giving it back to the man. I look back up with the clock in my hand, and the man lifts his head. His eyes devour my face.

He has a flat, strawberry nose to match his fat, red, broken expanse of a face. His facial expression mumbles with the sadness of a boy still alone in a world full of mothers. His mouth gawps but no words come out. He looks confused: the last space-hopper trying to remember if he needs to hop, or stay completely still to breathe.

Money and sharks never sleep.

He wants to say something extremely important.

He moves his head in a circle and starts getting up, a lengthy process, I suspect.

His bottom lip wobbles. A tear falls from his chubby left eye, runs down his face, hangs from his second chin, drops onto his third chin and then continues hanging. Giant tears fall from his fat face. I hush him to stop him bawling, but I can't. I watch on in shock. The large man on the floor cries like a baby.

I try shushing him several times in my most soothing shushing voice.

I don't know what else to do.

He blubbers less. He gains control of his bottom lip, but then he's off again.

Walking away from a person needing help seems entirely fine when the person isn't aware there is help to hand, but walking away no longer feels appropriate.

I look at the clock in my hand and observe its functions. A standard alarm clock. An option to change the song played when the alarm sounds. One of the song choices makes me smile, so I set the alarm to play the song. I don't expect the crazy guy from the tree to get, or understand, my unsubtle attempt at observational comedy, but regardless, I think the song might soothe him.

> *Hush a bye baby, on the treetop,*
> *When the wind blows the cradle will rock,*
> *When the bow breaks, the cradle will fall,*
> *And down will come baby, cradle and all.*

The man-baby screams louder.

I can't help any more than I have. I put the clock on the ground, as near to him as possible, while staying out of grabbing reach, which is remarkably close, such is the shortness of his arms. He stops crying and his face turns into a twisted, contorted rage. He looks like he's figured out after three years of trying, the square peg does go into the square hole, and it was me who told him it didn't.

I sense it's a good time to leave. He's not injured, physically at least, and he's stopped crying. I pick up my annoying dead deer of a bag, and walk away from the clock and the crazy man.

I have an odd feeling I've made a serious enemy for life who I should avoid at all costs.

I walk away trying to look tough, to send a message he shouldn't come after me, but with each step I take my bag jangles, making me sound like a fairy about to take off through the trees. As I walk back up to my usual tree I ponder that leaving my work and home might be a terrible idea. Perhaps, the worst idea I've *ever* had. Life is beginning to feel like it's a row of different coloured doors, which all lead into the same building.

I've walked away from everything good, which I thought was bad, and replaced it with everything I thought was going to be good: but it's a broken bag, a beard, a faint smell of dog shit, a park, and a fat man in a ginger wig up a tree.

I sit under my usual tree.

Bongo is broken beyond repair, and I have an imprint of a clock on my head thrown at me by a guy I don't want to meet again. Having the clock thrown at me, and my bag breaking, has got to me. My hands are cold and that's annoying me too. I don't feel as safe as I did yesterday. I'm hearing the words of my family and friends telling me that only crazy people live in parks. I thought if I lived in the park people would think I was the crazy person, and leave me alone, but I hadn't considered the *actual* crazy people living in the park. They know I'm not one of them. I should have listened to my family and friends. This is a terribly bad idea of insurmountable comparison. I had a job I didn't like, boohoo. I had no girlfriend, cry me a river.

In this city the purge of morality is the absence of meaning.

My job was degrading to my intelligence, but nobody said because we're forced into education we would be treated intellectually. I can't quit the park. Nobody can step off the bottom rung. There's nowhere to go. No further to fall back.

The realisation hits me, quitting a job is a luxury.

I've followed through in these trousers, all I can do now is wear them.

Night drops from the sky faster than a black curtain at the end of a play. The stars come onto the stage of the universe to have their moment in moonlight.

Starlight beams through darkness, making the night sky a bullet-ridden black door.

The moon is out, and I stare at its beauty.

If I had been the first man on the moon my first words would have been "OH, MY GOD! THEY'RE HERE! WHAT ARE THEY? OH NO, WE SHOULDN'T HAVE COME, WE SHOULDN'T HAVE COME. WE HAVE ANGERED HIM! HE'S COMING TO EARTH FOR OUR SOULS!" before screaming incoherently and replicating the sound of white noise.

Plenty of people have set foot on the moon, but nobody has played a joke on the entire planet.

I have to get my bags from the wood. I should have got them sooner, but I didn't want to risk the park keeper finding me on his last round, or someone seeing me coming out of the wood with my bags. I hope I can get in and out of the wood before other homeless men arrive. I move along the black fence and to the path. I follow the path up to the duck pond, past the abandoned house, and walk to the wood. Everything is silent as I walk. I'm alone in the dark.

A homeless shadow sits on the bench opposite the small wood.

I stop walking.

A second shadow walks out of the small wood and joins the other on the bench.

Homeless shadows make me sad.

The only people left in the park at night are the homeless and I.

I am the homeless.

We are the only people alive in the world.

I can't enter the wood from the front without passing them. I backtrack past the pond, back down the fence and walk around the long way, following the path so I can enter from the back. I watch the dark, homeless shapes out of the corner of my eye. One shadow keeps going in and coming out, but I can't see any bags. It was stupid of me to leave my bags in the wood. I had seen the beer cans and plastic bags, I *knew* people were using it. I want to avoid a conversation with homeless people on their eleventh strong lager of the day, and I don't want a confrontation, but if my bags have gone I'll have no choice. I need my sleeping bag. I need my remaining clothes. I'm alone, the night is dark and I'm scared.

I'm on the path that leads into the dark wood.

I'm at my closest to the two homeless men as I slip away: an old man, who with his last breath, finally admits love to his son.

I glance to my left before disappearing into the darkness. The two men are Inbin and Worzel. They rant alcoholic monologues which occasionally lap together, and when they do, each mistakenly conclude they're talking to the other.

What all conversations are, minus the booze.

I walk down the path running through the middle of the dark wood. If I walk to the end of this path it will take me straight to the bench where Inbin and Worzel are sitting. If Inbin or Worzel walk down this path as I walk up it, our shadows will collide, and the people in the houses backing onto the park would think my screams are foxes at night. I'm engulfed in blinding darkness. I put one hand out in front, while the other grips Bongo, trying to muffle his jangle as I shuffle along. I'm eleven years old and frantically searching the wall for a light after watching a horror film alone. But there's no light to turn on in the wood.

I feel my way through the darkness to the tree where I left my bags.

Find the light.

My bags aren't here.

Find the light.

My heart beats fast.

Inbin and Worzel have taken my bags.

No wonder they are waiting at the entrance: they are waiting for me. I don't have any possessions by society's standards, but that only makes my possessions more valuable, to me and to others like me. My eyes dart around the night, but I can't find any edges to the dark.

I'm being an idiot.

My bags *have* to be here.

I look in the direction of a snapping branch, but see nothing. I shuffle further along with my hands out, moving with caution from silhouette of tree to silhouette of tree, looking for my bags, but all I find are bag-shaped shadows, that disappear when I bend closer to see.

I hadn't considered hiding my bags so nobody could see them would mean I couldn't find them. I cough. My heart falls from my face and into the dark sea of black leaves. I bend over and pick my heart up and place it back in my mouth. My heart beats too fast. The taste of fear repulses me, old milk in new fridges. Another branch snaps, flapping dragon wings and a deck of cards shuffled. Somewhere too close to me, in these dark trees, a homeless creature with wings shuffles cards with clawed hands. The creature watches me through yellow eyes. Feasting off my fear, waiting for the perfect moment to throw a single card at my feet, the last object the creature knows I'll see.

I look for the path to start my search again. I can't see the path. I'm disoriented, confused which way is left or right. I'm impossibly high in space or implausibly deep in the ocean. I close my eyes for a moment and listen. I face the direction of the homeless men and their laughter: their joy, the sound of recent bag stealing. I walk toward the laughter, letting fear guide me. I'm Darth Vader in the moments before closing his heart down, deciding life is better spent causing pain than being its recipient.

I'm running, running through the black wood.

I'll surprise them, run full speed out of the trees, grab my bags and keep on running. I'm Forrest Gump without Jenny.

I close in on the laughter, chasing down the funny like a cat hunting rubber chickens. The irrational part of my brain kicks in. My thoughts tell me *someone* is behind me. Suddenly I'm running *away* from someone. I lose track of my concentration. A dark shape steps out from the path and stands in front of me.

There's nothing I can do.

I'm hit hard on the side of my head. I crumple to the floor.

My spine is ripped out mid Elvis Presley impersonation.

I wake up dazed. I stare up from the wet leafy floor at black branches clawing across dark sky: the front cover of a Halloween card, but with my cold fingers I can't find the edges to close it.

You're not looking at a card, your view is real.

I blink. The sky is still black. The laughter has stopped. The silence is thick. The hurricane has moved over me, and I'm on my back in the eye of the storm. My plan to rescue my bags has failed. My mind tells me to expect my hands to be tied, and to prepare to be eaten at the feast of the homeless, but nobody else is around. I stand up. There are no signs of life.

A wave of stupid washes over my beached face: nobody hit me, I ran into a thick branch.

I knocked myself out with a tree.

I feel the head on my bump. I brush the leaves off my jeans and jumper. My jumper crawls with bugs who think they've stumbled into an open window in a deserted property on Park Lane.

I find the path splitting the wood in half and walk down it, all the way back out to the way I came in. I'm too afraid to exit by the actual entrance in case I have to step over drunken men. I walk back down this path, and notice, to my right, a second path. The second path leads into a different section of the wood. A path I completely missed earlier.

I walked down the wrong bloody path.

I smile to myself, because I've been an idiot and I'm going to get away with being an idiot. I walk down the new path. Underneath the first tree I come to, exactly where I left them earlier, are my two bags, covered with my coat. I put my coat on first, and search my bag for my warm hat. I throw the bags over my shoulder and walk out of the wood the same way I came, the long way.

A great sense of relief washes over me as I walk through the dark alone.

If I hadn't knocked myself out by sprinting into a tree I may have stolen, in a rush, two bags from Inbin and Worzel. I would have become what my fears told me they were, fuelled by nothing more than a wrongly placed judgement based on expected behaviour, and a desperation to remain morally superior.

People die and people kill because they're afraid, but fear comes from a little part of the mind telling those afraid they have a right to judge, a *reason* to fear. Reasoning, the blueprint of mankind, is driven by a desire to prove moral superiority.

If Death has a parrot, his parrot is moral superiority.

Then again, I just knocked myself out with a tree, so what do I know?

I may look like Inbin and Worzel, but my brain is still very much The Observer on Sunday.

I walk along the path away from the wood. A creepy sensation washes over me, the type you get if you see something move in the dark. The sort you get when someone is watching you.

Maybe it's me.

Maybe it's impossible to walk across a park this late and not feel someone is watching you.

I turn my head slowly. I glance back at the entrance to the dark wood.

Standing in the entrance is a dark shape.

The dark shape stands beyond the reach of the overhead streetlight, in the area light goes to die in.

I keep walking along the path, determined to get back to my tree and curl up into the tightest, smallest ball possible until the morning comes. I walk faster, *don't look back*, but the more steps I take the stronger the temptation grows, until I tell myself I have to look back, or I won't know where the dark shape is.

Someone is coming up behind me.

I'm alone in the dark, and someone is coming up behind me.

I look behind me again, a quick glance, hoping to collect information without making the dark shape think it's being studied. The kind of look a beaten wife might occasionally shoot her abusive husband.

The dark shape hasn't moved. It stands still: a wolf before the silence of the lambs.

No one can help me. The dark creature knows I'm living in the park, and knows how many bags I own.

I walk faster, not fast enough to let it know I'm afraid, but quick enough to put more distance between us. I glance back one last time as I turn the corner. I only look at it for a second,

The creature with the pale face and a human shape stares at me from across the park. The dark creature brings a twisted right thumb to the left hand side of its neck, and scrapes its nail across its Adam's apple.

The creature's way of letting me know it's going to slit my throat.

Just because what's behind you isn't in front of you, doesn't mean what's coming isn't going to get you.

I'm not going back to the wood at night again, and I won't be leaving my bags there. I can't leave my bags in the abandoned house either, because there's a chance the pale-faced creature is living in the old house.

When I ran, thinking someone was behind me, maybe there was.

I find the black fence and approach the tall tree with the long branches I've spent the last two nights under. At night my only protection is invisibility and during the day, anonymity.

I name my tree as I walk.

I haven't said a single word since I walked into the park. I tried talking to Grace, but I spoke in raised eyebrows and facial tics she couldn't see, and then she put the phone down on me.

Perhaps naming trees in my head is a way of humanising my surroundings. So I feel like a real person, less afraid.

I name my tree, my home, Roald Dahl. I trust this tree. He's strong and has protective qualities.

Roald Dahl is a fitting name for a tree.

Maybe before long I'll be slapping his face.

As I reach Roald Dahl I hear voices in the night. A young Italian couple. The two young lovers have climbed him in the darkness to watch the moon.

I have to find somewhere else to sleep, somewhere new, and likely, not nearly as safe. Bad timing.

I walk away from Roald Dahl, down to the bush I hid my bags under in the first few days. I sit down on a patch of wet grass by the bush. I'm struck by the realisation I can't get any consistency, routine or pattern. I own nothing. I have the right to nothing. Everything is public. Nothing is mine.

I'm free, but I'm now living any kind of dream. Every

prisoner in jail is free inside his cell. Every person outside of a cell is a prisoner to the ignorance of their freedom.

A week ago I slept with an eye on the clock and woke up when the clock told me to. I arrived for work at the same time, left at the same time and ate at the same time. I ate the same sandwich, from the same shop, served by the same girl who woke up at the same time she always did, to take the same journey she always does, to the same place, to give me the same sandwich, before leaving at the same time as always. I wanted to *know* the girl who handed me my sandwich every day with a smile, because she smiled at me as she did. In cities built on power and development, rare commodities are the simple things, and the simple things in life, a door held open, or a sandwich passed with a smile, produce beautiful moments reminding us it's good to be alive.

I never said a word to my sandwich girl because routines are safe, and breaching them for original conversation is not part of routine, so what we want grows increasingly impossible to ask for. Eventually we stop asking for what we deserve, and finally we convince ourselves we don't deserve what we want. In exchange for fitting in, we stop dreaming. No wonder when every adult, if they close their eyes, can remember being told as a child to grow up and live in the real world. Those who talk about living in the real world don't even enjoy living in the real word, because the adults who tell children to grow up and live in the real world always do so with jealousy in their voice: they're the children who never learnt to play, the adults who campaign for signs reading *no ball games*.

As I sit now in the cold park on wet grass, I'm having withdrawal symptoms. I miss the system.

Sometimes you need to sit in the wrong place to see the right view.

I've thrown myself into anti-routine. I'm stressed.

What am I meant to do now I'm not copying everybody else?

If you aren't chasing your dream, your dream is being chased by a nightmare.

On the first night in the park I slept under a huge tree that stood tall, right in the middle of the park. I name the tree Stephen King. Falling asleep in the night with Stephen was fine, but waking up with him forced me into a hullabaloo with the park keeper. Stephen is too famous, too central, too visible: I can never go back to him.

He's deadwood to me.

Thanks to the Italian couple, I don't know where I can sleep tonight in (relative) safety.

Having no settled place to hide my bags is pissing me off too. No two days have been the same. I'm in a transitional period between the depressing real world and a potentially happy, fantastic one. The transition was never going to be entirely smooth. Finding a routine in this park is like trying to pin a giant tail made of carrot to the back of a donkey.

I push my bags toward the back of the bush. Nobody will find them in the dark.

If I'm naming trees I might as well name bushes too. I once read a Jeffrey Archer novel on holiday and it was so bad I felt like punching myself in the throat until I died. This bush looks pathetic in comparison to Roald Dahl and Stephen King, and continuing my *authors who affect me* theme, I call the inferior bush Jeffrey Archer, though I use the term 'author' loosely when associated with Jeffrey.

I stink.

I can't remember when the last time I washed was, and I've been sleeping under trees and crawling in and out of bushes. I can no longer avoid the issue.

I'm going to have to shower in the park.

I nervously look around the park watching for moving shadows, or any sign now isn't the time to get naked and have a public shower.

Any sign will do.

I'm ready to interpret any slight variation in wind strength as a personal message from the gods I shouldn't proceed.

There is no wind.

No sound.

No movement.

I scratch my face, under my chin, and feel uncomfortable in the skin that I'm in.

My head is clammy. My buttocks feel like two drunks pushing each other at a party where everyone else is on MDMA. The hair on my neck rubs at the material on my top. I want to tear me off and start again.

My arms itch, my eyeballs feel dirty.

I look around one last time.

I pull my smaller record bag out from inside Jeffrey the bush and remove my washing bag: pink stars on a white background. I unzip the bag and remove my green tea tree and mint shower gel, the kind which tingles and irritates during use.

To shower I'm going to have to remove all of my clothes and stand naked in the park.

My pubic place in a public space.

I leave my shower gel by my feet. I hang my towel from one of the branches. I remove a bottle of water and leave it next to my shower gel.

I remove my trousers and top, then my shoes and my socks. My toes curl away with the cold.

Cold night wind burns my arms, my head and chest.

I stand in the middle of the park in my boxer shorts. My legs set ablaze with ice.

I place my hands on the waistband of my underwear. I see myself at work typing letters into a machine. I breathe in. I exhale. My warm breathe turns to ice in the wind.

I pull my boxer shorts down. I stand entirely naked in the park.

I've made it, Ma, top of the world.

To a member of the public I am now either a sex offender or mentally ill, plain and simple.

No grey areas.

I unscrew the lid on the bottle of water. I hold the bottle of water above my head. I brace myself. Then tip the bottle over me. I tip the open bottle upside down. Ice cold water hits the top of my head, and cascades down my naked body and exposed skin, like an ice statue under a waterfall. For the briefest of moments I am only sensation. I swallow water. The park fades away. There is darkness. Cold. Terror and freedom unite as I am parted, each drop of water a wave. I reach down by my feet. I grab the shower gel and squeeze it into my right hand. I spread the green gel all over my shivering body. I rub the gel into my skin as fast as I can. I rub under my armpits and under my balls. I run a hand between my arse and down both of my legs. I am vulnerable like this. My focus is on me and not on the park. I have to focus on me, to get through this ordeal, this embarrassment, this humiliation, as fast as possible. But the park continues to live and breathe without me. The park is a wild animal, and my human process, my need to feel clean again, shines a torch on me in the darkness.

I look up, like a rabbit waiting for trauma. I've moved a few steps away from Jeffrey Archer.

A man wearing a hat and a warm coat looks back at me.

His dog sniffs the lamppost nearest to him.

I move my hands down from my chest to cover up Professor Merrydinkle, a name I've decided to use instead of saying penis, because some people take offence at reading the word penis, so therefore I'm not going to mention the word penis, or any penis-sounding words.

Keep walking.

Don't leave the path, please don't leave the path.

I want to be invisible. If there was a button I could push to no longer exist, I would push it. Trying to be something is so much harder than never having been.

The man leaves the path, but stops after his second step. He looks at me. Anger fizzes over his face, making his face wobble like his head is a bottle of lemonade trapped in a tumble dryer.

The guy *has* seen me.

The man shakes his head. He looks like he wants to shout, but the words and concepts being computed by his brain are too big to fit out of his mouth. We lock eyes. I feel nothing but shame. His eyes are full of disgust and hate. There is no human empathy. There is only judgement: them and us, pity, condemnation. All things perceived to be beneath, are instinctively registered as separate.

His face stops exploding. He steps back on the path. He walks away: his eyes bubbling, the dog's tail fizzing.

Shivering, withering mentally, shrivelling spiritually, I continue to rub the gel into my naked body. The gel combines with the cold water, creating a sloppy mush of white foam and bubbles. Some bubbles fall to the grass and for a moment reflect the world, before popping somewhere else.

I pick up the bottle of water, now half full. I tip most of the remaining water over my head. Ice becomes me again. Cold water floods away the soap from the city of my skin.

I bend to wash my feet. I remove the gel from between my toes and ankles.

Everything changes. I don't see it coming. I feel a force smack into the side of my head. I feel a surge of aggression in my shoulder. I'm confused. I am no longer standing having a shower. I am looking out from the bush. My face aches, like I'm waking up with a hangover. My arms feel scratched. My shoulder and body is heavy. My back hurts from where I have landed.

I look out from the floor of the bush, and up at two young Italian faces, smiling.

They are young, still teenagers. The girl has brown hair that falls straight to her slim waist, and her skin has a continental softness, wild olives before they're picked. The boy looks younger, full of beauty and insecurity. His hair is thick and covered in gel, his eyes scream with the impatience of a boy looking to prove he's a man to the world. The girl has her hand over her mouth, I can't tell if she's covering a smile or a look of shock. The girl's other hand, I notice, is around his wrist, as if we're in some kind of western and she expects her quick-to-anger husband to be the first to fire his gun.

The boy takes a step forward. The scratches in my arm sting. I'm naked, entirely exposed. The boy steps closer to me, as he does, my entire being curls slightly.

He stands over me. I prepare to be kicked. The boy makes a noise in the back of his throat. He brings from his brain to his mouth a large blob of snot. I hear the noise of the spit leaving his mouth, but I don't see it coming. I feel it hit the back of my hand. I cover my face.

Another sound, like a percolator making coffee, comes from somewhere beyond the bush, which suddenly feels like the entire universe away from me. This percolator is female. The girl is preparing to spit on me too.

Do something. Why aren't you doing something?

The second ball of spit lands on my leg. I feel it crawl and fall down my skin, parting my body hairs as it moves, like an excitable slug through a bin.

They laugh. The boy and the girl. They are excited by cruelty.

The laughter becomes smaller, more distant.

I lower my hand from my face. They have gone.

No words had been spoken. I am not deemed worthy of dialogue.

We had communicated through the international language

of violence. They saw someone vulnerable, someone who could not defend themselves, so their cruel hearts and instincts kicked me into a bush: a snapshot into world politics.

The truth, if I can confront it, is I know my dream to become a writer is impossible and will never happen. The people outside of the machine are always more likely to connect with my words than the people within. The truth is: I'm not in this park to follow my dream. I'm here because my landlord put my rent up. I could no longer afford to sustain my private depression. My debts were growing. My place of employment could have helped me, but I was met with the cold back of the system. So I left, deciding it was better to be homeless than participating in the social collective delusion of success and happiness through the medium of a desk job.

And now, I am here. Naked in a bush. The beautiful warm shores of my past long washed away.

I feel saliva of people on my skin.

I should get my clothes on. Go back to Roald Dahl.

Maybe tomorrow would be best spent hanging from one of his branches.

I stand and use my towel to wipe away spit. I touch my face to see if I can feel any bumps from his punch. I put the towel back on the branch. I feel no pain from the punch. I can't feel any bump. My arms are scratched. The last of my pride has been stamped away and set ablaze. Maybe that's a good thing.

I guess I'm okay.

Unless I zoom out a bit, for a broader perspective.

Zoom out far enough and we're all completely fucked.

Maybe *that's* what the television is for: the great distraction.

Death is what happens while you are busy making other plans. Lennon had reality upside down.

Best not to think about it.

I stand. I pour the last of the water over my head. A river of ice dribbles slowly over my skin. Soap and watery bubbles flow into the dark grass between the toes of my feet. I feel cleaner, yet at the same time dirtier than I've ever been.

I wrap my towel around me and hurriedly dress.

I put on my boxer shorts. Then my jeans.

I dry my feet. I put my socks on, then my t-shirt and jumper.

My body shivers under my clothes, as I wait for my jumper to resist the cold of the night.

Fully dressed, superficially cleansed, I walk back to my tree, Roald Dahl.

Have I crossed a line, or dropped beneath one?

I reach Roald Dahl. I place my bags on the ground. I get out my portable bed and shuffle inside. The cold air dissipates in the warm belly of my sleeping bag. The puffy bag wraps around me and feels like a hug.

I lay on the ground, and through the leaves I look up at the stars. I wonder if Oscar Wilde wrote *we're all in the gutter, but some of us look up at the stars* sitting by a warm fire, in a large house surrounded by brandy and unnecessary puppies.

My face is cold. I breathe in the universe above while feeling the sticks pushing into my back from below. I feel protected by hanging branches.

Tomorrow is another day, but only if you live through the night.

Maybe being homeless is not about finding a routine; maybe it's about finding my own meal instead of the world being put on a plate.

Now I no longer fit in a hole, I see the sunlight pouring through the cracks. There was no view before, a sense of conformity, of purpose, of belonging and safety, but no view. No stars. Every night, spent looking up at a roof.

What does it say about how seriously humans take life, if we're born into this world naked but buried in a suit?

I'm recalling emotions again, and reminded of how many varying and conflicting emotions we are capable of having. A friend once told me the *real pain is feeling nothing at all*: and that's the truth.

Tonight, I'm feeling *everything*.

I curl up tighter in my hug. I close my eyes. Tomorrow is another day.

A branch snaps. I open my eyes. My thoughts run to the other side of my mind. An angel is stuck in a spider web, screaming her last wish to fly one more time.

I see the creature with the pale face silently watching me from somewhere in the darkness.

The creature brings its right thumb to the left hand side of its neck, scrapes its nail across his Adam's apple.

Letting me know it's coming to slit my throat.

Dorangel Vargas

The year was 1965 and his soon-to-be mother, Sugar Vargas, conceived him in a temporary builder's cubicle on the M25.

Sugar Vargas was a good person. She worked hard. She held down three jobs. She was a cleaner, a fantastic chef and at the weekends a pet shop employee. She was a large, fat, proud black woman who possessed in her facial arsenal a beautiful smile and long thick black hair she never tied back because, as she would say, life is about letting go of what others hold back. When she laughed she slapped her hands on her lap and her giant breasts clapped together. The combination of slapping and clapping made her sound like two coconuts being bashed together by an advancing army of French horses marching toward an English train driver sitting cross-legged chewing a pen, who had just completed his crossword puzzle.

A good laugh, which combined the unexplained with relief and achievement.

Everyone who heard Sugar laugh became jealous of how much fun she was having, which didn't stop her looking anxiously for French horses once she moved from guffaw to chuckling. She smelt like pineapples in soapy water in the winter, and in the summer like dry pumpkin pie and curdled milk squeezed from sad cows with broken ankles.

Everybody agreed they enjoyed her winter smell more.

She spent her early life despising being called Sugar, and her later life wondering why she didn't mind it anymore.

One night, after getting lost driving home from the pet shop, she found herself parked on the hard shoulder of the M25, a worried look on her face, and twenty-seven bright yellow budgies in the back of her car tweeting, "we don't know where we are." But Sugar didn't speak budgie, she never could.

Two men knocked on her car window: large, fat, white men who had long lost their hair and never had much sense of anything else to lose. One was called Nigel, the man Sugar would later think was the father to her son Dorangel, the other was never known. I will call the other man Chubb. Let's pretend Chubb was a fishy man who had a fetish for looking through keyholes. Nigel persuaded the lost Sugar he could help, but only if she went with him into the temporary Portaloo.

The police made no arrests for the crime, but the lead investigator wrote in a statement the message took at least four hours to write, and no less than six cats.

Chubb stared through the keyhole of the Portaloo witnessing events, as Nigel squirted into her belly a life called Dorangel.

Sugar got back in her car in a daze. As she drove away all twenty-seven budgies, fifty-four individual budgie eyes, stared menacingly at Nigel and Chubb through the back of the car windscreen: eyebrows furrowed, bright eyes set to attack mode, wings bawled into fists down by their sides. Sugar failed to hear that the budgies, in shock, had stopped tweeting. Horror was etched on their faces, their beaks and eyes hung open like they had been sat in a room full of young dogs.

Sugar returned home and cried, but despite the horror she'd endured she didn't call the police. She waddled around her flat like a daddy longlegs with missing legs, putting lots of energy into forgetting her nightmare, while never getting anywhere.

Nigel was with her every time she went to the toilet and every time she got in her car.

She used to enjoy using the toilet at work. It was an excuse to leave the kitchen in the hotel or the front desk of the pet shop. After the rape, every time she entered a toilet cubicle, her brain made back flips inside her head. Twice she was found banging on a toilet door screaming to be let out, and twice work colleagues had to talk her into unlocking the door from the inside.

The only toilet she trusted after the assault was the toilet in her home. And even then she never locked it: the door was always open.

One morning a colleague in the pet shop asked her if she was pregnant. Sugar's brain did a back flip, and twenty-seven budgies in the pet shop window wept visible tears nobody noticed, because everyone stood over Sugar as she'd fainted.

When Sugar woke up, the doctor said he had good news: she was pregnant.

Nobody had ever given her anything, except Nigel, so she kept the child and told anyone who asked that the father had died in a fire inside a toilet on an oilrig. He left a cigarette burning on top of the toilet roll holder and was unable to escape. Nobody questioned her story. Her few friends thought it was due to grief that she told the story of Nigel burning alive in a toilet cubicle so feverishly. Sugar loved the thought of him burning alive. Her pleasurable revenge, she thought, for not going to the police. In the nine months between conception and birth, Sugar quit her other jobs and worked full time in the pet shop. Since Chubb and Nigel, she trusted people less and animals more. She liked the idea of being a mum more than she liked the idea of having a boyfriend. She put on weight she would never lose, grew bingo wings that never flew (or played bingo) and her ankles became so sore they justified her failure to move. When she was eight months pregnant, a white man walked into her shop wearing a builder's overall. He wanted to buy a puppy for his daughter. Sugar noticed a tattoo on his arm and darkness under his eyes. She recognised Nigel immediately. Nigel never noticed Sugar.

Sugar was eight months pregnant and looked different. Sugar had seen Nigel's face every night in her sleep. Nigel had never looked at Sugar's face properly even at the time his face was touching hers. For him, Sugar had never been a face or a person, just an object. Most nights he was drunk. His imagination was limited to a black screen and a noise he ignored, his conscience calling the phone in his brain, which he never answered.

Sugar had not been a consideration before, during, or after insemination.

The young budgies silenced. These budgies were the children of the budgies who witnessed the original horror. These children had been told the tale of the night on the motorway by their parents.

Their silence was a rage surpassed only by their eyes, all fifty-four of them. Nigel's face was slimy and long. His face reminded Sugar of a pelican trying to swallow a giant toad: two toad legs desperately peddling backwards, slime dripped down the pelican's beak of his expression.

"I am wondering if you have any puppies."

Nigel smiled a green, toad-leg smile.

Sugar threw up. She couldn't control it. She threw up all over Nigel.

"I'm sorry. I'm a little bit pregnant."

Sugar noticed Nigel had a deep hatred toward women.

He was wired, wrong: weird.

"There is a toilet out the back, you're welcome to use it and there's a special puppy just arrived, I'll give it to you at a discount, for the trouble."

"I bet you would give it to me cheap, wouldn't you, love?"

Over the counter Sugar threw up all over Nigel again.

That time she could have held it back, but she just didn't want to.

Nigel stormed through the door at the back of the shop and into the toilet: a single door, with non-spectacular white walls.

As regular a toilet as anyone could go in to remove sick from their own face delivered by their victim of nine months previous.

Sugar walked past the toilet and into the small kitchen for staff at the back of the pet shop. She put four brown slices of bread into the toaster. She pulled the lever down. The bread warmed. She always ate toast after being sick, as she felt it was the safest food to give to a sensitive stomach.

With her right hand (she was usually left-handed) she pulled a knife out of its holder.

She walked slowly to the toilet. She stood outside patiently.

Inside the toilet, Nigel removed the last bit of carrot from his ear.

Nigel didn't wash his hands. He took a moment to stare into the mirror.

One of life's great conflictions is beautiful people (outside and in) spend a lifetime avoiding their eyes in a mirror, because they think too much about who they think they see.

Yet Nigel spent hours staring at himself, not thinking about anything, just the surface of him.

Nigel opened the toilet door.

Twenty-seven budgies drew one collective breath.

Tick.

Sugar took a second to register the surprise on Nigel's face, but her second was over too soon.

Nigel took a second to register the knife in Sugar's hand, but his second was a lifetime with no end.

Tock.

Sugar inserted the knife just below Nigel's ribcage until she felt the knife against an organ. And then she pushed through the organ, exploding whatever it was, she kept pushing until the knife was stopped by bone: most likely his spine.

She withdrew the knife, pulling it back out through bone and organs.

Blood poured from the wound.

Nigel's eyes widened.

Sugar plunged the knife into the middle of his chest and through his heart, where she left it.

"Sugar."

Nigel's last word was the sweetest he'd ever spoken.

Red poured from his mouth. His lungs drowned in blood.

Nigel slumped against the toilet door.

He breathed out, but did not breathe back in.

Nigel was dead.

And up popped the toast.

Only Nigel wasn't dead.

The police discovered the builder who walked into the pet shop that day was not a Nigel but a happily married father of three called Phillip. Phil was a lad, a builder, but a good father and a husband. Sugar was not convinced, but DNA tests would prove she had killed an innocent man. Phil's wife snipped the last thread of Sugar's righteousness when she told Sugar her husband wouldn't have said *sugar* how she thought he had. Phil was a builder with one exception, he never swore. His mum had been so strict when he was a child that for his entire life he used 'sugar', 'fudge' and 'passport' as his swear words.

After meeting Phil's wife, Sugar knew in her heart she had killed the wrong man. Shortly after that, the person Sugar had been, dissolved like toffee dropped from a child's pocket onto a hot tin roof.

Dorangel was born in a prison that, in one way or another, he never left. He was born on the 30th July 1966. He exploded out of his mother at the same time Geoff Hurst volleyed a ball with venom into the back of the German net confirming England's one and only World Cup victory. As the commentator screamed, *"The people are on the pitch. They think it's all over. It is now,"* the pregnancy ended for Sugar and life began for Dorangel. The doctor who delivered the oddly pale baby did not want to deliver the oddly pale baby. He wanted to watch the game. The doctor was uncaring, impatient and unsympathetic throughout the birth. The first hands that touched the pale baby, did not want to touch the baby.

The baby arrived early and never apologised.

Dorangel's face was a scrunched up ball of ugly before he was cleaned, and after he was cleaned he looked like a set of dentures hammered into the face of a jellyfish.

At the age of sixteen minutes it was clear Sugar's son hadn't been put on this earth for his looks. His nose was a penguin with a broken back. His skin was ghostly white. His ears were too low or his head was too high. His chin poked out like a bag of clothes dumped outside a charity shop, and he was fat. It did not help his looks that on his fourteenth minute alive his mother tried to kill him. When Sugar realised her son was white she couldn't see the eyes of her son, only the dark spirit of Nigel.

So, on her son's fourteenth-minute birthday, she placed a pillow over his face and tried to blow out his life, like a candle on a flaming cake. She was caught and sedated. When she woke her son was no longer in her arms, and never would be again. In her drowsy state Sugar spoke to her pillow like it was her son. She cradled the pillow and whispered she was going to call him Spice, so they could be known as Sugar and Spice and all the things in life that were nice. She was known from then as the crazy bitch with a son for a pillow, and was moved to a home for the mentally unstable. Sugar would die three years later in the mental hospital she wound up in, quite young at the age of forty-five, at the hands of another mental patient.

She was killed for slipping up, and slipping on the wrong slippers.

Her unnamed son remained unnamed. He was known only as the number nineteen sixty-six until the day after his mum's death, when he was allowed to visit her body in the morgue. His first conscious memory of his mother was staring at her glass eyes and dark skin, which looked like wood and felt like cold marble.

After he'd seen his mother's body he refused to leave the morgue.

He was nudged out of the room but returned.

The mortician was a cold, rational man who thought the boy may as well learn the un-sugared truths of life. The boy stood in the doorway of the dead and rather enjoyed himself. One of the doctors at the morgue called him Door Angel in passing, another leant down and held his chin and asked another colleague if she'd ever met someone called Dorangel before.

And so nineteen-sixty-six returned from the morgue as a very young Dorangel Vargas.

Dorangel Vargas was eventually placed in an orphanage.

Age 7

When Dorangel was seven years old he trod on a dog's tail. The dog, a big dog, turned and bit Dorangel in the face. Most children, likely all children that young, would have run away crying. Young Dorangel stood his ground and stared at the dog for a moment. He stepped forward and removed the dog's nose with his teeth. The dog whimpered away and hid under a cabinet. Young Dorangel chewed the nose in his mouth like he was chewing gum, eventually swallowing it. He whistled down the corridor, and thought one day he would eat the dog whole.

He'd never been happier.

Age 11

When Dorangel was eleven years old the home paid for a cage of budgies to be placed inside the front entrance, as they thought yellow birds would brighten up the entrance and make the orphanage feel more like a family home. When Dorangel walked near them, the budgies stopped talking and stared at him with menacing intent. They were not the budgies from the back of his late mother's car, or the children of those budgies in the pet shop who witnessed the stabbing of innocent Phil. These budgies were not related or family, but the world of the pet shop budgie is small and exceedingly dull, so the tale of Sugar had fuelled budgie conversation for several lifetimes. When Dorangel walked up to them they bit their tongues so hard they drew blood and then opened their mouths, to show their tongues to him.

Dorangel didn't like the budgies. He knew their silence was a scream in his direction. They seemed to know his thoughts. He envisaged the budgies sitting in a paddling pool looking smug in a sunny garden he felt they didn't deserve.

He spent his days imagining all of the wonderful ways he could kill budgies.

He made a list:

How to Kill (ded) a buggy. My Liszt.

Cook them in a sandwich.
Drown them in a bath (with weyts).
Washing Machine
Iron
Shake/bear/octopus/in a cage
Explode them
Suck thier brains out
Pop their heads off
Coffee or brussel sproatz
Chainsaw
Dentist?
Give them homework?!

Dorangel dreamt of death and morgues. In one of his dreams he stood in a doorway looking at people in white coats with cold hands and toneless voices. In front of him was a silver table, and on that table was a body covered in a white cloth.

A lady bent down, touched his chin, and smiled at his unusual name. He walked to the silver table, but he was too small to see the body under the cloth. He helped himself to a stepladder. He climbed until he was looking over the table and down at the body. He gripped the cloth with his left hand (he was usually right-handed). Several big people in white coats ran in his direction, but they'd seen him too late. He pulled the sheet back. He stared into the face of a dead budgie the size of a horse, its yellow feathers now grey.

He looked into the giant budgie's glass eyes. He stared at himself staring back into them. Dorangel clasped the edges of the budgie's beak with his small plump hands.

He prised open the mouth of the bird.

The budgie's tongue was bleeding.

He woke up with a start. He hugged his pillow close. Even in dreams, he thought, *budgies are out to get me.*

Age 13

One morning, when Dorangel was thirteen, Nurse Cavendish removed the cloth covering the budgie cage. Her scream woke up most of the children in the orphanage, many of whom then went back to sleep, having spent most of their life acclimatising to the sound of varying degrees of horror. It was the longest scream she would ever scream. All twenty-seven budgies had hung themselves. Each budgie dangled from a piece of string, their lifeless wings down by their sides. Their eyes looked like glass, and she could see her reflection in them.

Nurse Cavendish discovered twenty-seven tiny suicide

notes tied to twenty-seven feet. They housed some very troubled children.

The director read out the suicide notes at the funeral service in the orphanage garden.

"I could no longer handle the depression."

"I was trapped, my life wasn't going anywhere."

"I was unable to achieve what I was instinctively born to do."

"I'm paranoid. I think people are always watching me, like I'm on show."

"I can't stand the colour yellow."

"Born to fly. Made to sit."

"The other twenty-six budgies were dead, and if you found only me alive I would've looked highly suspicious."

The one person who noticed twenty-seven budgies had died and the director only read out twenty-six suicide notes, was Dorangel. As everyone watched the dead budgies lower into the ground, Dorangel watched the director lower the last suicide note into his trouser pocket.

"Dorangel, can I see you in my office please?"

Dorangel sat in the office of the director of the orphanage for the first time. The director was a tall bespectacled man with short grey hair, a wiry frame and bushy beard. He had a permanent expression on his face like someone had just given him a parking ticket when he didn't own a car. He was thought of as being thoughtful, as he was a man of few words, but the people who knew him understood this wasn't because he thought a lot, but because he hardly thought at all. He had little to do because the orphanage was highly staffed by good people who knew their jobs. Some days he sharpened pencils, others he would stare out from his large bay window trying to remember what he was thinking about before he started to think about what he was thinking about, but couldn't because he hadn't been thinking about anything.

But to the casual observer looking in, there stood a great man looking out, having a think.

Dorangel watched the director looking out through his bay window, his back to the boy and his arms behind his back. Dorangel was concerned. The director was thinking about something, and he'd heard the director was a highly intelligent man. The director turned and faced Dorangel. He pulled from his back pocket the twenty-seventh budgie suicide note.

He looked up at the boy, then down at the note, before clearing his throat and reading aloud the words.

"I killed myself because of Dorangel Vargas."

Dorangel argued it would make no sense for him to write a note blaming himself, and it was logical whoever really killed the budgies left the note trying to blame him so the spotlight was not on them. The director didn't care much and quite liked not sharpening pencils, so he took the young boy's reasoning as truth, even though he couldn't be certain.

He decided to keep an eye on young Dorangel.

Age 14

When Dorangel was fourteen he buried the noseless orphanage dog alive, instead of picking strawberries. When he returned covered in dirt with no strawberries he was sent to the director's office. The director smiled, frowned and grimaced all at the same time. As Dorangel spoke the director put down his newly sharpened pencil. He listened attentively to the boy explain he'd picked hundreds of strawberries, but the dog ate them all then ran away. Dorangel noticed the director's face only looked normal when someone talking distracted it from its usual expression. The director sensed the juxtaposition between his face alone and his face in the company of others, and so their meetings suited both parties. Dorangel proved his innocence via the director's failure to care if he was guilty, and the director got to wear a more relaxed facial expression for a few moments.

Age 15

The orphanage bus was returning from a trip and fifteen-year-old Dorangel sat next to Margaret Taylor. Margaret Taylor had no friends either. She was nicknamed 'No Gaps' by the others.

Her nickname had nothing to do with her teeth, which were gappy.

Pale Dorangel, the boy who never spoke, disappeared for lengthy periods and always wore black, fascinated Margaret 'No Gaps' Taylor.

Margaret Taylor mostly annoyed Dorangel. There were some occasions when he didn't mind sitting next to Margaret Taylor because Margaret Taylor could talk for England. Dorangel sat on these trips in silence, listening to Margaret. Margaret would talk about any and all sorts, and her impressive ability to fill silence meant Dorangel couldn't hear the voices.

The silence in his head was a pleasant sensation for Dorangel.

As long as Margaret spoke he couldn't hear voice one telling him to eat her face, he couldn't hear voice two telling him to crash the orphanage bus, he couldn't hear voice three screaming at him to bang his own head into the bus windows and nor could he hear his fourth voice casually suggesting, while leaning back on a leather chair smoking a pipe, that normal people don't have to be distracted from listening to four voices.

Margaret 'No Gaps' would speak for so long, she would wake up talking and not stop talking until she talked herself to sleep. If she couldn't sleep she'd stay awake until her voice became croaky and hoarse, and would only fall silent when her tongue wriggled free from her face, running away to live under a bridge. Margaret Taylor was ginger. Dorangel saw fire when he looked at her, and he quite liked flames. Her hair was wild and scraggy. Dorangel imagined her being electrocuted. Her face was full of ginger freckles. He saw himself stabbing her to death with a fountain pen. Her skin was pale and white and never made

Dorangel think of violence, instead, he looked at his own skin and thought they were the same. She spoke with an elegance that pointed to being born with a silver spoon in her mouth, but her failure to control the pace of her own word distribution, coupled with the spoon indents in her forehead, indicated that not long after the silver spoon was placed in, it was ripped out with brutal force and used as a tool to beat her over the head with.

Dorangel thought she smelt like old running shoes tied to the back of a car driven away from a church by a couple forced to marry by their parents.

Sometimes, very late at night, Dorangel thought he would like to eat her tongue with his own.

On the orphanage bus, Margaret Taylor offered Dorangel a ham and cheese sandwich. Margaret's bare finger touched Dorangel's exposed leg. The touch was so light, it almost wasn't a touch at all. Regardless, Dorangel's legs tensed, his stomach tightened, and a burning sensation overwhelmed his lower half. Dorangel, confused, doubled over like he'd taken a bullet to his stomach. Margaret Taylor screamed. The orphanage bully, who was three years older than everyone else, sat in the seat behind them.

He knew what had happened, so he stood up on the bus and told everyone.

Dorangel ran from the orphanage bus to the sound of thirty children chanting:

"Dorangel touched Margaret's sandwich and got so excited he made a ham and cheese sex baby."

When he finally made it back to his room, he listened to voice three and bashed his head repeatedly into his bedroom wall until he blacked out.

From then on at the orphanage, Dorangel, who was already an outsider, was cruelly mocked. He became the boy who wanted to shower with sandwiches. The children waved their sandwiches at him and asked him. They asked what filling he most wanted to marry.

Margaret Taylor's light touch put him off girls. The orphanage turned him off food.

He expressed himself to nobody. The less he expressed, the more he compressed himself until eventually he had to explode. He took his rage out the only way he had ever known, by killing animals.

Food and girls reminded him of being shot in the stomach, which made him feel shame. Animals made him feel whole again, killing them gave him a purpose.

Dorangel stopped eating normal food. When he started killing animals on a regular basis his hunger and curiosity combined. He ate what he killed.

He ate the animals raw.

Age 16

At sixteen he was addicted to eating animals. He was on one cat a day. Sometimes he would kill an animal in the night just so he could eat one in the morning before he got out of bed.

Age 17

At seventeen he would eat a cat before breakfast, skip breakfast at the orphanage, then go to lessons. During lessons his thirst for animal flesh would return and he would eat dead mice discreetly from his pockets at the back of the class. Nobody went near him because he smelt like a chip trapped in the fold of a sumo wrestler's armpit. He got angry if he couldn't eat, and would use that anger to find more food. If he'd eaten, his thoughts calmed and he was able to focus on voice four, calmly questioning whether he thought it normal he listened to four voices and ate animals alive.

Age 18

By the time he was eighteen Dorangel was eating two cats a day, and for a weekend treat he would eat a whole dog. No animal was sacred, no animal safe: birds, rats, squirrels, hamsters, mice. Any creature with legs that wiggled, eyes that bulged and bones that crunched, found their way into his mouth.

Age 21

He was knee high in mangled bunnies after deciding to build a mountain out of dead rabbits, sit inside, and then eat his way out. His rabbit mountain plan was to celebrate his twenty-first birthday. A horse wandered into his eye line. His plan changed, and he celebrated his twenty-first birthday by eating an entire horse.

Age 22

He ate his first entire cow. The cow took him a month, but he ate the whole thing: eyeballs, nose, and brain. He decided, as he swallowed the last eyeball of Groplopodopiondolopodus the cow, that small animals were easier to eat and far more manageable. Even the cows name had stuck in his throat.

Age 25

Aged twenty-five he was massive. His diet of animals had made him grow to almost seven feet tall. He was at least two feet wide. He was homeless and deranged, but never returned to the scene of a murdered animal. Dead animals were a minor concern for the police. The RSPCA collected photographs and typed letters of concern, but had nowhere to send the letters, so put them in a file and read them out to themselves. The file, complete with the photographs, was put in a cabinet in one of their offices in Hackney, where it collected dust and was ignored.

Dorangel lived in parks, forests and woods. Apart from one dusty file, nobody in the outside world knew he existed.

Dorangel may have made no mark on the human world, but he was slowly eating his way through the animal kingdom. Tales of his massacres spread to every park and forest in England. At night, young animals refusing to go to bed were told by their parents: *you better go now, or Dorangel Vargas will bite off your head.*

The Battle
Of Bodmin Hill

In one forest in England, animals had been going missing for days. All the animals knew Dorangel the human bin had arrived. The animals of Bodmin decided to eat, before they were eaten.

The circle of forest elders stared at the fire and waited for the oldest and the wisest of them to begin the meeting. Billrumionarkpodian, an old horse with an eye patch and a scar down his long nose, really did have a long face these days and everyone knew why: his wife had been missing for an entire week. She was probably dead. Billrumionarkpodian placed posters around the forest, on all of the trees and all of the branches, but he received no news on her whereabouts.

The ants held a meeting. They had seen his wife. The ants waived their antennae at the beetles, who pinched the mice, who squeaked at the rabbits, who thumped the ground to the otters, who swam a note to the foxes, who screamed to the sheep, who bleated to the crows, who cawed to the owl, who twit ta'woo'd back to the crows that a meeting should be arranged to tell Billrumionarkpodian what the ants saw. The crows cawed to the sheep, who bleated the note to the foxes, who screamed to the otters, who swam to the rabbits, who told the mice, who squeaked the message to the beetles, who pinched the ants, who held a colony meeting and decided to march to the beetles, who took all the other animals with them to meet the owl, who twit-ta-woo'd for Billrumionarkpodian to join them and bring all the animals he could. The twit-ta-woo signalled the beginning of the most important meeting ever held in the wood.

Billrumionarkpodian, the old horse, arrived in the clearing leading a sea of bugs and beasts. He waited patiently. He nibbled his bottom lip nervously; forest meetings were almost never held.

The wise owl hobbled out onto her branch and lifted a wing. The animals and bugs stopped clicking, clacking and buzzing, and silenced as one. The wise owl was so old her voice was squeaky, clunky and crackly. She sounded like a witch clutching a 1900's typewriter falling from a building into a crowd of scuttling bagpipe players. The wise owl told Billrumionarkpodian in her clinky clunky voice she was sorry. His wife was dead, eaten by the wildest animal of the forest: the human. Billrumionarkpodian neighed sadly. A giant tear, an empty snow globe, strolled slowly down his long face. Billrumionarkpodian thought he would tell a joke, to lighten his mood, but it was hopeless.

"A horse walks into a bar and the barman says, 'Why the long face?'"

"Because my wife is dead."

The wise owl told Fardangliarn the sheep that her husband had been eaten alive. Fardangliarn baa'd so much as her wool absorbed her tears. She expanded, until she fell over, and couldn't get back up.

By the end of the meeting every animal in the forest was crying. Even the wise owl shared her tale of grief. Her husband failed to return home a week before and reports from the beavers stated the head of her husband had been seen floating down the river.

The animals decided to attack the human. They gathered sticks and stones and flew, galloped, marched, slithered and bounded toward the hideout of the man with the full intention of biting, stinging, pecking, mauling, spraying, sliming, and impaling him. They reached the clearing where Dorangel had set up his temporary home, and as he slept, they surrounded him. The wise owl hopped up onto his chest holding a stick. Dorangel felt something on his chest: a small weight, like the indication of a future heart condition. He opened his eyes. As he did, a stick poked into his eyeball, causing immediate discomfort.

He blinked. He looked down at the owl. He smiled at his luck.

This was the equivalent of a normal person being woken up by a pizza.

Dorangel picked up the owl. He bit her head off with a single chomp.

What was meant to be the animals' fight for revenge, their independence day, became 'The Battle of Bodmin Hill', which would later be remembered by the animals' children as 'The Bodmin Hill Massacre'.

Dorangel would remember the night as the weird one where he was woken up by all his favourite foods. He ate them all. There was so much blood. He was so full by the end of it, that for the first time in his life he was a little sick of eating forest animals.

He'd taken one kick from an old horse straight to the face. The once-ugly Dorangel was now uglier. The horse removed some teeth, flattened his nose and dislocated his jaw, leaving it hanging unnaturally from his pale face. Dorangel never sought help. He never put the jaw back and never visited a dentist or hospital. From the horse kick on, speaking was difficult, so the few words he spoke became grunts.

Fearful the amount of blood spread across the forest was too visible, Dorangel found himself a new forest, but his food no longer excited him as it once did. He imagined eating animals he'd never eaten before. These new thoughts made him feverish with anticipation. His wish list contained two animals he'd never eaten, or seen, two animals he simply *had* to consume. Dorangel found a poster on his travels advertising a travelling circus. On that poster was a picture of an elephant. He placed the picture neatly in the pocket that didn't contain a dead mouse. The elephant on the poster became like a girlfriend to him. He stared longingly at the picture for hours. He became obsessed with the elephant.

To him, the elephant was the most beautiful animal he'd ever seen. He had to eat one.

He dreamt about elephants. One night he dreamt the elephant's trunk was in his bottom and in his dream he liked it. He woke up from dreaming so angry, he tore the poster up. He hated the elephant for two days afterwards. When he calmed down he was sorry. He recovered what he could of the poster. A single piece the wind had not yet taken: the image of the elephant's trunk.

The circus came to town. Dorangel went to the circus, missing teeth and dislocated jaw in tow. He packed a knife and fork. He was a little misinformed.

Dorangel had never seen an actual photograph of an elephant. He'd never seen a documentary about elephants. The first picture he'd ever seen was on the side of an Indian beer, and the only other picture he'd seen was the picture on the poster he'd stolen. In Dorangel's mind these pictures represented the actual size of an elephant. He thought an elephant was just bigger than a mouse, a delicacy to cut in half and gulp down in two swallows. His misunderstanding of size and perspective often made him look silly. He once spent an entire night trying to eat the moon like it was an apple dangling in front of him on a string, because he'd heard it was made of cheese.

Dorangel walked to the circus with a knife and fork in his pocket and a small plate, with the full intention of eating the elephant he'd been obsessing about and fallen in love with. An hour later he was standing in front of the elephant cage, staring up at one of the biggest land animals on earth.

He stood in front of the cage and cried. He cried because he'd obsessed over the elephant. He'd loved the elephant but knew he could never eat the elephant. She was too large.

Perhaps, he thought, *she's large but made of jelly and so she'll be soft, light and easy to eat.*

Hopeful, he stabbed his plastic knife into the elephant.

The elephant did not move. The plastic knife snapped in two.

Security took a long time to realise the freak standing outside the elephant cage and crying over a broken plastic knife was not part of the circus. Dorangel was escorted away from the elephants and out of the circus. They let him keep his broken cutlery.

That night he ate as many of the animals in the forest as he could, not easy with a broken jaw, and then he ate some more. He blubbered like a baby as he stared at his tatty picture of an elephant trunk. When he had no more tears left to cry, he folded his picture of the elephant trunk and put it away in his blood-soaked pocket.

He knew he would never look at the picture again, not in the same way.

He rolled over to his side, surrounded by beaks and noses. He closed his eyes and slept soundly.

In the morning his focused changed completely, and the elephant, which he knew he could never eat, no longer interested him at all. His mind raged with a desperate desire to consume and eat the second animal on his list. His thoughts became obsessive. He would rather die if life meant not ending the life of the one creature he loved. He took from the same pocket he kept his dead mouse in his list titled *Things To Eat Before I Die*. He crossed a line through the first name.

He knew exactly what his entire life had been building up to.

He had a new reason to live.

He stared at his new, updated list.

As he read the words, saliva dribbled out of his broken face, and smudged the letters like tears on a page.

~~Elera~~

Afrikan Gray Parrot ✓ ☺

Day Five

Butterfly Wings Calm Heartstrings

My eyelids open. The morning chill punches through my eyeballs down into my body, pulling me back out through my sockets by my smaller intestine.

If you think of your eyelashes as sun rays and your pupil as the sun, every time you close your eyes the sun sets, and when you open them it rises.

The sun blinds my eyes and reminds me of the darkness last night.

I cringe at being naked in the park.

Being hit by a boy.

Knocking myself out with a tree.

People who think they aren't blinded by light are just as blind as those who live in the dark.

I place my hand underneath my woolly hat. My bump has eased. I feel a scratch like a paper cut. Having a paper cut after running into a tree makes some sort of sense. Perhaps the mark is not from the tree, but from the punch the boy landed on my head. I hadn't seen a ring, but it's possible he was wearing one.

Fingers dripping with gold, head full of lead.

I need to find a new place to hide my bags, as I can't risk leaving them in the wood.

I'm tucked up in my sleeping bag, but like every morning,

the desire for a lie-in is washed away by the fear of being seen having one. Because of my shower last night, I don't feel dirty, but the itching underneath my skin won't go away.

I reach into the bag nearest me and pull out my toothpaste and water. I clean my teeth on the floor while still in my sleeping bag. I brush up and down, white froth circles my mouth. I'm a worm with rabies losing his mind to the disease. Once I've finished scrubbing my teeth I take a gulp of water and swish it around my mouth. I then spit it out to one side, into the grass.

The grass bubbles like I've poured acid onto skin.

I stand out of my sleeping bag. My gloveless hands scream at me to cover them with anything, shouting I'd be dangerous if I only had a brain.

Like the scarecrow from *The Wizard of Oz*.

Only he wasn't homeless.

I roll up my sleeping bag and stuff it into my large bag. I look across the park.

This hole has no ladder to climb back out from.

I put on another jumper, then my coat. I walk with my bags along the black fence underneath Roald Dahl. I head away from the main park entrance. The black fence leads me down a short hill.

At the bottom of the hill Jeffrey Archer the bush is to my left. I continue walking right.

There's no path now, just grass. I walk around a corner and hit a dead end. A row of large black railings stop people getting in at night, or leaving the park too late. They strike me as odd. The front of the park has no gates. Beyond the black railings is a road, and on the other side of the road are large houses.

This area is a clearing to nowhere, a cul-de-sac of hope.

One bush sits in the middle of the area, a dead end around it from all sides, apart from the way I came in.

No pretty plants to look at, no reason really to be here.

The perfect place to leave my bags.

I drop my bags into the overgrown centre of the bush. I cover them with my coat and place branches over them. I need my coat to cover my bags: the price is the cold I feel in my bones.

I walk back up to the hill, hands light with the freedom of empty handedness. I take the path to the toilets. I reach the clearing at the top of the path. The duck pond and abandoned house loom over me, making me feel like an unwanted baby left on the steps of a monastery.

A silver mist covers the grass and trees, like fireflies over a thick stagnant pond.

Billions of tiny particles fall and rise. The fireflies dance the line of sanity over the wet green surface, creating a mist, making the morning wind visible.

The dark figures, engulfed by the morning mist, stand at different points on the grass. The dark figures look in different directions, like lost minds inside a mental facility.

I don't move. I don't want to startle them. All three dark shapes turn and face me at the same time. My heart beats too fast in my chest. I can feel cold sweat growing through the pores on my forehead.

The park keeper will be along soon.

The dark creatures must live in the derelict house. I've disturbed their morning ritual.

The dark creature in the middle of the mist is wearing a hood. I can't see his face. The dark creatures begin walking toward me. These creatures are too close to my bags, too close to Roald Dahl, too close to where I live.

The tallest creature steps briefly into the morning light. I catch a glimpse of a pale hand. This is the creature I saw last night: the monster who wants to slice my throat. His fingers are knives. His nails are instruments to take life away with.

I should run.

The pale-faced creature sways.

A figure blowing in the wind, with all the answers, according to Dylan.

There's nobody around.

I'm outnumbered.

The smaller dark creatures move into the sun. I recognise their faces: Inbin and Worzel. They look terrible. The time the world has not cared about them, has meant they don't have a care in the world. Dark souls, with darker pasts. Worzel points in my direction, with hands full of gummidge and eyes without love. Inbin raises an unsteady hand too. He waves at me, and smiles, showing me black teeth and yellow gums.

Cold air fills my warm lungs and melts inside me. Steam leaves my face.

I can't even say goodbye to my friends.

Inbin groans. Worzel shouts something, but I can't make out the language. The massive creature behind them removes its hood. I feel like I'm going to pass out. I want to cry.

They say we either fight or run, but that isn't true.

We freeze. The unexpected stops us dead in our tracks.

I am a rabbit in a world full of headlights. I am a little boy picking up a blue ball in the middle of oncoming traffic, the closing of eyes in the moment before goodbye.

A loud squawk from a bird of unusual size brings me back to life. My fingers move. I pick up the blue ball and run.

I don't know if they are following me. I don't know anything.

I run down the path toward the toilet. I burst over grass and gravel. I explode past trees. In the background, I can hear cars driving along the road. Normal people driving their normal cars to the places they normally go. And I'm here, running away from the mentally unstable.

I enter the toilet. I close the door behind me. I fumble at the lock. My chest burns. Sweat drips from me. I stink again. I dry heave. My stomach tries to bring up food, but there's nothing inside me. Maybe hunger is messing with my mind. I feel like

I've run a marathon. I hold the lock. I slide the bolt across. I'm either safe, or I've just trapped myself. I rest my forehead on the inside of the toilet door for a moment. I imagine a summer day and butterflies playing.

Butterfly wings calm heartstrings.

I detach my forehead from the inside of the door and turn around.

The toilet is completely dark. The light doesn't work. I sit on the toilet seat, in the dark, with the door locked. I stare at the back of the toilet door, hoping nobody tries to come in, like always. My heart beats so fast I wonder if I'm going to implode.

I imagine the homeless walking the path to the toilet, blood-covered axes scraping along concrete behind them.

I wait. No rush to leave. Soon the sun will warm the ground, and people will begin crossing the park on their way to work. I should be safer then. I'll stay here for half an hour. When people enter the park, the homeless men will disappear back into the mist they walked out from. And the pale-faced creature will return to the shadows.

On the upside, if I need to go to the toilet, I'm already here.

Positivity and perspective: the glass is half full and I know where it is.

The toilet door is hit from the other side with such force, the door shakes and the lock rattles.

My glass falls to the floor, and everything inside it that was, becomes no more.

I stay silent. Even though it's clear they know where I am.

The door is hit again, possibly kicked. The entire door moves. The lock rattles harder than before. I get up and push the door away from me with both of my hands. Anything to hold my ground.

"Is somebody in there?"

The voice of a woman: I relax. She is not the pale creature.

Maybe she has a phone. Maybe she can help me. I'm going to be okay.

I unlock the door. My fear fades to ashes after the flames.

I open the door. My eyes meet the wild glance of a woman in her seventies. She's lived through some shit, and it boils her skin. She wears small circular glasses. She has messy, long, grey hair and the kind of face cats find to die on. Her nose is the only part of her face not affected by years of being sad, and sits on her face like a party popper, forever waiting for something to celebrate. She appears a wick short of a candle. She spends her days on her front porch rocking back and forth in her wedding dress waiting for her husband to return from war, sixty years after receiving a letter from the government declaring him officially dead. Her veins are thick. She has custard for blood. Her body is yellow and lumpy.

She holds a dog lead.

"Have you seen Flump?"

The old woman is visibly distressed. I realise that there is something inherently creepy about an old lady looking for a lost dog. My mind tells me there is no dog. I step forwards to comfort her. The toilet door opens behind me. As I step forwards the old woman steps backwards.

The old lady puts a trembling hand over her mouth. I'm a monster coming out of a cupboard. To the old lady, after five days of living in a park, I have become a creature. For all I know, I could look pretty pale.

I hear the lawnmower that isn't a lawnmower rumbling close. The park keeper is beginning his morning rounds.

The woman lowers her trembling hand.

Her mouth opens but no scream comes out. She drops to her knees. I wish she would close her mouth, but she doesn't. Grey hair falls over her old yellow face. She gawps. Her thick veins bulge in her hands and arms. She might be dying, for all I know. I can't see any teeth in her face: an old lady with a rotten mouth full of gums.

The vehicle that isn't a lawnmower sounds like it's coming closer.

The old lady dropping to her knees at the sight of me, suggests I am now seen as a homeless person.

I want to comfort the old lady. I want to tell her I can help, but she's so distraught if I take another step toward her she's going to explode, covering me in custard like some out of control future Japanese television show. There's nothing I can do. I walk around her, and out of the exit. I walk down the path, and along the black fence. I follow the black fence until I'm away from the toilets, the duck pond and the abandoned house.

The park keeper will be with the old woman in a moment. He'll help find her dog.

I feel my beard. It's pretty long, about ten days' growth. My clothes are dirty. I am bald, but the hair on the side of my head has become longer and appears scraggy. I've become a second glance. The people we take an instinctive second glance at we avoid, once we've processed the reasons for the instinctive double-take. Whereas bland featureless faces we can know for years, without ever properly looking into them.

I hope the old lady recovers and finds Flump.

Worzel is close to Roald Dahl. He's standing on the other side of the black fence, in open space, and his bags are at his feet.

Are they looking for me? Are they looking for my bags? Am I being hunted?

He's standing straight, tall and thin. From here I can see his suit is ripped. White foam bleeds from his shoulders. His hair is dark, long and matted. His beard is older than he is. His eyes are in his head, but his thoughts are his vision. He spins around squealing the word *buttercups*. Normally a man *squealing buttercups* would be funny, but this morning everything is a little sinister at the edges, and a little dark in the middle.

When not a safe distance from the peculiar, it's harder to see the funny side over the sinister. Lots of clowns in a field might amuse, but being stuck in a broken lift with one would be terrifying.

I'm at the cosmetic point where my fellow homeless believe I'm too normal to be trusted, but to everyday ordinary folk I look like I live in a bin. I'm neither here nor there, as to be with the homeless I need to drink Super Kestrel, and to get on with common folk I need to shave and wash.

I am Colossus Sosloss Abstemious, a clean bum: a rather unnatural state.

I walk down the hill, find some grass and lie down.

I dream about robots telling me what love is.

The sun is now out. The old woman no longer screams.

I walk back to Roald Dahl and sit.

Lots of wandering around, lots of not knowing where to be.

Lots of walking from point A to point B, then back to point A.

Lots of drumming my fingers on the top of my brain.

Lots of not knowing what to do, now I have the freedom to do anything.

Wars are fought over freedom, people die in its name. But dogs wear collars, and their tails never stop wagging.

A man with dumpty legs and humpty arms rolls, oval shaped, underneath Roald Dahl and over the ground where I usually sleep. His two dogs follow him. Either the dogs' legs are comically too short or their bellies scrape along the ground because they're too fat. The dogs waddle and toddle behind their egg-shaped master, old tumble dryers rocking back and forth on broken drums. The longer the dawdler and the fat dilly-dallying dogs diddle-daddle across my bedroom floor, the greater the chance of them deciding to eject a brown pickle in my bedroom. Dog number two squats his back legs, and with an expressionless face, expresses a brown pickle over the exact spot I've been resting my head on for the last few nights.

The owner has kept walking. He has no idea what's happening.

The dog looks up at me, tongue lolling to one side, as happy as Larry.

As proud as punch.

He circles his own poo, sniffs it, and then looks up at me.

He smiles. The dog winks at me, then runs off down the hill. *What a bastard.*

I observe the massive, curling shit in the middle of my bedroom. I have plastic bags but they're hidden away with all of my stuff, so I can't get to them now without risking being seen. I'll have to remove the giant turd later tonight, when it's dark and hardest to do.

The heat from the burning sun prickles my skin, causing warmth to spread over the surface of the body I'm in. People all over the planet must be running for cover and shade, drinking water, fearing the midday sun. Not in England, where we sit out with dogs who meow and wear saucepans for hats. I sit for hours in the sun. My beard grows silently, my skin slowly turns brown: living dangerously.

I watch couples enjoying the sun. I feel alone, the only pop-up book in a respectable library.

Work isn't classified as being out with people, but it is. On the silent tubes in the morning there's a sense of belonging. Everyone might be a stranger, but we all go the same way, strangers together. I'm in no group. I'm not at work. I have no common sense of belonging. No words are spoken, like on the tube, but the silence here is not communal. There's no togetherness here in my silence. This silence is personal and restrictive.

We are born alone and die alone, together. So we are separate and we are one.

I walk to the toilets, it's around 4pm. I walk up by the black fence, to the duck pond and past the abandoned house. There's a guy standing outside the entrance. The gate to the toilet is locked. This is the first time I've seen the toilet locked during the day. The guy talks. He's feverish with the power that comes with knowledge, like only a person can be when they think they know something they're certain everybody else does not.

"Did you hear what *happened*?"

The man is tall and dressed in a suit: gelled hair, long features. He's young but has told too many lies. The ghosts in his past haunt his eyes and cast shadows on the skin beneath. Dark rings, smooth approach. He sells for a living, but the one thing he can't sell is he to him. He has a long nose, long fingers and drooping sad eyes. The fingers of a chess champion. The eyes of a chess champion's wife. Relationships land on him to die. He places his right hand on my shoulder. He extends the long fingers of his left hand and points as he talks. A witch teaching a class of young princesses the health benefits of eating apples. His eyes don't hold still: they dart around and avoid mine, two prisoners avoiding the searchlight escaping prison at night.

"The *police* just left. An old lady lost her dog. Some homeless guy snapped her dog's neck, cut the dog up and nailed its head to the back wall of the toilet. This guy comes out of this toilet, covered in dog blood, and she looks behind him and sees her dog's head. Her dog's head, can you believe *that*? What sicko would do that? Some foreigner probably!"

He's Fox News, *on a good day.*

I don't know what to say, or my first words in days would be now. The man tells me the police told him not to tell anyone else, but they told him they had to show up because of the hysterical woman. He tells me it was a waste of their time, a job for the RSPCA, not for the thin blue line.

I nod my head.

He says he knows: *same shit different day.*

I think given enough different days, shit changes.

The man laughs and squeezes me on the shoulder, the

presenter on a game show. I've just lost the holiday of a lifetime. He winks, like the dog from earlier, and trots away.

The man's turd might be metaphorical, but in his own way, he's just dumped on my day.

I don't like him. I don't like his story.

The part about the guy leaving the toilet and attacking the woman is an exaggeration. I was the guy who left the toilet. When I took a step toward her, she screamed. Was a dog head nailed to the back of the toilet door?

Between the darkness of the toilet and my distracted state it's possible, but it's more possible the young man was exaggerating. I thought the old woman screamed because of my beard and unruly dress, but it *may* have been because of something else.

Perhaps she was looking behind me and not at me.

If the story is true, the police have my description and think I killed a dog.

The sun will set soon. The last place I want to be seen is the toilets. I need to get out of the park, and I need food, so I head to the shops.

A Mini Shopping Experience In A Faraway Sainsbury's Local

The shops are the place adults with kids get to give other adults with kids the look that says: "What have we done?"

I walk by the tills and down the aisles. The eyes of everyone follow me. Everyone expects me to steal something, or at the very least head straight for the alcohol section. I can hear the thoughts of strangers screaming look at him. Even the kindest eyes judge me for my weakness. The eyes of the people reflect the thoughts their minds whisper to them: he is pathetic. We all have troubles in life. He just completely folded beneath them. I hope he doesn't have children. I bet he does have children, but he never sees them because he's too afraid to be a parent. Look at him, alcohol has a lot to answer for, so does addiction, but that prick has indulged himself at the expense of anybody who ever dared to love him. There is no love from any of the eyes. No compassion. This is what happens when you return to society as a bit of an outsider. The pack turns. I've made my decision, all bridges burned. Nobody makes eye contact. All looks are sent from the corner of eyes. Nobody wants to confront their own fear; nobody wants to lend a hand or an ear.

The security guard follows me. The security guard is tall and has beady, bug-like eyes. He wears the same round glasses The Beatles wore. He has potted skin and oily hair: a teenage dream in a nightmare setting. I don't like the security guard, not because he follows me: I'm a tramp, with a long beard, my clothes are dingy and I'm wearing a coat that smells of wet dog. I don't like him because he looks so bloody miserable doing it. He looks like he hates his life. This Sainsbury's only has one aisle the staff at the tills can't see, so his job is securing one aisle. A narrow aisle. Not even the aisle people would steal from. The aisle with the alcohol can be seen by all the staff. The aisle he guards contains tins of beans, the gluten free section, sardines, hair removal cream and tampons.

His expression says he knows he could guard more than one aisle, but he's accepted he never will.

In Field of Dreams, to live his dream, Kevin Costner built a field when he already lived in a field. Building a roller coaster out of cat brains would have been a greater test of his desire to live his dream.

Sainsbury's has peppercorn steak slices for one pound and bananas are eighteen pence. I don't like the slices, they make me feel sick afterwards, but the man inside me can't say no to the combined words meat and pie. I pick up a packet of sliced apples, six bananas, the pie and a cheese and spring onion sandwich. The depressing security guard follows me down his one aisle, and breathes dead lifeless air over me. I'm at the self-service till. The security guard watches me feed each food item through the machine. Out of the corner of my eye I watch him watch me.

I'm about to blow out the candles on my birthday cake, but before I breathe in he blows them out. He punches me in the face, grabs the cake and runs out of the front door cackling like an evil goblin sent from hell to turn good memories bad.

I feed the last pie through the machine. The till bleeps, and tells me there's an unexpected item in my bagging area. But I look at my bagging area, and I can't see an inflatable parrot or baby from Indonesia playing the piano. My heart beats faster. The security guard looms nearer. A shadow falls over my day. I rescan my pie. The robotic noise silences. The security guard looms away. The shadow leaves my face. I hurriedly feed coins into the machine. I leave the shop. The grey leaks out of my ears, seeps off my arm and floats back over to him.

I'm not judging the security guard, but do what makes you happy, not what makes you sad.

Smile sometimes: it won't add years to your life, but it will add life to your years.

I walk along carrying my bag like a dead deer, listening to the coins jangling. They mock me with each step I take, but because of the coins I just spent, they mock me a little less.

I have a green tea in the café to try and look normal, for a moment. I have a peculiar awareness that normal is a lie. I attempt chatting with the staff. The girl with short blonde hair serves me. She knew me a week ago. From the radio behind her, an eighties' love song plays. The song is familiar but I can't place it.

We used to talk and smile seven days ago when I was wearing a suit. Now I'm dressed in a beard and smell of dog shit I don't even get eye contact. I ask her how her week is going, and she looks to her friend behind the counter as if to say: I think this creep is hitting on me. Shall we call the police?

I realise the great sadness of this life: all the people we see in our working life, every single one of them, from the people who serve us our tea and coffee to the people we sit next to, none of them are awake. This girl has never spoken to me: I've only ever been another customer to put through the till. I feel like an idiot. I was going to ask her out.

There is nothing more deceptive, more grandeur, than the delusion of a single man.

The End Of The Mini Story About How People Treated Me Outside Of The Park

Back in the park I walk by Stephen King, the big tree I spent my first night under. A man is urinating against him.

I walk up the path to the black fence, and follow it along to the comfort and protection of Roald Dahl.

Something is different about my favourite tree. Before I left to get food his branches fell all the way to the ground, giving me privacy and a feeling of safety. That feeling may well have been an illusion, but it felt real.

One of the park keepers, I suspect the midget who hates me, has cut his branches shorter. They no longer fall to the ground. The protective leaves have gone. A gaping hole remains. I walk down to Jeffrey Archer. His lower branches are gone too.

I'm concerned.

I have an image of the park keeper taking the police to where I sleep and cutting down branches. I can see him taking away my favourite places in the world, foaming at the mouth as he does, barking about how *he's sure this will flush me out.*

A message perhaps: an act intended to make me feel uncomfortable.

Time to move on, son. No you haven't committed a crime, but

the likes of you make people uncomfortable, so you can't stay here.
Don't make this harder than it has to be, just walk under the carpet,
I'm holding it up for you, so you can no longer be seen.

I feel a sense of injustice. Aggressive action has been taken against me without conversation.

The sun has gone. The day is getting too dark for me to find another place to sleep.

I will have to stay under Roald Dahl tonight, far more exposed than usual.

I retrieve my bags from the bush at the bottom of the hill. They're untouched. At least the park keeper doesn't know where I'm hiding my bags.

Friday dusk becomes Friday evening. The park is feverish with life. A young Asian man screams into his mobile phone, not stopping to listen: a young man with his heart in his penis.

I clean my teeth. I'm battered back into my sleeping bag by the cold. I get in my sleeping bag and look out. Without the leaves stopping people from clearly seeing in, I can clearly see out. My view is expansive. I'm on top of a hill, and can see the city of London spread out in front of me. Unfortunately, the entire city can also see me. I turn on my phone to check my messages, almost no battery. The light from the screen beams brightly in the dark.

A call to the wild.

A homing beacon to a dog killer.

A silent flare.

If someone is prepared to kill a dog, they're dangerous.

My battery dies, no more phone. I'm alone in the dark. Alone in the world.

Music plays, young people shout. I say music, it sounds like pirates forcing children from the world of classical music to run barefoot across a dark field full of hedgehogs and broken glass. Behind me is the abandoned house.

The abandoned house concerns me more.

Two shadows walk toward me. The shadows see me, change direction and walk down the hill. Teenagers looking for a place to grow older together faster than they should, desperate to become adults, because the only thing they know is being a teenager is no good. They will eventually learn they wasted the good bit.

I'm caught between the abandoned house and the party at the bottom of the hill. I fear any moment I will be held down by drunken youths, beaten and set on fire for their amusement.

I tuck my sleeping bag around my head. I bring my big bag up to my side so I feel protected.

Shouting comes from the abandoned house. A glass smashes at the bottom of the hill.

I try to fall asleep. I listen to the sounds of the abandoned house.

I hear cracks and snaps from ambiguous shoes. A scream curdles the night. Screaming foxes either in the process of having, or trying to mate: or a woman attacked.

I anticipate the next scream will be a cry for help.

Before we are born and after we die there is black, perhaps the same black: and so from all death comes life, and from all life, comes death.

There are no more screams.

The ducks are silent. They don't beg for bread at night.

Day Six

Beautiful: be you to the full

I walk up colourful stairs singing a song about chocolate. At the top of the stairs I look around. I see Oompa Loompas. I'm Willy Wonka.

I look down. Beneath me, in my chocolate sauce river, is an unexpected guest. Standing naked, waist high in chocolate is a woman, and not a woman of the usual Oompa Loompa stature: a beautiful woman, Brobdingnagian in size when compared to an Oompa Loompa. Dark hair bobs above her shoulders. She has a tanned complexion, a subtle undefined Japanese look. She speaks the language but in the wrong accent. She looks confident, like only a woman could look waist high in a chocolate lake. She blinks cocoa flakes. Many years ago she was taken advantage of financially, and lost lots of money on a sandwich venture in the Far East.

Her past is not relevant: she is here, in my chocolate river, and she is perfect.

Her neck is long and slender, and her body is toned.

If Cleopatra ran a sandwich business, in a language she didn't understand, and lived in a chocolate river, this would be her. I stare at this woman and don't look away.

She holds my look.

The phonetic message in the word beautiful: be you to the full.

I dismount the colourful sugar-coated stairs.

I'm next to her. I place my arms around her slender waist.

"I want to be with you every day. I want to love you every day from this one."

"That's so eighties."

I have no idea what she means by telling me my concept of love is from the eighties, but I don't want our first conversation to be a disagreement, so I tell her I was born in the eighties. She tells me she's thirty-one and wants children. I wonder if this is a test, but don't care. I tell her she should have them with me. She blinks, chocolate flake eyelashes tumble over ice cream skies. Her face is the cherry on the cake of her skin. She tells me, with no doubt in her words, she wants to live in Derry.

I'm not sure what she means, but I tell her I'll live anywhere with her.

She tells me she hopes her chocolate river is transferable. I tell her not to worry, we'll hire a van.

We dance slowly, waist high in chocolate.

Oompa Loompas come from behind sweets, cookies and chocolate pennies. They surround the chocolate pathway above. They swarm over the chocolate hill. They sing the Oompa Loompa song, with the lyrics altered:

"Oompa Loompa Oompa de doo, Colossus Sosloss is moving to Derry the second biggest city in Northern Ireland and he is procreating a mini Colossus called Floccinaucinihilipilification."

I have no idea why I would call my first born such a ridiculous name, and then my love speaks, whispering into my ear. She tells me that Floccinaucinihilipilification is the name she wants our first child to have. I say the name is terribly long. She tells me it means short, small and little. She tells me it's destiny. The name balances the meaning of mine. I see a world of complicated form filling, telephone calls to people in call centres taking hours, a boy at school asking his teacher for another pencil because he's run out of lead before he's finished writing his name. Thinking fast, my world suddenly all apples and unsteady carts, I ask if we could possibly call our baby Flocci, for short. Her eyes turn from snowmen to boiling puddles. She shakes her head. She tells me Flocci means a small tuft of woolly hairs. She asks how we could put a child through life as a small tuft of hair. I tell her okay, our first child will be called Floccinaucinihilipilification, which means small, and we won't shorten it. I'm ignoring the thought in the back of my head that this beautiful woman is too demanding to be beautiful. If I have to prove my love to her for the rest of my life, either she doesn't love me, or there was never much love inside her in the first place.

I lighten the mood by whispering into my new love's perfect ear.

I tell her I know the owner of the chocolate factory. I'm being cocky because the owner is me.

I tell her I can get her a job away from the factory floor. I tell her I'll move her into one of the offices, where she might be more comfortable. She laughs and tilts her head back. As her mouth opens I notice her dental hygiene is an area of concern, a consequence of working in a chocolate factory with no dental insurance. The Oompa Loompas sing she's going to eat me, and there's nothing I can do.

Her hands are behind my head. Her leg is in the air. We tango.

She brings her head forward. I see rows of black teeth. They are shaped like points, shaped for meat.

She sinks her black teeth deep into my cheek. She bites down hard and pulls back with the strength of a shark. She rips away my entire cheek.

Half of my face is gone.

Blood covers her mouth and teeth. Her eyes turn from green to white. My cheek hangs from between her teeth. She moves her face closer to mine. Her white pupils reflect the moment children find out about dying.

She holds the back of my neck. My face is an inch from hers.

She opens her mouth. She leans back, and swallows my cheek in one gulp.

I watch the more attractive half of my face swallowed by my future wife. She blows the breath of part of my own head back up my nose.

She opens her mouth and sticks her tongue out so I can see that she's swallowed. Her hands move from the back of my neck to the front. Her fingers are powerful. She could crush the bones in my neck by applying effortless pressure. I'm an egg in the grip of a vice. My blood flows from my neck, over her claws, and drops into the chocolate river. The emergency contamination light above the river swirls and beeps. My once-perfect chocolate river now contaminated. She lifts me off the ground. We might need counselling after this.

Her voice is dead and hollow: the last dodo shouting into an empty cave for friends.

The reading out of enemy names on a war memorial:

"*Turn around bright eyes.*"

Her face cocks to the right. Her nails dig further into my throat. My feet dangle in the air. I'm a child trying to reach the top shelf in the kitchen for Mum's biscuits.

"*Love is like a shadow on me all of the time.*"

Her words make a curtain fall over the window of my soul. I can't feel anything. I can't think.

The sun darkens in the sky.

And everything fades to white.

This is the cycle of life. I have a sense of dying and being reborn. I am aware there is only ever life and creation. Nothing has an end, not how we think of endings.

I wake up in my sleeping bag. I'm still in the park.

I remember my dream. The song I heard playing in the café yesterday was *Total Eclipse of the Heart*.

There's an early morning mist, but the sun has already started its shift, having spent the night setting fire to other parts of the planet. I have no idea what my dream could mean: one day I'm going to have a child with a ridiculous name with a beautiful woman I love who will want me to live in Derry, where she'll eat me alive to the sounds of Bonnie Tyler.

Turn around bright eyes: the last words before I woke up might have been my subconscious warning me about the police, the angry midget park keeper or even the old lady looking for her Flump. They might all be trying to find me.

Dreaming of being eaten by the perfect woman is mentally disturbing, but the good news is I've made it through the night without being physically assaulted.

I brush my teeth. I rinse and spit, not with water, but with mouthwash. My teeth have never been cleaner.

I hide my bags in the same bush as yesterday. In the part of the park tucked away in the corner.

I head to the toilets. The sun is high and the day hot. I follow the black fence under Roald Dahl to the path and walk up to the duck pond.

The creature is studying something on the ground. A hood covers its head. The beast is all in black. It must be eight feet tall. I can see its hands. They look human, only its fingers are claws. Sharp nails, never cut, curl away from its finger tips like swords. The monster has ghosts for skin: it's a black cloud on a sunny day. All of the bad things rolled up into a ball, and kicked into the face of humanity. Its clothing is thick and heavy, too warm to wear under this sun, a suit of armour in a tanning salon.

I step slowly toward the toilets. As soon as I take my first step, it looks up. It sees me.

The creature sways slowly to the left, and back to the right. Its large hood covers its face, which I'm glad about. I don't want to see its face ever again: the image of yesterday will never leave my mind.

I look forward. I don't look back. I move quickly.

The toilet is open, thankfully. I enter and lock the door behind me. I check each wall for dog heads. There are none. The toilet is remarkably clean, unrecognisable from yesterday.

Monsters do exist.

The toilet's been scrubbed but the cosmetics fail to hide the dark truth, like lipstick on Myra Hindley. The taps are polished, but the only water that leaves the faucet is boiling. The walls have been painted, but the smell of piss remains. I sit until my heart rate slows. I cautiously open the toilet door and step outside. I walk into a large white leg. I take a step back. I study the white horse. The homeless creature sits on top. It raises its hand. It spreads its fingers as wide as possible and leans toward me. The creature swipes across the space in front of my face. I think it has missed. Then I realise blood is pouring from my neck. The creature has sliced my throat with his long knives for finger nails. He swipes at the space in front of my face again. I'm swirling around in a circle. I see the creature. I see the ground. I see the horse. I see my body, which has fallen against the horse, covering the animal in red with the explosion of blood from my open neck. I see the toilet. I land in the toilet bowl. The creature has dismembered me. From here, I can only see the ceiling of the toilet. I notice now, that whoever renovated the toilet forgot to fix the ceiling. The panels are still loose and the tree still crawls across the surface.

The water from the tap burns my skin, bringing me back from my imagination and into the world of the living. I undo the lock. I open the door about an inch. I peek through the gap in the door.

No white horse.

No monster with knives for fingers.

I open the door. I step outside. No creature in black.

I walk back along the path and across the duck pond. My throat starts to close. My Adam's apple is too big for my throat. I reach the area where the creature was standing earlier. The dark shape has disappeared. My throat expands.

I sit under Roald Dahl. I wonder if I'm being paranoid. I tell myself I'm not, and then ask myself how I can be so sure. I don't know the answer, so I go back to wondering if I am.

I want to talk to my imaginary friend to get some advice, but the last time we spoke he accused me of talking to him like he wasn't there.

A creepy silence follows the creature. The creature has pulled the world's tongue out. No sound, nothing emanates from it. Sound vibrations hit it and crumble.

I feel alone, isolated.

Not speaking for six days means I've forgotten how to communicate. I've been spoken at once or twice, but never *to*. All because of how I look. Not once has someone engaged me by holding eye contact, indicating they want a response. The guy by the toilets yesterday was nervous. His eyes darted like burning flies because he didn't want to make eye contact with a homeless guy. Perhaps he thought he could be talking to the guy who killed the dog, which would explain his departure before I could speak.

I notice a single red ant on me. Then I notice millions of them. Ants don't travel alone.

Small in size, no egos.

Millions of red ants devour me. They carry my body parts separately into their holes.

I walk over to the large tree on the opposite side of the park. This tree is far away from the duck pond, abandoned house and pale creature. The faraway tree won't hide me at night, but the base of the tree is soft and comfortable. I sit at the tree's base.

I'll sit here for the rest of the day, until sunset: a moment of calm during an out of control acid flashback. This is a beautiful tree, no leaf out of place. The trunk is so dark it looks varnished.

The Faraway Tree is an Enid Blyton book I read when I was very young. I don't remember much about it, but I remember it was my favourite book at the time. I call the tree Enid Blyton.

I lean back on Enid's trunk. The faraway tree is now extremely close, and Roald Dahl is the tree far away.

The sun is so hot lizards wear tin foil hats to reflect the heat. The crows want the tin foil hats for their shiny collections, but are too hot to do anything about their wants.

I could load a shotgun with another world filled with glaciers, fire that into my brain and live there for ever.

Naming the trees I like after writers is a subconscious coping mechanism for being lonely, an attempt to create the illusion of company and friends.

But all it's doing is reaffirming I'm alone.

I look out from Enid Blyton. An old oriental man moves his hands, with grace and strength, from one side to his other. I'm not certain what martial arts he's performing, perhaps Kung Fu.

I'm in awe at seeing this ancient practice so closely, and not through a TV screen.

I swap the beginning letters of each word around and get Fung Ku, an oriental man saying thank you.

I ask the man if he can teach me how to fight the creature with the ghost for a face and knives for hands. He tells me, face beyond ironing, to varnish the tree, clip the tree, wash his car, do his shopping and tidy his house. I fight the creature with the pale face, it eats my leg. I hop away crying, like an emotional pogo stick. The old oriental man laughs, tells me I never had a chance, he just wanted help with his shopping.

I'm imagining talking to people, imagining a life, as it happens around me and to others.

I am sitting on grass in a park but I mentally never left the office. The tree is my office chair. The park has become my window to stare out from: my best life is still playing out in my head.

My eyes leave the old oriental man. I look at two women. From their accents they are Polish. They are both wearing bikinis. My thoughts begin to turn, against my will. I kick a ball over to them. The ball hits the first girl in the nose, bounces off *her* nose straight into her friend's, breaking both their faces: from nice oil paintings, classically drawn, to Picassos on the lawn.

They don't give the ball back.

Psychologically I've lost all arrogance. From my new position of social bottom feeder there's no woman I'm not finding alluring. I'm aware it's entirely safe to think these thoughts, because no woman will reciprocate the glance of a tramp. And if a woman did, I would have to look away, because she would have to be mental.

I drift into sleep under Enid Blyton. I float on a raft down a river of what-the-fuck-have-I-done and once-the-rope-is-wet-the-raft-will-split-and-I-won't-survive-the-life-beneath. The oars are my memories, the murky river where I've been. My raft floats to the riverbank. As I'm securing my raft to a tree I look up in time to see the butt of a long rifle thump into my face.

I fall asleep in my dream and wake up in reality.

A single blob of rain runs down my face.

Smears of clean: traces beneath of who I could have been.

Another blob lands on my hand. A dark cloud looms ominously, the head scientist in charge of building the first atomic bomb on a final cigarette break. The few drops of rain coupled with the grey sky are enough to make the two girls and old oriental man leave. Lightning flashes across the sky. The sky buckles in pain. A wind howls across the park and whips around Enid Blyton. Bright yellow leaves blow onto my grey jumper. A rumble in the distance belches across the sky like God is suffering from wheat intolerance.

None of us are free. There's nothing to fight for, no war to believe in, no guns need firing in the name of freedom. We are born in a body, and dying from the moment we first breathe in.

Life is a prison, and we're all in prison together.

And that's beautiful. That's our freedom.

We forget, too easily, how easily led we are.

There's always a storm happening somewhere.

I watch two older Indian men wander with a blue bag containing four beers. Respectable family guys dressed in jeans and bland tops. Their hair is still in the side partings their mums sent them to school with. Both are married and local to the park. Maybe they are neighbours. I watch them sneak along like window cleaners on a rainy day, obsolete together. Both men are grabbing a moment away from their families, a moment they can just be men, like it was before domestication. I'm alone, aside from the two Indian men wrestling back a notch from their lives, but they don't know I'm here, and if they did, they would step away as I stepped closer.

I notice a clock by my elbow.

In this park, a clock on the floor is an indication of a fat mental patient up a tree. I look up. The obese man in a ginger wig from two days ago is up in the tree asleep. Now he's asleep, I'm less intimidated, and get a good look at his face. He is probably in his fifties. His fat, strawberry nose is still flat and his skin alarmingly red. A lobster in a tree, scaring birds into thinking the end of days is here. He has no facial hair, which is a shame because a beard would cover his cratered skin. His wig is lopsided, and underneath it I can see what looks like another wig. And underneath that wig, he appears to be wearing a swimming cap, but it could just be his bald, pale scalp. His shoes and socks are on the ground. His t-shirt is brown and heavily stained. His trousers are red and baggy and tied on with rope. His face looks like a moon.

He is Moonface in the faraway tree.

He is so heavy it must have taken him hours to get into the tree, and the climb would have been dangerous: a thirsty Tyrannosaurus Rex on ice in roller-skates trying to carve ice sculptures of fairies using a chainsaw.

Remembering how precious the clock is from our last encounter, I don't touch it.

Moonface opens both of his eyes. His look gobbles up my spine and soul. I can't seem to walk away. He has the controls.

"TRAINS!"

Two days ago this word seemed misplaced and didn't affect me, an oily duck down a seal's back, but after recent events with the horrifying pale creature with the knives for hands and this morning's dream about being eaten alive by the love of my life, hearing Moonface shout *trains* is bloody terrifying. His voice is deep but has a gargling sound to it, like his tongue is on backwards in his mouth. He's a child blurting out his first words. His palette holds no colour. His paintbrush is just a stick he repeatedly jabs into his own eye. He looks, and sounds four forks short of five forks.

He reaches out toward me like a fat monster from a low budget horror story.

"TRAAIIINNSSS!"

He hisses like a snake trapped inside a steam room. Moonface is all of the animals, cages, staff, location, customer base and marketing drive short of a zoo. To attempt dialogue is pointless.

Moonface could be the lookout for the pale creature with the knives for hands. I imagine the creature creeping up behind me, his fingers waggling, the knives flowing behind my back. This could be all part of some grand plan to eat my brains for lunch.

I turn around sharply, bright eyed. No one is there.

I look back up at Moonface. He giggles. He puts four of his fingers down his throat and attempts to regurgitate. I've seen enough. I step away from Enid Blyton, and I keep walking.

I walk back to the black fence and up to Roald Dahl. I leave the faraway tree faraway from me. I have a feeling that somewhere between the pale creature and Moonface, a messy fate is closing in on me.

Moonface is still screaming for trains.

A knife will slip through my sleeping bag tonight and into my stomach. A hand will clasp over my mouth. The word 'trains' will be the last word I hear.

I try and ignore the image of my brains being eaten by a tumult of terrible tramps, a shocked look on my face: the top of my head open, Moonface and the pale creature fighting over who gets to eat my superior colliculus.

Thunder cracks into lightning flashes. Rain falls. A man walks his dogs hurriedly toward me, trying to get them onto the ark before the end of humanity.

These six days have been long enough for me to reflect, in silence, on the language I choose to project. I would like my first conversation in six days to be full of noble words, or phrases reflecting truth and honesty. I want my first conversation to represent the first step to becoming a better person.

I'm resetting a computer to delete a virus.

The man turns. He approaches. He speaks with a wonderfully educated voice which smacks of colour and vigour. His voice tastes like dark oaks, red berries, a hint of spice and a smattering of southern France.

"Forgive me for the intrusion, but it's not a terribly good idea to sit under a tree, on top of a hill, in the middle of a lightning storm."

I want to tell the man not to be so *terribly* dull and to join me under the tree to test our joint fortunes on this wonderful day, but before I can gather my thoughts, I'm already talking.

My voice is too eager to be heard. My brain is too tired to get in the way.

I tell him, and I actually use the word terribly, what a terribly good point he's raised. I thank him kindly for his advice. The man waits for me to move.

I move. I don't want to. I'm just being *terribly* polite.

I pick up my bags and walk away from Roald Dahl. I walk along the black fence.

The man finally continues walking in the direction he was heading. I don't want the man to walk back and find me under the tree I told him I agreed it was a good idea to leave, so I wait in the heavy rain for ten minutes.

I stand in the rain, picking up the soggy pieces from my first complete attempt at communication in six days. It utterly betrayed my actual thoughts. I even mimicked his voice and style of speech, as well as agreeing with him when I didn't. I reset my computer with the best intentions of removing the virus, but instead I've doused it with petrol, set it alight, taken the whole thing and dropped it from the top of a high-rise.

I walk back up the hill to Roald Dahl. Three Indian men sit in my usual spot, two men from earlier and a new friend. I'm tempted to warn them about the dangers of sitting under a tree in a lightning storm, but they would probably just laugh at me. I move as near to Roald Dahl as I can. I get soaked by the rain. I sit on wet grass and listen to the three men talking and drinking beer.

"So how do you do it? Once a week, every week, you two meet up for a beer and you don't get into any trouble for it. Come on now, they must be getting suspicious, isn't it so?"

"The first time I go shopping at the beginning of the month I buy the whole month's food."

"Which he stores in my garage, so it is."

"Yes, which I store in Badal's garage. But my wife, she thinks I go every Saturday to do our shopping."

"And she does not suspect? She says nothing of this, is it?"

The man laughs.

"No, she suspects and it makes her completely mad. She tells me it would be a lot easier if I took the car one Saturday at the beginning of the month, and shopped for the whole month in one go, and then stored the shopping in Badal's garage. That way, she says, the kids could see more of me."

The men laugh, because they know the reason they're all meeting in a park, is to avoid their children. I move to get my bags while the park is empty. I look for somewhere dry to stand, but find nowhere. The storm eases. The men move. I move back under Roald Dahl. I use my towel to dry my skin. My body shivers. I'm a drowned rat with a human for a face. I snuggle into my sleeping bag and think of a warmer place. I wait for sleep to take me away.

A police car drives slowly through the park. I wonder if they're looking for someone matching my description on suspicion of murdering a dog.

My eyes are heavy.

The police car drives slowly back along the same path but in the opposite direction. They're looking for someone. They have an old lady holding a dog collar, and a midget pressed against the wet glass inside the police car, looking out for a bearded dog killer.

I close my eyes as the light fades. I wonder if I'll be woken from my sleep by the police handcuffing me, or Moonface's fat hand over my mouth muffling my screams.

Day Seven

The First Twitch Of Professor Merrydinkle

I wake up and rise with the falling temperature.

My body has shaken me awake. The cold morning air burns my hands.

I have to get up before a person sees me, because it's easier to ignore who I'm becoming, if nobody sees who I am. My eyes are my alarm clock. The threat of detection is more powerful than any coffee, or desire to arrive at work when expected. The expectation of overwhelming shame, is unbearable.

Last night, frustrated at being in the same clothes, and tired of my skin, I took off my clothes and slept naked. I wasn't too cold, and being separated from my clothes made me feel cleaner. Now, I'm freezing. Another idea good at the time, eroded over night.

I stand naked, with my lower half still in the sleeping bag. The cold morning air demoralises my expectations of the day. I bring a hand over my eyes and it's 1865. The village elder Don Xung has ordered my disembowelment, and there's no time to make a papier mâché replica of my own digestive system.

I scramble for clothes. My movement is hindered by my lower half in the sleeping bag. I'm a snail crawling through a hole smaller than its shell.

How does a snail know it's not a slug if it can't look over its shoulder?

I hop nearer my clothes. I pick up my t-shirt. I need both of my hands to put it on. I let go of my sleeping bag. The bag falls down by my ankles. I'm in freezing temperatures, naked in a public park again. I put my t-shirt over my head. I grab my boxer shorts, put my socks on and jeans. I move fast. I hop up on one foot, then the other. I'm no longer naked publicly. I look around, fully clothed, nobody is walking, nobody is looking: nobody knows.

I pack up my sleeping bag. I hide my bags under the same bush as yesterday and the day before.

My first stop is the toilets, better to use them when there's no chance of crossing paths with a child or a parent. I follow the black fence along past Roald Dahl and up to the duck pond. The early morning mist, present on the last couple of mornings, spreads itself menacingly across the grass, like black paint spilling over a child's painting of rainbows. My morning eyes adjust. I have no idea what I'm looking at. I'm standing on the path, the toilets and abandoned house are to my left. The duck pond is to my right. At first I think it's a large bag. I wait, not wanting to make a sound, caution naturally guiding me after my recent experiences. My heart beats faster, my hands sweat, I'm acutely aware of how cold I am.

Fear.

My father punched in the stomach by a fourteen-year-old child.

My father hunched over, clutching his stomach.

The creature is hunched over, *Its* back is to me. The tall dark monster is crouching in the mist. *It* is dressed all in black, *Its* life a funeral. My throat narrows. My Adam's apple expands. I'm locked in a cupboard. The world is now very small. There's just me and 'It' throughout all time and space. I lose control of my breathing. My body is not mine to control.

I hold my throat and close my eyes. I feel weak. The colour drains from my skin.

Think of winning, think of strength.

Thoughts tumble back into my frozen brain.

Move fast, move quietly, never come back.

Move before It turns around, bright eyes.

I hear the rumbling of the park keeper, on his vehicle that isn't a lawnmower. I turn my head in his direction. His beautiful big head appears in my sights. I breathe. I'm pleased to see him, pleased to see anyone. I stare at him. I wait to give him a nod so he can see my fear. I wait for him to notice the dark shape, but he's sitting up high on his machine and wearing ear protectors.

The park keeper stares ahead with the serious expression of a man thinking serious thoughts in a serious fashion. He doesn't want to engage me or the other homeless man.

I'm completely alone.

The park keeper is paid to drive around in his weird car and that's what he's going to do. He wouldn't get extra money for stopping and asking what's going on between a homeless man and a monster, so he isn't going to. He drives by the abandoned house. He turns left, out of sight, leaving me behind: a bad soldier. I'm left with a deflated feeling of being expendable. I'm a spare part for a machine that no longer needs me.

My eyes fall back to the creature. *It's* no longer hunched. The giant black shape stands, and glares straight into my soul through eyes like black holes. The monster removes *Its* black hood. I tried to block out the face I saw the other day. I didn't even write it down, in the hope that by not writing it down, the memory would change. *It* is closer now than before. The early sun splashes over *Its* face. This is the type of horror that stays in the memory and never fades.

My stomach expands and spins.

It is pale, *It* already looks dead. *It* is bald, and *Its* face is mangled.

Something is in *Its* mouth.

Its lips are fat. They sit in the middle of a haggard face, like two slugs kept alive by salt dripping from the tongue.

Something is in *Its* mouth.

The creature has a massive nose. *Its* beady eyes sit too high on his head. *It* has no ears. *Its* face doesn't droop or sag. *Its* cheeks aren't flabby like the face of Moonface. *Its* cheeks are taught: *Its* skin is tight. This is a massive creature, but *It* is not fat. *Its* jaw appears to hang off to one side. *Its* head is swollen. Two large lumps, like moons, rise up from *Its* temples. They look like small horns. *It* looks like *Its* head was dropped from a great height and shattered on impact, and was then stuck back together using old tape. A scar runs from between *Its* dark eyes, all the way down *Its* nose, over *Its* lips, over *Its* chin and down *Its* throat: like at some point *Its* entire skull has been split with an axe, right down the middle.

Something is in *Its* mouth.

It has never laughed.

Laughter fears the creature.

It is a skinny snowman built by blind children, and once built, *It* ate the children who made *It*, leaving the blood of the blind all over *Its* face.

Crazy eyes.

The creature turns back to what *It* was doing, nonchalant to my presence, a manager walking off with the receptionist's pen.

I gather my senses. I pick my hands up with my teeth, my hearing and eyes follow. Lastly I grab my sense of smell and taste from the branches near to me.

I shuffle nervously back down the path, a person with agoraphobia forced out of their house because of a fire. I collapse underneath Roald Dahl exhausted. My adrenaline rush fades. I shake.

I don't like this park. I don't like this experience. I'm intimidated, scared and cold. I smell like wet grass, my fingernails are dirty, my beard itches and I don't think I wiped my bum properly the last time I took a poo in the haunted toilet from hell.

The creature had something in *Its* mouth.

I'm sure he had something in his mouth. There's only one way to know. I have to go back. I can't spend forever running away.

Twenty minutes later, I tentatively return to the duck pond. I walk along the black fence to the path. I walk up to the duck pond. There's nobody there. The dark figure has gone. I stand in the same spot where the giant creature crouched. There is blood on the grass. A lot of blood. The creature dragged a body to this very spot. Or killed something here not long ago. A couple of ducks wander close to me. Out of a desperate need to talk, I blurt out my first words this morning:

"Good morning, Mr and Mrs Duck! Did you see what just happened? Blood everywhere. Look at it all over the ground! Blood! Real blood too! There's been a killing."

It feels good to talk, even to ducks.

"What's wrong with you?"

Surprise pushes a noise from my throat I've never made before. A desperate, feminine shrill. I'm a choirboy who knows he's soon to be hurled, flaming, from a broken roller coaster into a queue of ordinary, decent church folk waiting patiently for candy floss.

"I said, what's wrong with you?"

The angry park keeper would like nothing more than to run me over in his vehicle.

"I'm fine, not my blood thanks."

My response angers the little man further. He wobbles in his seat. He removes his seatbelt and climbs out of the chair.

The vehicle is quite high. I wait patiently as he struggles down from the height. Even though I suspect he's getting down

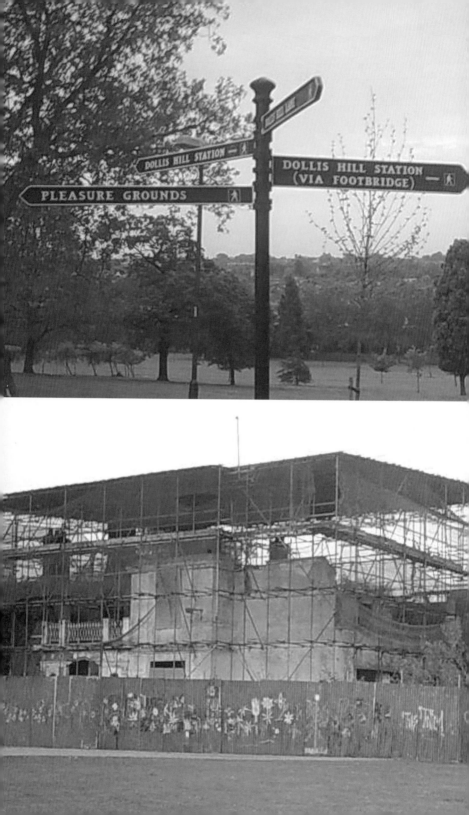

from his machine to hit me, I bow to social graces. I take a step forward and take his elbow. I offer to help him down. He shrugs my hand away from his arm. He turns, and jumps the rest of the way to the ground. He lands heavy, for a small man. I know it hurts him, because it's the equivalent of me jumping from a tree. He says nothing, but doesn't look up. He doesn't want me to see his pain.

I don't say anything. I wait. My fingers tap my upper leg.

He stands and brushes grass from his knees. He looks skywards. He shakes his head, as if he can't believe the life he's living, as if the grass stains are the final straw in his day, the cherry bomb on the anger cake.

"I mean what THE HELL is wrong with you?"

His face is an angry scribble, drawn by a teenager in a hurry.

I thought he was checking if I'm okay, but he's questioning my mental health.

Where confessions end, emotions begin. I decide to be open with him.

"This has nothing to do with me, I just saw the blood and…"

"Shut up. I'm done with you. You hear? You talk to your sleeping bag. You're up here talking all crazy stuff about blood to a couple of ducks. Man, I tell you… "

He's ranting. He is shaking with fury. He should be holding a pitchfork.

We're getting on like expectation and opportunity, which is to say, we aren't getting on at all.

"Before you turned up nothing EVER HAPPENED! I'm sick of picking up dead *fucking* animals."

He takes a step toward me. I think he's going to head butt me in the stomach, with his massive head. I close my eyes. Nothing happens, so I open them just in time to see him waddle by me in my peripheral vision. He grabs a dead squirrel impaled on the black railings. He pulls out a plastic bag and lifts the squirrel. Blood and a long blue stringy thing fall from the impaled bum of the squirrel. There's a noticeable chunk missing from the squirrel's stomach. Someone, or something, has taken a bite out of it.

I cover my mouth and turn. I'm going to be sick. The act of impalement doesn't bother me as much as the mouth on the squirrel.

The thing is smiling.

The park keeper returns to me. My hands are on my knees. I'm staring at the floor, trying not to throw up. He whispers into my ear:

"You're up here jabbering nonsense at two ducks boasting about what you've done. The police told me to keep an eye on you and I am. You hear me, you homeless fuck. This is a nice park, a nice family park. I know you killed that dog, and ate the face of this squirrel."

He waves the dead squirrel in front of my face. Half of the squirrel's head has been eaten. The squirrels right cheek, eyeball and forehead are all missing. There are bite marks all over its being. The squirrel's left eyeball is open, and bloodshot. The squirrel's chest is open: its heart is missing. And the grin, the little unfortunate animal is having the time of its life!

I can't hold it. I throw up. I throw up all over his ridiculously shiny shoes. He waddles three or four steps backwards. He puts the dead squirrel in his plastic bag. I'm not sure the memory will be so easy to dispose of. With my right hand over my mouth, I bring my left hand up and wave it in his direction, indicating he should stand back. I'm about to throw up again.

He looks surprised, then angry. He drops his bag and charges at me headfirst.

He smashes his giant midget head into my face, at the exact moment I throw up again.

I throw up over his head, and swallow one of my teeth in the process. The park keeper jumps back. He screams. He moves one of his stubby arms across his giant forehead. He smears white sick across his face. This isn't going to improve our relationship.

Vomit: The V is for the Victory of what you omit.

"GET OUT OF HERE! If I find ONE MORE DEAD ANIMAL I'M CALLING THE POLICE but not before I find you with some of my friends and BEAT THE FUCKING SHIT OUT OF YOU!"

This situation has spiralled rapidly out of my control. I don't argue. I run back down the hill. There's no denying from the park keeper's perspective all the evidence is so alarmingly and hilariously against me, I'm fortunate not to be arrested. He saw me this morning by the pond but didn't see the creature. He saw me standing next to a dead squirrel, and heard me talk to my sleeping bag and to the ducks. And he has a report matching my description from an old lady who thinks I'm the person who killed her dog.

I put my hand to my mouth. There's blood. My front tooth is in my empty stomach, and what was in my stomach is now on a midget's face, and it's not even 10am.

I sit under Roald Dahl. I think about the pale creature in the dark hood.

The creature looks like Death. Maybe it is. The creature is here, and things are dying.

I lick the gap in my teeth. I worry about Death taking up residence in the same park as me, and the angry midget who thinks I'm committing its crimes. I don't want to call the pale creature Death. If I call it Death, I'll be too afraid to do anything. Every waking second will be spent trying to not have a panic attack.

I decide to call the creature Squirrel.

It has eaten a squirrel this morning, so the name is fitting, but not as psychologically petrifying. My brain prefers to imagine a bushy menace, rather than the bringer of the end to all mankind.

The last words of the midget park keeper were clear: if he

finds one more dead animal in the park I'm going to get arrested. And beaten up. This seems a likely scenario, considering this morning Squirrel has killed a squirrel, and two days ago he killed a dog. From the park keeper's reaction I'm certain Squirrel killed an animal yesterday too. The park is likely littered with dead animals, or living animals soon to be dead. My choices are either beat up and stop an eight-foot monster called Squirrel, or get beaten up by a five-foot park keeper with short-man syndrome.

Both options are completely shit.

This is what happens to passive people, their passiveness makes them a donkey, and everyone else sticks their tales of woe to them. We live in a society where if you aren't *seen* doing good, people think you must be bad. By doing nothing I've become the victim of other people's issues. The park is an incubator, harvesting the deranged nobody else wants to deal with, or the law can't arrest. Because these people never talk, loneliness and isolation has enhanced their bizarreness. These people are behaving unlike anyone else, because they have no one to copy.

In Gladstone Park the crazy have been allowed to express themselves.

Moonface wants to hurt me. He thinks I'm trying to steal his clock. The park keeper thinks I'm eating his animals, and there's a monster we should all, as a group, be concerned about, but I'm the only one who has seen him. And nobody is going to believe me, because I live in a park, so I must be crazy.

Two ducks waddle near me. I have become a duck magnet. Maybe they can smell dough in the wind around me. These ducks sound unhealthy. They wheeze as they waddle, their bodies have become too fat for their brains. They are also a good ten minutes from the duck pond. They've left the pond, certain beyond their perfectly groomed pond is a bigger, better pond than their parents and other ducks could ever imagine.

They've packed little satchels of bread, which they carry on the end of small sturdy sticks.

They're going to find the promised pond, then call for the rest.

But it hasn't worked out that way for these two ducks. Instead, they're too far away from their pond to know how to get back, and for all intents and purposes, for all their utopian ideas, they've found a homeless bloke with a beard.

I see a lot more of myself in these two ducks.

I consider showing them back to their pond, but with Squirrel killing anything he wants to eat, the ducks are no safer there.

I could *walk out of the park and never come back.*

I have nowhere to go. I've not only burnt my bridges I've gone back into the ashes with a shredder and hand fed each ash through, one at a time. This is my life now. A single cloud briefly covers the sun.

What kind of creature eats a squirrel when fat ducks are waddling around clutching asthma pumps?

Animals in the park must regularly die from natural causes. If I can be wrongly accused by the judgement of the park keeper, then I too could be wrongly accusing Squirrel. I try to consider an alternative scenario.

A Quick Alternative Explanation For The Missing Heart Of The Dead Squirrel From Earlier

The small fluffy squirrel was sitting in a tree, minding her own business, uploading a tweet:

Clive bought me new lipstick but I've put it on and it's not my colour. Bloody Clive! He never gets me what I want, but what he wants to see me in. Men!

As the lady squirrel hit the *tweet* button a blood clot, arriving late because it missed the earlier vessel, entered her heart. She slumped over her laptop. She fell from her tree, splitting herself in half on the railings below. Confirmed dead by impalement by the animal doctor, they found paperwork in her pocket stating it was her wish to be a heart donor to squirrels less fortunate than herself. So in keeping with her wishes, her heart was removed.

The laptop fell into the pond, never to be discovered.

An hour after her heart was removed, Squirrel, a monster with a keen interest in nature, found the dead animal and tried to save it by replacing the missing heart with its monstrous own face. After that failed, the charming and helpful monster attempted experimental last ditch revival of brain activity by eating half of the little animal's face. And it was at this point I stumbled onto the scene.

The End Of The Mini Explanation

I have to consider it possible Squirrel found the animal already dead from natural causes, and then decided to eat it because the creature hadn't eaten for a few days. Homeless monsters must have narrow options. Plus, the park keeper was so angry it's easy to believe he got the wrong end of the stick about events. He is all emotion, and no logic. I can't take his account as fact. He has a stubborn, bumbling, tired presumptuousness about him like an old beach donkey who wants to sleep, but keeps getting woken because children keep pulling his ears. This haggard, impatient manner is conflicted by the pride the park keeper displays in his work. He's the person who is the easiest to read. I know what he's thinking, because he isn't.

If we all did not think, would we all not think the same?

I sit and watch the world go by from underneath Roald Dahl.

Two retired couples, with tennis racquets, walk toward the

courts. Two girls sit where two girls only ever sit, on the hill opposite me. In the distance I see the faraway tree.

A small child scoots behind his parents on his scooter.

Everything is normal.

Pleasantly normal.

I open my record bag and pull out a couple of plastic bags from Sainsbury's: the food, from my visit to the shops a couple of days ago.

I pop half a cheese and onion sandwich in my mouth.

I stop chewing. I had forgotten about the fat dog with the large belly. Next to my right foot, no more than an inch or two from my little toe, seven inches high, is the large brown pickle the dog left me. I place the rest of my sandwich back into my Sainsbury's bag of food, and tie it up. I stare at the poo. Never a moment's rest. In my former life as a receptionist I used to deal with other people's shit for little pay. Now I deal with other people's dog shit for free.

I'm thankful I haven't rolled over the dog excretion in the night. I have to either pick up the dog poo or leave my favourite tree.

I grab the spare Sainsbury's bag. I place it over the poo, using the bag as a glove.

I retch as I tie a knot in the bag. I set it down and look for the nearest bin.

I find the nearest bin, drop the bag inside and walk back to my stuff.

My appetite has diminished. I leave my food and take my usual position in the sun.

The sun doesn't take long to cover my body and infect my mind with thoughts of kissing a woman. At some point I'm going to need physical tramp relief. If I was still working in an office, needing tramp relief would be the type of fantasy I could never tell anyone about, because it would involve cruising parks at night offering cash to the homeless in exchange for depraved acts. This is not that, this is the natural need to submit to the clock of nature. My location is highly unnatural, so I suspect nothing about this is going to be straightforward. If I'm remaining true to the dictionary definition of my current life situation, I actually need bum relief, but that sounds like something different. I guess other tramps, or bums, are so drunk and depressed they think little of relieving themselves sexually, or maybe it's because they do think of these things, but can do nothing about them, that they remain drunk.

The specifics of how I pull off my bum relief are a mystery. There's no Idiot's Guide to Masturbating in Public. Part of me wants it to remain a mystery. Another part, the part most men allegedly think with, most certainly wants the mystery resolved at the earliest possible convenience.

Not in the daytime. At night I'm less likely to be caught.

Late, late, late at night, but where? In my sleeping bag feels like a crime against myself.

I can't do anything now. I lay back and try to imagine something very unattractive, in an attempt to distract my mind from girls.

Unattractive Scenario: Full of Hair and Men

Two very hairy men sit in a small steam room in Finland. They are old men, retired. Their back hair is their chest hair, which is their feet hair. It's impossible to say where the hair begins, as it covers them both entirely, but it's easy to say where it stops; on their bald heads. One of the men has a giant wart in the middle of his forehead. The other arches his hairy bottom off the steam-room bench and farts.

Both men laugh.

These two men are slow developers. They still collect newts from dirty ponds.

"Almaark, put more coal on the fire. My hairy bum is not sweaty enough. My haemorrhoids itch."

Jonarm's voice is high, shrill and oppositional to his fat stature, like a fire alarm on an igloo.

"Jonarm, if you want more coal, put more coal. My bottom is so sweaty, one wrong step and I'll slide off the bench and into your wart."

Almaark's voice is deep and cumbersome, but on occasion his sentences stand on their tippy toes and dance just before the full stop. A ballerina bear, shot in the leg.

"Jonarm, you fat beast."

"Do we not both have weight and hair issues, and in my case a giant wart, and in yours haemorrhoids? Are we both not dimpled and pimpled? Does our skin not fall and dangle from us like the base of a homemade pizza being made fresh by an Italian chef? Do our stretch marks not share equal length? Do our breasts not reach our belly buttons?"

The steam is thick now.

They are just voices in a room.

"Jonarm, I should say… "

"No, Almaark, let me."

There's a pause. For thirty seconds the only sound is the sound of coal burning and rising steam.

Both men speak at once. They both speak the same words.

"You have lovely eyes."

Jonarm silently moves his hand along the wooden bench toward Almaark. Almaark, always the shy one, lifts his fingers in the air about an inch off the bench, ever so slightly. Jonarm moves his fingers through the steam. His fingers touch the tips of Almaark's fingers.

LE END

I open my eyes in the park. I can't even trust my own imagination. Thinking about hairy men in a steam room tells me one thing: bum relief time, tonight, before I imagine something I can never unsee.

The sun is slowly setting and the air is starting to chill. The nights are getting colder. I already need my coat, but I can't get my bags safely from their hiding place until the park keeper finishes his shift, which is about 8pm. I prepare myself for a rather unpleasant few hours of pacing back and forth, and shivering in the cold. Apart from briefly being head-butted by the park keeper, and being stared at by Squirrel, it's been another day without human interaction. The sun drops further and it's now bitterly cold. I walk to get my bags early, but as I near the bush I realise I can't get them because kids are playing late in the tennis courts. I'm only wearing a t-shirt. The wind picks up. I am stressed. I hate being cold. The freezing wind grips my arms and slaps my face.

I leave my food and my small bag under Roald Dahl. I go and wait in the toilet, where I will at least be a bit more protected from the elements.

The park keeper closes the toilet at 8pm. My guess is 8pm is only an hour away: nobody is going to be using the toilet now.

I enter the toilet and take a seat. I close the door behind me. I have immediate shelter on all four sides from the wind. This is a definite step in the right direction.

When being in a toilet is a step in the right direction, it may be time to rethink your life.

I only have to wait here for half an hour then the kids will be gone, and I can get my bags. I look around, checking for dead animals. There are none. I look at the sink. I look at the walls and the branches breaking in through the ceiling. I'm bored. My eyes fall on the lock.

The toilet has a lock.

Professor Merrydinkle twitches.

The park is practically closed and it's freezing outside. And I have time to kill. Killing two birds with one stone makes perfect sense to me.

There's even toilet roll.

I can't wait for after, when the thoughts of sex have left my brain through my penis.

This needs to be quick. This is not for pleasure. This is a quick, functional process I might not even enjoy. I pull tissue from the rack. I turn so I'm facing the back wall of the toilet. I close my eyes.

I imagine a woman.

I tug Professor Merrydinkle.

In my imagination the woman gets on her knees. I look down at the top of her head.

This is good.

She has thick black hair. Her face is long. Her tongue laps out of her mouth and all the way over her head. Drool falls from her mouth, and she slobbers all over my trousers.

The woman looks up. She isn't a woman. She's a dog.

Not just any dog: the dead dog that was murdered.

My hand doesn't stop moving. I stare at the dog. The dog has no body. I'm receiving a blowjob from a dismembered dog head. Clumps of muscle and spine drip from its neck. Blood and flesh drop to the floor.

I try and pull the Professor out of the dog's mouth. There isn't enough time.

Professor Merrydinkle spits into the tissue.

I open my eyes. I look down at the tissue. I should have used more. I feel guilty and need to wash my hands.

I feel dirty.

The mind can flicker anywhere, if only for a second. I should never have relieved myself in the same toilet where the dog was supposed to have died in gruesome fashion. I want to start again, right away, so Professor Merrydinkle's future lessons won't be on a sliding scale of ever-increasing weirdness. If I don't jump back on the horse immediately this could be the type of experience which affects my chances of marrying in later life, or my future relationship with dogs. I wait for a feeling of peace, but it doesn't happen. Instead, I get an awkward feeling of not being alone.

I turn around. The toilet door is open.

The park keeper is staring at me. The keys to the toilet are in his hand.

Awkward.

I don't speak. The park keeper can think of nothing to say.

I put the Professor back in my trousers. I clear my throat. This situation is probably more for me to explain, than for him to approach.

"I forgot to lock the... "

"You've just ejaculated up the same wall you nailed a dog's head to!"

I think about explaining that I *actually* ejaculated into a tissue, because I'm not an animal, but this is not a situation for me to try and gain any advancement in moral high ground.

"I promith you won't see me again."

I sound like all the writers of *Sesame Street* trying to fit in a New York cab: part air, part spit and whistle. My missing tooth has given me an unpredictable lisp. The park keeper gives me both barrels.

"I just want to go home! Get out of here and GO AWAY! The only reason I'm not calling the police is because it will waste my time tonight, and you'll be let out in a few hours with a caution and be back in the park tomorrow. BUT tomorrow, first thing, I'm going to call the police to ask their advice on what to do, and one day I'll be walking up to you with a police officer, and when I do, you won't ever be coming back to MY PARK. Now FUCK OFF!"

I don't argue. I leave the toilet. I scuttle down the path and into the darkness. The people playing tennis have gone. I grab my bags and move to set up for the night under Roald Dahl.

I'm in my sleeping bag. The park is pitch black.

I'm in my sleeping bag and angry at myself. I cringe at what I've been caught doing. I'm not too worried about my mind wandering onto the dead dog. I hadn't considered the dog, facing that wall, I guess the possibility was always there, but getting caught means I now look like some animal-murdering sex pest. My missing tooth makes me sound, and look, like a family of clowns tucking a whoopee cushion into a turkey at Christmas.

I'm stressed about the morning, the possibility of being arrested, and my missing tooth.

I feel my brain walking to the kitchen and pouring itself a strong coffee, because it knows I'm going to keep it up all night being stressed, worried and angry.

I put my hand in my Sainsbury's bag to grab the remainder of my sandwich and pie for dinner. As my hand grips the pie, I stop. My face contorts.

My hand is gripped firmly around the edges of a massive dog shit.

I scream out loud. Even my scream annoys me, because with my missing tooth my scream sounds like a tug of war between bagpipes and a legion of broken dog toys.

I am the biggest idiot in the world!

Earlier I threw the Sainsbury's bag with my food into the bin, and left the Sainsbury's bag with the dog poo in with my stuff. I can't see my hands, but I can smell them. Being careful not to touch anything, I get out of my sleeping bag and stand up in the freezing cold. Instead of eating the second half of my cheese and onion pie and falling asleep, I have to get out of my sleeping bag, walk to the bin, dispose of a massive dog turd, and then take a freezing cold naked fucking shower in the middle of the park.

I stand. I'm close to tears with frustration. I cry.

I can't help myself.

I'm so stressed. The park has gone crazy. I'm hated by people who don't even know my name. I can't handle it. I can't handle knowing I have to take a shower in freezing temperatures. I can't handle the thought of washing.

I can't see the point of anything.

My mind is as dark as the night. My hands are covered in shit. ACTUAL SHIT!

I can't even wipe my tears from my own face, because if I do, my face would be covered in dog shit. I bury my head into my sleeping bag and scream. I move my head back. I breathe in. I place my head back in my bag. I scream again.

And again.

And again.

Fuck this world.

Those born into privilege get an unassailable head start. Nobody cares.

I quieten. My chest heaves. I grit my teeth. I do what I have to do.

I stand out of my sleeping bag. The cold wraps itself around me. An anaconda made from ice. The wind whistles. I can hear laughing. Am I losing my mind? Did I enter the park because of the reasons I think I did? To prove the universe is our friend, that we don't need the system to be happy, or did I enter this place because I'm fucked in the head? I don't know.

I'm naming trees and bushes after famous authors, wandering around a park talking to ducks. I'm fucked in the head. I'm probably fucked in the head.

I scream into my sleeping bag. This time I scream until I have nothing left in my lungs.

Even my air is borrowed. I don't even own the air in my lungs.

I rub my face against my sleeping bag, hoping to dry my tears, but I catch some of my beard hairs in the zip. As I pull my head away they rip from my skin, causing me pain. The pain sharpens me, for a second, before making everything else seem like a blur. The blur is better, and for a second I contemplate hurting myself again. I stand, careful not to use my shit-covered hand. I take the bag with the poo to the bin. I wash my hands, but I still feel dirty.

I have my tramp shower: cold water, naked skin, shivering, more screaming – but inside now – more tears, but these ones fall silently. I'm standing naked, crouching in a bush, hoping nobody sees my willy. I can't blame anybody for this but myself. This frustrates me even more. Washing is my most vulnerable moment, like taking a girlfriend home to meet your parents for the first time when your parents are animal rights activists, and your girlfriend is a Japanese fishing trawler with a dead dolphin caught up in the nets of her face.

I finish washing. I dry myself. I do something that isn't me, something I can't explain.

I walk away from the bush. I walk away from my protection. I drop my towel. I stand naked in the middle of the park. I raise my hands above my head. I still feel the cold, but for now, I simply don't care about it.

I feel alive.

I scream. I scream into the night. I howl back at the wind.

I laugh. I spin around in a circle. I stare up into space completely naked. Perhaps this is freedom. Perhaps the only freedom there is, is letting go of yourself. I cry. I'm crying and I don't know why. And still I spin, a naked, bearded homeless man missing a tooth, crying, spinning in circles, because this is what the system wants, isn't it?

Anybody who leaves the system is crazy. Anybody who quits the system to live in a park is crazy.

That's what everyone says.

That's what everybody thinks.
Fuck you all.
Fuck everything.

Day Eight

Little Big Head and Coloththuth Thothlothth

The girl runs playfully away from me. I chase her. I grab her gently. I pull her down to the ground. We tumble and laugh and kiss. I'm laughing. The sun is on my eyes, on my back and arms. I laugh. I laugh and I'm so happy. This is the happiest I've ever been.

I wake up in my sleeping bag. Early, 6am. The morning is bitterly cold. Everything is a little too white. I close my eyes. I try and fight the voice telling me not again, *not this again*.

The one good thing I can remember, and it was a dream.

I need to get back inside my head and get control of the wheel. Even my subconscious is trying to fuck me over. If something good doesn't happen soon, I'm going to break. If I'm ever going to get over what happened yesterday in the toilet with the dead dog head then it might as well be now.

I need to feel good. I need to feel something. I move my hand up and down in my sleeping bag. I'll move Professor Merrydinkle out of my bag at the appropriate moment.

Don't think about dog heads.

I have half a mind thinking I'm going to get caught, another half scanning the park for any early morning walkers, another half trying not to think of dead dogs, and another half questioning why I'm so bad at maths.

My old maths teacher was a bearded man who looked like Papa Smurf.

Behind avoiding dead dogs and bearded maths teachers are weak sexual images. They struggle to make an impression. Seeing these images is a frustrating impossibility, like trying to eat a pig through a straw. I continue moving my hand. I feel a surge of shame.

The school bell rings. Professor Merrydinkle ends his lesson. It's over.

This is not a moment of serenity.

I am not certain if I ejaculated to the image of my old maths teacher, a dismembered dog head, a woman, or all three. The thought I might have ejaculated to a female maths teacher with a bearded bespectacled dead dog for a head is a concern.

I feel guilty and paranoid. I'm certain I've not helped my problem.

I move my towel over to wipe the grass. I roll onto my back.

Why won't any good feelings come?

Sitting in the branches of Roald Dahl above me, is Moonface. He's staring down at me, a sloppy, proud grin across his red, fat face. A man who's memorised a treasure map then eaten it. And then followed the map to the treasure, and eaten that too. In his hands is his very own professor. From the look of it, his professor teaches at a much larger school. Dead dogs, male maths teachers and disabled people up trees: I will never touch myself again.

Events spiral out of control.

That's what they do, the winding up of anything takes ages, but when something starts to spin, it can be undone in no time at all.

Life moves faster than memories, otherwise we would look back on tomorrow.

Moonface shouts at me with the anger of the gods. His face is furious. His voice is a loud booming screech: televisions in cement mixers, nails running over chalkboards, large ships sinking from the surface of oceans, creaking and breaking under pressure, the dying men inside yelling as pressure pops their veins and turns their faces red.

I want him to shut up. I want to stop him drawing attention to us.

"WHERE'S MY COCK?"

He wants everyone in the park to see him playing with himself up a tree. He's like some hairless monkey on heat.

I hear the rumble of the park keeper's vehicle that isn't a lawnmower.

This is how my day is beginning after yesterday.

After last night. After my brain snapped and I lost my mind.

I'm going to get arrested.

He shouts again. His eyes bulge like the tips of rising moons over sand dunes. He continues saying *cock* until all his breath has gone. There's a moment of silence I mentally cling onto.

The wrong kind of help in a bad situation: an armband in a hurricane.

A man overboard in a bulletproof vest.

CPR equipment for terminal cancer.

I move fast. I start to pack away my stuff, but I have no time. The vehicle that isn't a lawnmower pulls up alongside Roald Dahl.

Thankfully, it's not the usual midget park keeper driving. I have some small hope this may not lead to my assault and arrest. The park keeper dismounts from the odd vehicle to the sound of Moonface screaming for directions to his man chicken.

This park keeper is roughly my height, and he has a kind face. He is bald, with slightly longer hair at the sides of his head, giving him a sort of almost monk-like quality. He is unshaven. He has a few lines on his forehead, so I think he might be a thinker. He has an open face, which to me says he understands ideas and situations first time around. He's never had to squeeze his face into someone else's idea, leaving him with a pinched face like he's forever chewing a lemon. He has blue eyes, which seem open to the ideas of others. He looks a bit like me, only cleaner, and in long-term employment. He gives me a look, a look which recognises we look a bit similar: we have entered the unspoken bald-hairy-man union. His face is almost wet, and his features are a little bit droopy. His eyes sag, his flat nose hangs over his chin. There is a sort of sadness to his look, like at any point he could be picked up, and he is powerless to stop being the toy of life. He is sweating, but looks comfortable with it, like sweating is something he never stops doing.

Intelligent people are often thought of as looking intelligent, but if you *really* look at them, they actually look ridiculous. Faces shut in doors from taking life too seriously. Real-life clowns, buckets filled with science, to throw into the faces of religious fanatics.

The park keeper walks up to me. His skin is almost translucent, but that could be the light he is standing in. He looks at my stuff. He shakes his head. He looks at the floor. He studies my sleeping bag, my life. He nods down at my waist. I feel a rush of anger at myself. In my rush to get ready, I've pulled my boxer shorts up too high and to the side. The edge of my right testicle dangles out from the side.

A single curve, hairs detecting the wind.

A wrinkled elbow: the bald head of an old person.

I want the world to swallow me up, eat me alive and spit out my bones.

I push my testicle back into my underwear, and pull up my trousers. I grab a jumper, and wrap my coat around me to fend off the cold. I think about making a joke about being sorry for the mess, I wasn't expecting guests. I'm concerned for the park keeper. At six in the morning, he has followed screaming, and found two naked homeless men.

He tells me most people call him Blobfish. He says it's because he makes small blob-shaped jellies for kids' birthday parties, to supplement his income. They don't really look like fish, but if he says they are Blobfish, kids love them. I can understand why he doesn't want to give me any personal details. So I nod my head. Now that I know his nickname, he looks like a Blobfish. He has a flat nose and a bald head, and a sad demeanour, like he's forever discovering he's out of toilet paper. The sweat that lines his skin, gives him the glistening appearance of a gelatinous mass. At least being told how he wants to be known feels like a normal beginning: the sound of a normal conversation awakening in unusual circumstances. I tell him I'm Colossus Sosloss, but when I speak, I say *Coloththuth Thothlothth.*

I need another tooth implanted into my gums. I can't live the rest of my life sounding like a Chinese soldier too drunk to realise he's not at the wedding of his general, but in the zoo next door, talking to a manatee about how to take over the world. Blobfish tells me he would normally shake my hand. I appreciate the gesture. I understand his reasons for not wanting to shake the hands of a man who can't control his own nutsack.

Moonface screams at the park keeper. Moonface accuses me of having his clock. Thankfully he's forgotten about his cock for the time being. Blobfish and I both look up into the tree at the fat naked bird exposed to the elements.

Broken wings, a dodo: good for nothing. Neither bird nor beast.

Saliva leaks from every hole in his face. A line of drool drips out of his mouth and hangs from his chin.

Blobfish tells me he doesn't care why I'm naked. He doesn't care if I've been masturbating to a disabled man up a tree. He says it's none of his business what turns me on. I try and protest, but I don't like my ideas or the sound of my voice, so I look down like I'm being told off by a teacher at school. Blobfish tells me how I get my kicks is up to me, but he can't have Richard sitting up in trees screaming at the top of his voice.

Moonface is Richard.

Richard, or Moonface, I'm not sure what to call him now. The name Dickface springs to mind.

Blobfish shouts up into the tree for Dickface to stop shouting. Blobfish tells Dickface to calm down, that he will find his clock. Blobfish asks Dickface to remember the first rule. I get the feeling this question is designed to make the fat, red man in the tree calm down. Dickface doesn't wipe the spit from his face. He chews his bottom lip. Snot from his nose hangs in a thick gloop, a slug trying to escape a radioactive plant in the middle of a meltdown. He looks down at Blobfish like a sulking baby asked to hand back a toy. He folds his arms and shouts back down: the first rule is don't throw excrement.

Dickface's balls rest on a branch. His penis dangles over the edge.

Blobfish looks annoyed with himself. He tells *Richard* to ignore the first rule. He asks *Richard* to repeat the law they have on swearing. The man in the tree looks down, confused. He shouts out two words: severe delays. Blobfish uses a soothing voice. Dickface calms. Blobfish keeps talking slowly and calmly. The man in the tree smiles, but his eyes still scream that they hate me.

Dickface whispers down to us. His face lights up.

The mental age of a child, set fast behind the eyes of an aging man.

Perhaps Dickface is an unfair name for him, but I feel it's too late now, and his name *is* Richard and he *does* have a face. Dickface asks us nicely now, his nakedness, him up a tree, folds of fat drooping between leaves. He asks us calmly, a well-to-do gentlemen checking his pocket watch to measure the distance between thunder and lightning. He whispers softly. He asks us if we have seen his clock.

Teas on the lawn, croquet at dawn.

Blobfish was expecting an apology, but he'll settle for peace and quiet.

Blobfish tells *Richard* he needs to talk to me. He tells Dickface to behave and put some clothes on. Blobfish asks me where I got my unusual name from. I tell him my parents.

Every time I pronounce the letter 's' I say 'th' so when I say parents, I say *parentth*.

I wonder if Blobfish has a strange name too. Or an embarrassing name. Perhaps that's another reason he goes around calling himself Blobfish. He asks me what's going on. I'm thankful for the chance to finally explain myself.

A soap box, a moment to cleanse my guilt.

I like Blobfish. He's in a position where most people would judge, but he's calm, open-minded, gathering information. He's approached this ordeal like I think I would. I want to sit in a two-man boat with him in the middle of a lake, rods over the side, catching fish, drinking beer and talking about our children. He's been gracious enough not to mention my missing tooth, or to ask me to repeat the words I'm sure sound like two harmonicas arguing over whose turn it is to do the washing up. I tell him I had a sex dream. I woke up with an erection, I masturbated. I then rolled over and found *Richard* naked in the tree above me. Holding his willy.

honetht mathturbated retholve thcreaming ith

"Before you thay it, you don't have to. I'm never touching mythelf in public again. I may never touch mythelf in private again."

"Well, that's a relief, Colossus, or not as the case may be."

I smile. I almost laugh. Blobfish smiles too. We get on, Blobfish and I, but I shouldn't be too keen, shouldn't come on too strong. I've had no one to talk to for some time, lots of time talking to plants and trees. I want to hug him, and to be hugged back.

I've forgotten comedy, it feels alien on me. I regret not laughing immediately because the comment was funny enough. A moment that could have been funny falls into regret.

I'm looking forward to laughing again, but baby steps. I'm in my first adult conversation in over a week.

Blobfish tells me I've been lucky.

I look around at the wet grass. I feel the cold on my face, in my bones. I feel the dirt shifting between my arse cheeks. I enquire how he thinks I've been lucky. He tells me he was driving around the park looking for me this morning, looking for me to tell me about *Richard*. He tells me the other park keeper hates me, which I know all about because of the gap in my teeth. He tells me the other park keeper didn't want me to have the information he is about to tell me. But Blobfish says I have a right to know, if I'm in the park, I have a right to be as safe as possible in the dark.

I'm not sure if I want to know.

Blobfish says the other park keeper is called Edward, in case I wanted to know. *Big Edward* they call him. He laughs as he tells me. He says he knows it sounds like *Big Head*, but the world is full of friends who prove their friendship by saying the most terrible things.

That's true, I think.

Blobfish says they call him Little Big Head, and Edward is fine with it. He never complains, and laughs when he's meant to. I think *that's not really the same*. Blobfish says he's sorry I got my front tooth knocked out, and that I sound like a door that needs closing. I say I appreciate him trying to bring peace to the park, but a sorry from Little Big Head would go further that a sorry from him.

When I say sorry, I say thorry. I'm sorry for my thorry.

Blobfish tells me Little Big Head thinks I buckled over in laughter, and then waved him in for a fight so I could be sick on him.

That sounds bad, I admit.

I explain I threw up because of the dead squirrel being waved in my face.

Acthident thtop thick

Blobfish nods his head. I want to hug him again. Sit him down and write in a letter I hope we can be friends for ever. He steps back from me, perhaps seeing a look I didn't know I was giving, a slap in the face.

Waiting for a date who never shows.

The moment your best friend makes your girlfriend laugh harder than you ever could.

He explains I need to understand: I'm homeless, a mess, and look crazy. I've been seen talking to wildlife, plants and ducks. I don't want to listen anymore, I want to push him over, run away and have a cry. He doesn't want to be my friend.

Nobody will ever want to be my friend ever again.

I want to reach over and pull his tongue out, twist it into a knot, and hang him from a tree.

He tells me Edward has anger issues.

There are two sides to war. Both are wrong.

I thank Blobfish for explaining Edward, because what other choice do I have? He's broken my heart and won't ever know, but I have to thank him anyway. Even that goes wrong:

"Thankth for explaining Edward. Hith behaviour ith underthtandable."

"What?"

"Underthtandable."

"I don't understand you?"

"Underthtandable."

We share an awkward pause.

Blobfish looks at me. He *still* doesn't understand the way I've said understandable. I've said it three times, but this lisp, this *fucking* lisp. He talks over our silence, leaving the elephant in the room.

"I'm here to tell you whatever you do, don't ever, ever, ever, even if you think you're helping, don't ever touch Richard's clock."

"Right."

Well, I'm fucked then.

I've crossed the moors during full moon.

I've fed gremlins after midnight.

I've fallen asleep at the wheels of my own nightmare.

I've touched the clock of Dickface.

Blobfish tells me he used to work in an office, but he left his job because he had a breakdown. He visited the park, and slowly started to feel better inside his head. He says he thinks I might understand, and I think as he's talking to me, he's also giving me advice. I tell him my life was similar. I worked in an office. I tell him it's possible I had a breakdown. He tells me if I'm living in a park, I've definitely had a breakdown. I don't know, but I guess there's a chance he knows me better than I know myself. Blobfish tells me he was walking through the park, when a man threw shit at him from a tree. That man was *Richard*. Richard, sitting above, asks again for his clock, but he's being well behaved now, so we ignore him completely.

Blobfish tells me the police can't do anything about him. He should clearly be in a home, but there isn't the space and he doesn't want to go.

Blobfish tells me Richard's three favourite things are his clock, the trees and the trains.

His clock is the love of his life. The parrot to his bell.

I'm told *Richard* freaked out in a shop because he thought bananas shouldn't be yellow, and to mark his protest he took off all his clothes and refused to move.

All this happened in aisle four, TESCO's.

Blobfish says when *Richard* is inside buildings, he carries all the furniture outside, until he's emptied every room in the place. So he's a pain to look after for anyone. He's happiest up trees, so people turn a blind eye. He stays in the park. He fell out of a tree once, breaking both legs and ankles. *Richard* thought the ground had bitten his legs, so he's afraid of the planet.

Blobfish tells me Richard has learning difficulties. He's obsessive, compulsive, and violent when it comes to his clock. A walking time bomb. A hulking ape they can only control sometimes.

Finally, I think, we're getting to the point of all this.

Richard, still naked in his tree, asks again if we've seen his clock.

Blobfish tells Dickface he's getting my clock.

Dickface and Blobfish both think I have the clock.

Blobfish says the last person *Richard* thought took his clock, he battered in the face with a branch until there was nothing left to remove. *Richard* was taken away for that, but he returned to the park a month later, after the system had yet again decided they didn't have the space or the staff to do anything with him.

Blobfish tells me he understands how homeless people who have nothing, steal from others, and how when nothing is a commodity, something as simple as a clock can become gold.

Dickface croaks *clock* like a surprised frog. Until that croak the frog thought it was a hippopotamus, and expected to remain silently anonymous.

Blobfish goes into detail about the man *Richard* attacked. He uses words like skull, skin, removed, coma and clock.

But I still don't have his clock.

I'm about to tell Blobfish I don't have the clock, but before I speak, he tells me what he's getting at. His point rounded, the final dot on the end of his sentence:

"I know you don't have the clock."

I'm surprised. I tell him I'm relieved, that for the first time in days I've been delivered good news. Blobfish shakes his head and tells me not to be a fool. He tells me this is probably the worst news I've received in years. The worst news I could bring him, because it means *Richard* hasn't lost his clock. It means *Richard* has his clock. *Richard* is in a moment of psychosis. He is likely obsessed with me because I made eye contact at some point.

Blobfish tells me *Richard* is using me to act out delusional thoughts.

He tells me this has nothing to do with a clock.

This is all about Richard's violent tendencies and obsessive nature spiralling beyond his, or anyone's, control. Nobody can protect you at night, not in this park, says Blobfish. Nobody can stop Richard coming into the park to find you, because there are no gates at the main entrance.

There is no way to close the park at night, he says, no way to keep the crazy people out, or the bad people in.

I've never been more alone.

I say *shit*, but the word squeezes through the gap in my teeth and sounds like *thit*.

I ask Blobfish if he has any advice, any hope for me at all, or if I should just take my face off now, hand it to *Richard*, and be done with it.

He tells me *Richard* has the strength of a gorilla, but the brain of a volatile pea.

Dickface.

He tells me *Richard* can be distracted by moving him from one thing he likes to another.

Dickface.

All I did was fall asleep, and I wake up to this.

Blobfish says he knows, but God forbid he didn't say anything and something happen to me. Now if something happens to me Blobfish doesn't have to feel guilty. I'm not entirely convinced he's here for me at all. I thank Blobfish for the information. I would rather have it than not. Blobfish tells me he'll do what he can, but nobody can be watched all of the time.

I ask Blobfish about the giant creature with the long nails and pale face in the park eating *animath*. For a second I see a look of concern. He wipes a puddle of sweat from his forehead.

He tells me he doesn't know much about any of that. He tells me Edward thinks it's me. Blobfish tells me it must be me, but he doesn't want to upset me and get in a fight. And here it is, the wall: the instinctive distrust between those who have, and those who have nothing at all.

Blobfish looks up at the tree. He asks Dickface if he wants to go and see the trains. Dickface looks down and shouts *trains* like a little boy chasing bubbles. The face of Dickface contorts. A large fart shakes the leaves from the tree. An uncomfortable smell turns them to sticks.

"BROWN TRAINS!"

If Dickface does kill me, I would have been murdered by the biggest idiot on the planet.

I pack up my stuff. I leave Blobfish with Dickface.

The bitter cold of the early morning is lifting. The hot sun rises again. Considering my life might be cut short by any manner of circumstance, I decide to hop over the black railing and hide my bags in the wilderness. Maybe after I'm dead, someone kind will find my bags, and decide that in some small way I mattered.

With Little Big Head watching my every move, and now obsessive Dickface after me for his clock, my bags need to be in the safest possible place. Now they are.

I take a long walk back to Roald Dahl, making sure there's no sign of Dickface or Blobfish. Nobody is there. I sit down safe in the knowledge Dickface won't start hunting me for a few hours, at least until he's done obsessing over trains. I understand now, more than they ever could, what people said about being homeless being dangerous.

Although I like Blobfish, I hope I never see him again. If I do, he might be trying to find my teeth, nose and eyes in the bloodied grass, to return them to my face, like a real-life game of Mr Pop.

The Greek version of Mr Pop should be called Mr Popolopodous.

Grace, my old work colleague, is coming to see me later today. She sent me a text before my battery ran out on my phone, having a go at me for not telling her I had moved into the park, calling me crazy and telling me she was going to come today and bring me food.

She called me a selfish bastard for not telling her when we spoke, even though I'd called to tell her, but couldn't get a word in.

I'm not going to tell her about the pale-faced creature called Squirrel, Dickface, Little Big Head or Blobfish. The bottom line is, with nowhere to live or go, I need to stay in the park.

With Little Big Head cutting trees back and trimming bushes, my hiding places are shrinking. Before long Dickface won't need to find me, I'll be left out in the open.

At least in this moment, nobody is trying to kill me.

I lean back against the trunk of Roald Dahl. I try and relax in the shade.

That expression on Blobfish's face flashes through my mind.

The worried look he gave when I mentioned the guy in the park eating the animals.

I've seen the same facial expression once before, in a book called *The Lying Fat Bastard Unicorn King*.

The Lying Fat Bastard Unicorn King

The lying fat bastard unicorn king was king of a starving town called Reflection. It was a town that had no mirrors, but whose banks offered reasonable rates for first-time buyers of mortgage protection. Every animal and person was dying of hunger, including the unicorn king. They desperately prayed for help, because they'd even eaten the leftovers from all of the bins.

One day the unicorn king was wandering through the enchanted forest thinking of many things, praying to God he might stumble upon a new branch of the popular supermarket Morrisons.

The unicorn was thin and close to death. His crown weighed more than his too-skinny head.

The unicorn king happened upon a stream where he took a drink. As he raised his thinning head from the pond he noticed, with thinning eyes, a witch of considerable size. The fat witch stood in front of him with a basket full of delicious-smelling food. The unicorn begged, but the witch offered him only a deal, but it was to be a poisoned chalice: like the McDonald's Happy Meal. Being so close to death and looking like a mop with a loaf of bread for a head, the unicorn king listened to what the fat witch non-rhymingly said:

"I will leave a magic fridge here for you that will be stocked with the greatest food from all of the worlds, from the finest caviar to the most basic garden bean. It will overflow with food. You can come and eat from it every day, but only you. If you tell anyone you have the fridge, or if anyone ever sees the food, the spell will be reversed. And your fridge will be empty, and all the other fridges in the town of Reflection will fill."

The unicorn king agreed and ate till he threw up, and then he ate some more until he blacked out. Then he woke up and ate again until he passed out, and while he passed out he threw up. When he threw up it woke him, which was fortunate because he could have suffocated, and he ate again what he'd previously regurgitated.

Every day the unicorn king returned to the fridge. Slowly, day by day, he started to gain weight, while all those he reigned over became weaker and weaker. The people of his kingdom started to whisper, how can our king be so fat, when we are so much thinner?

The whispers turned to shouts, which turned to revolution. The people screamed at their unicorn king in the streets. They begged him to bring them food, or to offer them his solution.

The unicorn king replied he wasn't eating, and that he too longed for a sandwich with meat in.

"Unicorn King, Unicorn King, our children are dying, we beg you to show us the way out from thin."

Fatter still, the unicorn king became, walking out of town to his fridge on the hill. Then one day, the unicorn king was gorging from his secret fridge, eating all the chocolate cake that he could. While his mouth ate from the lower part of the fridge independently, his unicorn spike speared a large chicken pie that sat on the top shelf benevolently. When the fat unicorn king removed his head from the fridge he failed to see the pie secured on his spike, which offered to all who saw it, undeniable evidence their fat unicorn king had been lying. The people of Reflection found the strength to come to their windows and throw their shoes at his face, and call their fat unicorn king a lying disgrace.

The very next day the lying, fat unicorn king returned to his fridge, but it was bare. Every fridge in the town of Reflection had been filled, and it was the townspeople's turn to get fat through the medium of wonderful meals.

The witch kept her promise. The people had seen a pie from the magic fridge in their town, so the spell was reversed, and in an interesting turn of events, the unicorn king was now cursed.

The fat unicorn king, still with the chicken pie attached to his head, returned from his empty, secret fridge to find his town enraptured with laughter and celebration. He thought his people were suffering from starvation dementia.

All of his people now ate well, as the fat unicorn king began to look rather frail. The unicorn king collapsed in the street. The fat people he once led gathered around at his feet.

"Please?" begged the unicorn king. "Please, somebody give me some food. I'm feeling rather hungry and you're being rather rude."

"Unicorn King you're only getting back what you gave to us. Besides, if you want to eat, you only have to eat the chicken pie attached to your head."

"Townspeople of Reflection, I'm sorry for not feeding you, but such cruelness is not needed. Please, please somebody feed me. I AM YOUR KING, and my sins I've conceded."

Across that day, and for the next week, hundreds of townspeople told the king his solution was the chicken pie stuck to his head.

But because of how evil the now slim, lying unicorn king had been, rather than take them at their word, he became paranoid and bitter. Wasting away from starvation, he addressed his town of very fat people (who no longer drank water because they preferred gravy), in one last attempt of rebellious bravery.

"Townspeople, I lay on this ground starving and now I die, do any of you know why?"

"Yes, our king, because you've refused to trust us, and so you've ignored all of our chicken pie advice."

"NO! You've refused to feed me and soon I'll be dead!"

"But, our king, you really do have a chicken pie stuck to your head."

The witch, you see, had stocked up all of the fridges in the land, but not before leaving a note on every fridge door:

"This fridge will be stocked fully every day, but only on one condition. The unicorn king must save himself before you save him. He has a chicken pie stuck to his head. This must be the first food he eats. Once he eats the pie, the townspeople of Reflection can bring him anything they wish. But he must eat his own pie first. Nobody can touch the pie, but you can tell him it's there."

"P.S. Witches don't rhyme."

The thin unicorn king cried out one last cry:

"Please, please don't leave me to die."

And one villager stepped forward while eating some custard, and to a cheer replied,

"Let's leave him. He might not be fat, but he's still a clear bastard."

As the unicorn king died, the final look in his eye was the very same look Blobfish gave me earlier when I mentioned the guy eating animals in the park.

It was a look that told me Blobfish knew I was killing the animals.

I am the pie and Blobfish is the unicorn who doesn't believe in me.

Yesterday a dead squirrel was found impaled through a railing, and the day before a dead dog head nailed to the back wall of the toilet. If the pattern has continued, then somewhere in the park, right now, is a dead animal, a *murdered* animal no less. The animal could be anywhere or in any condition: a pigeon glued to a tree, a cat taped to a park bench, a dead fish nailed to the back of a dead duck nailed to the back of a bleeding badger, a strangled toad, or a hedgehog struck though the heart with his very own spikes and left to wander injured until he bleeds to death, his body eventually found on top of the sundial by the park entrance.

My problem is, if Little Big Head finds the dead animal first, he'll call the police. He'll be able to report to them I'm responsible for three deaths. After three dead animals, the police are likely to act.

There's little point trying to find the animal because if there is one, the poor thing could be anywhere. My chances of finding it are slim.

Grace arrives. I watch as she walks in my general direction. She walks quickly, pointing to impatience. She has to get to me quickly so she can leave sooner.

The type who walks down escalators.

We hug. She cries.

What's happened? There's been a car crash, she's got cancer, someone's committed suicide, she's been attacked? She sobs into her hands, keeping a safe distance from my smell. I ask her what's wrong and she tells me everyone is saying I've gone crazy. I laugh, and think that's what they would say, because if they didn't think like that it's everyone else with the mental problem. She tells me she's missed me. I tell her I've missed her. I tell her to stop being an idiot with the tears, because I thought something serious had happened.

Thomething therious.

She calls me an emotionless goon.

Not last night Grace, last night I was the goon of emotion.

I note it has taken, on this occasion, two sentences for her to tell me to shut up. Not my record, once she told me to shut up before I had said anything, like she knew what I was thinking and didn't want to hear it. Grace steps forward and playfully hits my chest, a chest I've tactfully left on display because I've spent so much time in the park under the sun, and starving, that I'm actually looking pretty lean and tanned.

The brain rots inside though, all the important parts nobody sees.

I tell Grace I've missed her, and in a way I have. We ate lunch together every day for over two years, and on some occasions, when Grace had nothing better to do, we would see each other on weekends. She tells me I look good. I don't cut off the top of my head and show her the darkness inside my brain. Perhaps she would fancy me if I wasn't homeless, jobless and mental. She tells me I look good compared to what she thought I'd look like. She said she expected me to be dying, but I don't look *that* bad. She says without my beard and with a full set of teeth I might not look like a mental patient.

I thank her.

Thankth.

She tells me I look like a mentally disturbed yeti.

I tell Grace I swallowed my tooth because a midget head butted me, and she laughs.

We walk around the park because she wants a tour. I'm an excellent tour guide. I tell her I'll show her everything, but I know the tour won't include going near the railway tracks. I tell her I've named the trees and the bushes, and last night I thought I was losing my mind and screamed out loud a lot. She thinks for a second, tilts her head, and laughs.

She hands me a large, plastic Waitrose bag she's been

carrying. The bag is full of food and drinks. She tells me it's all for me. She says she made me sandwiches, but doesn't know if they're any good.

I look in the bag and her sandwiches are rolls, odd shapes for sandwiches.

I leave my bag behind a bush and carry the bag full of rolls and cheese. I can't walk around holding my broken bag like a dying deer and carry the food.

My small bag will be fine for an hour or so. There's nothing inside it to take. Nothing I need to survive. Not now I've just been handed better food.

We walk by Roald Dahl. I tell her I sleep under him at night. We walk by Jeffrey Archer. I tell Grace Jeffrey is where I used to leave my bags before they shaved him. We walk by Stephen King. I tell Grace I slept with Stephen on the first night but I can't sleep with him again because a member of the public pissed all over his face. We walk all the way over to Enid Blyton and the faraway tree where Grace is surprised, and a little disappointed. I have no story about the tree she thinks has the best name.

Grace tells me the London Marathon almost killed her.

I don't tell Grace the park will likely make a ghost of me too.

We walk to the abandoned house. I joke this is where the homeless zombies live who might kill me. When we reach the duck pond I stand on what's left of the blood stain, so she doesn't ask questions that lead to the story of Squirrel.

On the path leading to the playground we stop. Grace turns around. She tells me she has a date tonight so can't stay for long. She cocks her head to the side and asks me what's wrong, because my facial expression has changed:

"Oh please, don't tell me you're jealous of my date?"

Tell me you are, please tell me you are, she means.

I try to remember what my normal face looks like and do my best impression of that. I hear myself speak, like I'm listening to myself from another room with a glass up against the wall. I tell her I'm not jealous, and suggest she goes and buys us ice cream.

She thinks it's a great idea, and tells me not to go anywhere.

Nowhere to go, I'm already here, I think.

Grace walks merrily to the ice cream van parked outside the playground at the end of the path. Not quite far away enough for her to clearly see what I'm up to, but just close enough for her to see I'm up to something unusual, should she decide to look back. Behind where Grace was *just* standing, on top of a bush, is a dead fox. A noose is around its neck. A plastic bag is over its head. Several human mouth-sized chunks are missing from its stomach.

Think fast.

Little Big Head can't see this fox. He'll call the police. I'll be arrested. For that reason, I'm relieved to be the first to discover the animal. No children have seen the animal yet. No child should.

I look back down the path to see Grace being handed two ice creams. The usual bag I carry with me is under Roald Dahl. My only option is the bag I'm holding: the large plastic Waitrose bag Grace brought with her.

Think.

I take the plastic bag off the fox's head. I empty what I can of the food from the Waitrose bag into it.

The rest of the food I tip into the bin. A waste, but I need a bag big enough to put a fox in, and that bag is the bag from Waitrose. I hide the bag that contains food. I feel bad for Grace, she's gone to a big effort for me, and I've put most of her food in the bin.

I'm left with the large, empty Waitrose bag.

I grab the fox by the rope. The fox's head pulls up. For a second the fox looks surprised to see me. I sweep the fox off the top of the bush and it drops into the bottom of the Waitrose bag.

I put the bag on the ground. I push fox tail and legs into the bag. The fox is all the way in.

Grace yells something about ice cream melting. I turn. She skips toward me without a care in the world. She hands me an ice cream, and gives me a puzzled look like someone just asked her what the gross domestic product of Japan was in the period 2005-2007. She asks me what I'm up to. I tell her I'm looking at the food she made for me, and thank her for bringing me so much.

Thankth.

She tells me she doesn't mind carrying the bag for a while, but she doesn't really mean it and knows I know she doesn't really want to. So I decline, but not for those reasons.

I walk with Grace. We stroll along. She walks by my right hand, so I carry the bag in my left.

I ask about the guy she has a date with.

We walk casually in the sun. A peaceful day, by all accounts.

I have a dead fox in a Waitrose bag.

I have a dead fox in a Waitrose bag.

I have a dead fox in a FUCKING Waitrose bag!

"Mum and Dad met on a blind date and well, he's just *really* nice, you know?"

"Colossus?"

I have a DEAD fox in a FUCKING Waitrose bag!

"Colossus?"

I have a DEAD FOX in a FUCKING Waitrose bag!

"Colossus?"

It could be worse, I guess. Instead of a fox, I could have found ten hamsters speared on a stick like a hamster kebab. That would be worse, walking around with a dead hamster kebab. That would have to be illegal.

This is almost fine in comparison.

"COLOSSUS!"

I apologise to Grace for not paying attention to a thing she's been saying. I tell her sometimes my mind runs away with me. She tells me to shut up.

We walk up to Roald Dahl. We sit down outside his shade, in the warm sun. The entire time I am wondering how I'm going to explain that I've turned our picnic into a dead fox.

I put the Waitrose bag behind me and sit between it and Grace.

What am I going to say when she asks me to pass her the bag?

I could hit her in the head hard, and put her in the bag with the fox. Perhaps, a tad extreme.

"Pass me the bag. I'm starving!"

I ask her what she wants. Grace tells me she wants a sandwich. I look into the bag behind me. Two dead fox legs stick out from it. The face of the fox stares out of the bag at me.

I tell Grace she didn't bring me any sandwiches. She tells me to shut up and pass her a roll. I look back in the bag at the dead fox staring back.

There is only way out of this, feed her ego.

Fuck.

I tell her she is right. I'm completely jealous of her date. I wish it was me. I tell her I'm only being honest, and I'm sorry.

I feel sick rise in my throat, but I'm able to stomach it.

Jealouth honetht thorry.

She laughs and calls me an idiot. Then she insists I hand her a sandwich.

Oh, fuck you life. Fuck you right in your stupid face. I cannot believe I am going to have to escalate this conversation into an area of complete ridiculousness.

I have no choice.

I look Grace in the eyes and soften my voice.

"Forget the sandwich for a second, Grace. I'm trying to tell you something."

Grace looks back at me. She leans away.

Fuck. Here goes.

"I love you. I've always loved you."

Goodbye friendship.

The Waitrose bag kicks me in the back.

Grace looks at me. She doesn't know what to say.

"Colossus, I mean. I have a date tonight. We are *friends*. I mean, you are *homeless*. And *old*. And *bald*. I mean, no, just no, just *ewwwwwwww*."

Thankth.

The Waitrose bag kicks me again. I need to get rid of Grace before she sees the bag move.

She needs to go now.

I lunge toward her for a kiss. My front teeth scrape the edges of her right eyeball. She pushes me away. She holds her face. She asks me what has got into me. She is angry. Her face is flushed.

She has completely forgotten about wanting a sandwich.

Grace stands. She tells me I'm acting like a complete dick. She says I've lost my mind. She tells me that it might be true what everyone is saying about me. She tells me someone should report me to the council, to get me some help, for my own good. She tells me she doesn't like the new me. She says she's leaving, and will have to seriously consider if she ever wants to see me again.

Oh, no.

Thank God.

She walks away and I watch her go. I know she'll turn around to see if I'm watching her walk away, because she wants to know I live in her pocket, so I keep looking, keep playing my part. But she doesn't look back, which is worse than her looking back to see if I live in her pocket.

But she's gone, that's the main thing.

I look at the Waitrose bag and it kicks again. A hairy leg kicks from inside the bag. Having a dead fox in a bag to get rid of is one problem, having a not quite dead fox in a bag is entirely different. The fox, with half his stomach missing, is suffering greatly. Unfortunately for me, fate has thrown me into the great moral dilemmas of life: can we be cruel to be kind, or is that just another way to be cruel?

5pm. Daytime, busy park. Not the ideal time or location to finish off the life of a dying fox.

The fox in the bag whimpers, and sounds just like a gargling baby human.

I can't allow another life to suffer.

I need to kill the fox. Then hide the body where it can never be found. I could put the bag in a bin. Job done, bag hidden: fox gone. Out of sight, but never out of mind. I would always know what I did, and how long would the fox take to die? How long would it suffer at the bottom of a bin?

Blind people are not lobotomised. We see through memories, and think through eyes.

There's one place I can safely kill.

The juxtaposition between safety and kill: like having a safety button on a gun.

The one place I can safely kill, is the last place I want to go.

The old abandoned house.

I've avoided the building at all costs because it only contains all of the bad things. My choice is stay safe and the fox suffers, or risk being harmed in the old abandoned house by the pale-faced creature called Squirrel.

Not Death.

Not good choices.

I have never wanted to harm or kill anything in my life.

The bag kicks again. Every second I wait in my hot soapy bath of luxurious indecision, must seem to the fox an entire lifetime of being skinned alive and dipped in vinegar.

I decide to do the wrong thing for the right reasons. With the Waitrose bag in hand I walk up the hill. I walk along the black fence and up to the duck pond. I follow the path around the duck pond to one side of the abandoned house. I find the broken slat. Without looking back, I bend down and, hunched over like a humpless Quasimodo, I step through the broken slats, and inside the grounds of the home of a monster.

The ice cream van in the park pierces the sky with a burst of showdown music from a cowboy film.

I imagine two cowboys eyeing each other up on a quiet, dusty street. Their hands hover above the handles on their guns. Both men wait to see who will draw first in their duel to the death.

The ice cream van usually plays *Greensleeves*.

I stand inside the grounds of the abandoned house. I look around. This is it, the territory of the devil.

Overgrown weeds make this area difficult to walk through. I am not inside the house. The broken slat has opened into a small overgrown space that runs down the side of the house and around the corner. The front door to the house is not here. There is only crumbled bricks and glass that has fallen from the smashed windows above. I hold the bag tightly. The old building is supported by scaffolding, the old house's Zimmer frame.

On the other side of the corrugated iron slats which separate the house from the park, I can hear birds singing and children playing, but on this side, where I am, there is only silence.

No birds sing from the trees. No children dare play here.

I place the bag with the fox on the concrete. I put my back against the crumbling wall of the old house. I walk slowly, taking only cumbersome steps. My feet are canoes. I reach the end of the wall. I poke my head around the corner. There is nobody there. At the end of the path, on the right, is the front door to the house. The door is missing. The entrance to the house is a wall with a section missing.

There are no signs of life.

Not here. A graveyard of time.

A hand to a gasp, never stopping the sound.

Two bricks are missing from the wall a few feet from me. I move toward the hole. My heart pounds. I am the cat. This is suicide by curious. If I'm killed by the pale creature, at least I won't have to kill the fox.

Is that why I'm doing this?

My canoe feet feel larger and even heavier. Walking is impossible.

On the other side of the corrugated slats the birds stop singing. The children stop playing. No sound comes now, not even from the park.

I bring my heavy, left foot down. I snap a twig. The twig snaps, breaking in two, sounding like a tree falling over into a school.

I stop. My heart sounds like a tiny helicopter landing inside a giant megaphone. I can hear my breathing like I'm inside a space suit. My peripheral vision broadens as my adrenaline floods my senses. My subconscious mind is preparing my body for a fight, my hearing is more acute. I'm a rabbit in the jaws of a bear. I bend down. I put my eyes to the holes in the wall, and look into what I expect to be hell.

Its eyes stare back from the other side.

Its hand grabs my throat through the gaps.

I smell before I see. The stench of death fills my nostrils. Six black nose hairs turn white. They bend, wither and discuss how things were better in their day, back when you could leave your mouth open and nobody would steal your teeth.

I don't know what death smells like, but I think this is it. A musty, sweaty smell. A smell that cannot be likened to anything else. The chemical smell of erosion and desperation clings to every molecule in the air. Every breath I take is a reminder of my own decay.

I place my hand over my mouth and nose.

There are two single mattresses on the floor. A broken chest of drawers rests on its side, as if pushed over by escaping clothes. A damaged staircase leads to the second floor. There are two doors on this level. The rest of the second floor has fallen to the ground, like a bomb has hit the building and destroyed half of it.

Both doors are shut.

There are no dead animals. Nothing incriminating. No proof of life. The smell is coming from somewhere inside, most likely from behind the closed doors. The police should come here.

I've seen enough.

I retrace my heavy steps back along the wall and walk back around the corner. I pull the fox from the Waitrose bag. I lay her on the concrete. One of her eyes blinks; a human thing.

I look for a brick, but I can't see one. Several long, heavy scaffolding poles lean up against the old building. I pick the shortest. I imagine this will take three or four swings.

I lift the pole above my head.

This fox will be the first and last life I kill.

I tighten my grip on the pole.

I exhale.

The wrong thing, for the right reasons.

I bring the pole down into the head of the fox. The fox's head explodes with a pop. Blood spurts everywhere, beyond the fox and back at me. The blood is dark and thick. The blood covers my jeans, the concrete, the weeds, the scaffolding, and the wall of the house. Bits of brain stick to bits of plant.

The fox's ears are missing. Most of its nose, I presume, is under the pole. The fox's one good eye now stares unnaturally out to the left. Her other eye is no longer in her head.

The fox is certainly dead.

I hear something scrape against a wall. The scraping comes from around the corner.

I drop the pole.

The scraping is coming closer.

I freeze.

This is a running moment. I've run a lot in this park. I've run away from many things. I know I'm good at running. This is a running moment, but my feet are syrup. The floor has turned to sponge pudding.

The scraping is nearer. I know what the sound is.

The fingernails of the pale creature, long like knives, are running along the wall of the house.

It is dragging its nails along the wall, as it slowly walks toward me.

It is just around the corner.

The scraping stops as *It* takes its nails from the wall. The monster has stopped before turning: a momentary pause, before it kills me.

My legs are dead. I'm all upper body, I feel like there is nothing beneath me. All I can move is my eyes. My eyes look down at the bloody mess at my feet and then to the corner.

Change your mind, Squirrel. Please, go back into the house. I don't want to die.

The nails scrape along the wall again.

It is almost upon me. The pale creature. Death: here to deliver my last moment.

And so it comes.

Death.

The creature with the pale face, the monster with ghosts for skin.

The demon nobody thinks exists but me.

The first thing I see is the black of its coat, followed by the sides of its dark hood. I look down and see its long bony fingers and pale hands. Nails like razors. It turns, and I look into its black holes for eyes. There are no pupils. No white bits. Just dark saucers. I look up at Death. It looms over me. I try and remember it's called Squirrel. But, this creature is Death. Its hood covers most of its face. I can only see its disfigured jaw and its scar that runs down its chin and throat. I want to be sick again.

We wait.

My hands are down by my side. I wiggle my fingers to check I'm still alive and not completely paralysed. The creature moves its claws, which are down by its side too.

The ice-cream van pierces the silence. A burst of cowboy music bellows all around us.

I'm in a showdown with Death.

I wait for it to swipe my face off with its claws. I imagine it knocking me to the floor, feasting off my skin, dragging my body around the corner and feasting on my body for several days.

It breaks eye contact, if indeed, it has eyes. As it looks away I feel part of me is missing, and I wonder if its attention has stolen my soul. It bends over and picks up the parts of the dead fox that are left. Mainly a bloodied body and a mashed head. Death puts the fox parts in the Waitrose bag. It turns to face me, and for a moment, I think it's going to attempt communication. The part of its face I can see, looks like it's been kicked in the face by a horse.

Death steps toward me.

I'm going to die.

It turns away from me.

Maybe I'll live.

The creature groans. It is in pain, suffering. Only nobody can put the creature out of its misery. The world is too afraid to go near it to help, so it lives alone, walking the earth, being chased out of towns like Frankenstein's monster. Maybe it *is* Frankenstein's monster. I feel for the monster. I don't believe monsters are born, I feel they are made. Whatever has happened to it, was so awful, it has shunned the world. The creature has never even learnt how to speak. The reason why we are so fearful of Death, is that it cannot communicate. I wonder if it could learn to speak, what it would say.

Death, Squirrel, the creature, whatever I call it, the *thing* walks away from me: it scrapes its nails along the wall of the old house. It walks slowly, with its head bowed, as if suffering a great depression. It pauses for a moment, and I have an acute feeling that it doesn't want to leave my company. I understand depression and isolation too, I am also an outcast of society, and we live in the same park. In a weird way, Death is my neighbour. I guess even monsters need company.

I almost reach out to it, this monster, and I think, for a moment, it almost reached out to me.

It continues to walk slowly. I am certain if I called, it would turn.

It stops.

I breathe in sharply.

The creature bends to look closely at a bush. Hanging from the centre of the bush, by the optic nerve, is the eye that popped out of the fox. The eight foot beast makes an approving groan. This groan is filled with more joy than its last, but the joy is hollow: it has travelled too far down a lost road. The creature plucks the eyeball from the bush, and places it into the bag.

I try and imagine it as Squirrel, not just by name, but in vision. I try and imagine a giant squirrel in front of me picking out, and picking a cherry and placing it in a basket. This vision actually helps me. As the beast walks around the corner, I see a squirrel walking away from me. The more I imagine Death as a squirrel, the greater sensations I start to feel again in my body.

They say a good way to conquer nerves is to imagine people naked, well, I think I've found a better way. Imagine what scares you as a squirrel.

My legs are part of my body again.

I run out of the abandoned house, back across the pond and along to Roald Dahl.

I pull my knees under my chin and I cry.

I cry because I killed a fox.

I cry because in my whole life I've never been so scared.

I scream into the ground because I'm seeing the beauty in monsters.

I scream because I just killed an animal, and that makes me a monster too.

Day Nine

Single Planet Syndrome

There's so much life in this bar I feel more dead just being part of it.

At the end of the bar is a giant screen, the final of a big sporting occasion. I'm sitting on a bench. To my right sits a beautiful girl who seems to know me. She leans back laughing and clutching a plastic glass. Her long black hair flows to her lower back. As she leans away from the table, I instinctively look down. I see the edges of her black bra under her white top.

The lighting is unusual, orange and red. There are hundreds of wish lanterns on the floor and around the bars.

I'm in Shanghai.

A friend asks us if we want another drink. He shouts to be heard over the music and good times. He says he may be a while because it's so busy. We don't care how long he takes, because this is the time of our lives. I look to the girl in white, just her and I now, surrounded by hundreds of strangers. We are having the time of our lives, seizing forced moments of our making. The good of life: laughter, smiles, looks returned from strangers. Drinks are thrown into the mix. We are free to do anything as long as we aren't in control of ourselves. I seize the moment. I roll with the punches. This is my time to land a few blows of my own.

I tell her I wish I had pens for eyes, so my kisses would write *I love you* into her brain.

She laughs and tilts her head back, again revealing the black bra beneath her white shirt. My head is woozy. For a second, everything darkens: a planned blink.

I open my eyes. She's gone.

My friend has not returned from the bar. I look around. Everyone has gone.

I'm alone. I feel empty, like my heart has been taken. I've been deserted. I sit only with memories. There is a cage on the bar, and the wheel inside the cage spins, even the hamster is missing. There are holes in the dirt, but no worms. A blue balloon drifts into the sky, because the child who was holding on to it is no longer here. The bar is empty. No queue. The big screen now shows an empty stadium. There are no fans, and no players. The blimp filming the aerial shot of the stadium is on fire in the middle of the pitch. Nobody puts out the fire.

Everyone has disappeared.

I walk out of the bar and into the street. Car engines are running, but nobody is behind the wheels. Bikes lay on their sides, wheels spinning. A bike wheels across the road in front of me, leans to one side, and then falls into a market stall.

Fresh oranges tumble to the floor, creating alien movement in the land of still.

I approach a coffee shop. Cigarettes still burn, slowly baking greying ashtrays. The cigarettes are dying. The people who breathed life into them in exchange for their own have gone.

Whatever happened, happened in the blink of an eye. I'm the last person left alive.

I open doors. I scream hello into alleyways. I shout words, surrounded in darkness, down well-lit streets full of false brightness. I change hello and scream *turnip*, because after shouting hello to nobody I feel stupid. I walk into a shop. From the outside the shop fixes heels on cobbled shoes, but once inside, the shop is remarkably different.

The inside of the shop is Gladstone Park.

I don't want to wake up. I can't feel the cold of life. I can't feel fear in my dreams. When awake we are green and red bits glowing under a machine, lights turn off and on, and people of science convince themselves they know what's going on. Backs are patted, hand are shaken. Test, record, collect. They tell us what we already know. We are all dying, dying slow. When awake, there is a feeling of impending doom, and if you can't feel it, close your eyes, or open them further. When we're in a box underground, heaven is finally above us, but it's not in the sky, heaven is the planet we lived on, and all of the angels are people. Here, in a dream, it's just me floating in the back of my mind, among parts we don't fully understand.

I want to hang on to this.

I move further into the shop, past trees and grass, down hills and through bushes.

This is not a shop with a park in, but a park with a shop in the corner.

I notice a small blue door by my feet. Small for a person, possibly, but big enough if I become the smallest version of me. I get on my belly, open the door, curl into a ball, and roll forwards through the entrance. I leave my life in the park behind me, for something else entirely.

I unfold on the other side, stand up, and take in my new surroundings.

There is no grass here, no park. There is concrete. Grey corridors stretch away and come toward me. The place has the feel of a hospital: grey floor, white walls. No imagination. All art has been crushed by seriousness. There are no windows, no natural light.

I'm underground. I'm beneath the park: heaven is above me now.

At the end of the corridor a creature in a lab coat, holding a clipboard, makes notes on a chart.

Crouching low, I cross the hall. I enter the white door opposite to me. I stand. I face two foxes. They wear lab coats and look healthy. A look in their eyes tells me emotions are secondary to their bellies and coats, like two foxes fed with the spoils of war.

They are the size of humans.

I blink. The foxes are still in front of me.

One of the foxes speaks in perfect Queen's English.

"Please, Colossus, do sit down won't you, fellow? We imagine you have some rather pertinent questions."

The fox is voiced by Stephen Fry. I ask the fox if he isn't Stephen Fry in a fox costume, and if this isn't all some sort of elaborate hoax, filming homeless people who won't be missed, as their environment manipulates them into madness.

"No, no. Stephen Fry has one of the clearest voices on your planet and it makes this process more efficient if we speak in the clearest dialect for your basic human sound disambiguators."

The logic is sound. The voice of Stephen Fry does relax me.

The fox on the left looks at his chart, pushes his spectacles up his long nose, and tells me they did the most humane thing they could, not for them but for us. He tells me I might not understand, but they know more than I do, and confusion is the nature of the stupid.

I ask them what they're talking about, and they laugh.

The fox on the left tells me he knew I'd say that. He tells me they ran tests. He tells me they don't act on impulse: they put the entire plan through the wash, dried it, and put it through again. Then hung it up on the line, and studied it from both sides. To be certain, to *know*. He tells me they observed the human race for years before knowing what their mission was. They tell me I would agree with their decision, if ever faced with the same empirical evidence.

The other fox speaks. He looks the same only he doesn't wear glasses. His black nose is wet. He has a white mark through his red fur in the shape of two axes crossing.

He speaks in the voice of Stephen Fry too, which is a bit creepy.

I suggest to them it would have been funnier to get Hugh Laurie to do the voice of fox number two. They tell me humour is irrelevant. I tell them it would have been a nice dynamic, a nice little moment, a nod to history. They tell me I'm getting sidetracked, which is all part of the problem with mystery. Fox number two tells me they discovered people are built with clocks. Their research showed them all people are walking time bombs. He tells me, cheery fox that he is, that time means every person living and about to live, dies.

It's a matter of time, but time is just a matter.

He tells me I'm not able to see the bigger picture while part of the drawing. He says that planet earth sits in a big plastic bag, and everyone on it is taking their last breaths. I tell them I don't understand. They laugh again. I ask them if humour is irrelevant, why laugh?

They assure me that what I think is laughter, is pity.

I ask them again to tell me what's going on. They raise their eyebrows. The fox on the left steps forward.

"Dear boy, we thought it obvious. We've wound the clock forward. Everyone on your planet is dead. We left you as the only one on it."

To end the suffering of the dying, the second fox says.

I ask the self-righteous foxes why they kept me alive. The fox on the left tells me they kept me alive so I can truly understand what being *alone* is. The fox on the right tells me people spend their lives complaining about everything, and one of the most common complaints is the feeling of being alone. He shakes his head, and says they've studied the thoughts people have in their lifetimes with the thoughts they have in their last moments of life. The first fox says the results show people live their entire life lying to themselves, and only a few minutes being honest.

Remarkable, says the first fox, how so many people living on a circle, could find themselves approaching life the wrong way round.

I scream. I call them all manner of things: murderers, cold-hearted killers, devils in fox costumes, doom bringers, death stickers, chasers of children, and vicious-clawed racist idiots in white coats.

They tell me by being left truly alone, I'll be the first person to understand nobody ever was.

The first fox tells me humans are a self-indulgent race of spineless excuses for intelligent life forms, we prefer to wallow in warped ideas of loneliness and misery.

The second fox corrects the first. He tells him humans *were* a self-indulgent race.

The first fox waves his paw, as if correcting him is an act without meaning.

When he gets the details wrong they're irrelevant because he knew what he meant, when others get the details wrong he changes the face of their planet.

The first fox tells me their studies show all people think they can write a book, are touched with genius, troubled. He says their studies show all humans want to be noticed or thought of as different by everyone else who wants to be noticed and thought of as different. He asks me if I see the irony. I ask him if he finds himself a bit whiny. The second fox shakes his head, and reminds the first fox he should be speaking in past tense, because people are no more, a feature of yesterday. The first fox, impatient, asks a rhetorical question:

"There is a human present, is there not?"

The first fox asks me what the hell we kept fighting for, like war is my fault.

"There are only two of you."

I say.

"And you can't agree. Multiply that by six billion and you would fight wars too."

The second fox takes over. The voice of Stephen Fry is now serious. These two can't lose moral high ground. They kill to be loved, but that's not their thinking.

Fox number two tells me they couldn't release my race from its suffering without letting one person live to realise how good we had it. How loved, how lucky, how overpopulated, how popular, how bloody envious every creature and non-creature was of the opportunity of man.

How cruel of you, I tell him.

"That's what happens when you only have one earth. 'Single planet syndrome' it's called in the universe. You get used to being selfish."

The other agrees, and nods his head. He states if we had two earths, maybe the human race would have learnt to share. Both foxes look at me, and say I can thank them now.

I ask them what for: for killing everyone else, or for letting me live?

For opening your eyes, they say.

And I do.

I wake, freezing cold, pain in my bones. My skin is frozen. My nose and my face has gone. A bird lands on my nose and sticks, warm claws fuse to ice skin. Bird wings flap in my face, unable to fly, the alarm clock of nature. *What time is it?*

I panic.

People are moving across the park. I've overslept. A simple act, but one full of danger. I watch an old lady, head down, scarf wrapped around her. She is determined to make it to wherever she's going, faster than she can possibly get there.

I shouldn't have killed the fox.

Everything is dying. There is no cruel to be kind, only cruelty finding new ways to convince us to let it free from its leash. In my dream I had a full set of teeth, I was lisp free.

There is no Dickface in the tree above me this morning, a different kind of relief.

I get out of my sleeping bag. It's too cold to wash with water, too cold to get my hands wet with soap. I use wet wipes. I clean my body and face: a wet cloth rubbing over dirt, half removing it, half spreading it over new bits of skin. Two separate wet wipes, one for body, one for face. No expense spared.

I brush my teeth, white froth spills over green.

I hide my bags over the black fence, somewhere deep and in the wilderness.

Last night I removed my blood-stained jeans and threw them into the bin. Nothing says future mental patient like drifting around homeless wearing jeans covered in the brains of a fox. So now I'm wearing my last pair of trousers. These trousers are jeans, and they are not warm. They are cold and hideous to see, and three sizes too big. They are beige, the worst colour on the entire spectrum. These trousers make me look like I've strapped two Shar Pei dogs to each leg. My legs will soon be dirty work vans with *clean me* inscribed on their windows by people too young to drive.

My full beard now contains blonde, ginger, white and black bits. I'm now a homeless guy to avoid. I've become a gamble: school kids will dare each other to go near me. Fearing if they get too close I'll eat them.

I keep my coat and jumper on. There's no sun, grey clouds loom above, teasing the people below. A chill to the air reminds everyone the weather is changing, but not for the good. I go and sit on a nearby bench. I pull my coat tightly under my chin. I put my cold hands in my pockets. I wish I was made of oil, so I could light a match to myself.

The murder of the fox, because that's what it was, burns into my subconscious.

That's a good thing, I think, because I'm still me. If I didn't care, I'd be someone else entirely. Then again, before yesterday I didn't believe in ending life, and today I've killed.

My dream, my crazy fucking fox dream.

The meaning of the dream feels: even though the fox was dying, I killed it.

There's not much humanity in being human(e).

I watch morning runners, casual walkers, people walking to work, and early morning dog walkers. The people wearing suits walk faster than those not in them. Those walking slower notice the rising sun. Those in the suits, don't. Those in suits walk with their eyes fixed ahead. The system broke their backs first, and their necks followed.

This cold makes my bones creak, my eyelids stick and my hands grey.

I sit, closing my eyes like I'm on a bad ride. Sometimes I think I am.

I wait until I think it might be 8am, and head to the toilets. Something to do, something to move toward, something to kill some minutes. The duck pond is empty.

Death is not swaying in the mist.

Maybe it never was.

Why think that, what does that even mean? I'm coming apart at the seams.

I use the toilet. I wash my hands, and then dry them off. I wash them again, and then dry them again. I can't wash away the memory of the fox. I leave my hands under the warm tap until the water is hot. The water burns through the invisible layer of ice sitting on my skin. It burns me until my hands turn red. The boiling water blurs everything to a mist in my mind.

Blood on my hands.

I wish I could put my head under the tap, so I can burn away the ice around my brain, and feel my thoughts. Find who I am. Remember something good that I did with myself.

I leave the toilet and walk to Roald Dahl. I sit under him, a little warmer now I've walked a bit. I ask the tree how he is today. He says he's always brilliant, because he doesn't have a brain. He says I should stop asking me questions out loud, because that never ends well. I tell him I didn't think I was, and he laughs, but only to me. He says I'd better watch out, there's trouble coming. I look out at the park. Walking toward me are Little Big Head, a little girl and a tall giant of a man.

Here comes that trouble.

I run through a field of poppies toward Little Big Head. He lifts me above him and twirls me around. We spin to the laughter of the man and the girl.

"This is him, right?"

Little Big Head points his stubby finger from his stubby hand attached to his stubby arm controlled by his stubby brain. He nods his stubby head toward me. His beady eyes feverishly dart from the giant man and back to me. Little Big Head's question is leading. He dares the man to give him a different answer to the one he wants to hear. This is Little Big Head's chance to get me out of his park. He's drawn the dots, and all he needs is someone, anyone, to go along with his game. No question has been asked: accusation and statements point in my direction. They leave his fingertips and stain my face.

The man standing next to Little Big Head is tall. He is dressed in a suit and presented immaculately. He has short, gelled hair. The clean look of a man who showers, shaves and aftershaves daily. A boxer's face, and a face like a model. Good looking, no doubt, but God came down, put a flat hand on his face and squished it slightly before announcing he was done. A protector's face, unfortunate for me, as he's positioned himself between me and the girl, meaning he sees me as the threat.

Can't blame him for that, not really.

His suit is black. His shirt is white, his tie pink and his shoes are well polished. He's just walked across the park, but not a blade of grass has taken residence on either of his shoes. In contrast, the little girl is covered up to her knees in mud. She has even managed to get a blade of grass on her face, which sticks to her forehead with a look of horror on its surface.

Little Big Head must be having trouble removing my sick from his too shiny shoes, as this morning he is wearing wellington boots.

The immaculate man speaks to the little girl. His voice is like frying pans bashed together underwater: deep, slow, a little laboured. He speaks three or four languages and finds English the ugliest and most derogatory to his intelligence. There is impatience in his voice. He knows he's at the beginning of a long process. He places his hand, a family-size pack of crisps, on the girl's shoulder to reassure her she's safe to answer. His hand touches her shoulder, a crisp packet crumples.

Little Big Head asks the little girl, with anger in his voice, if I'm the man.

He points at me again, as if I'm in a line-up with other men.

Small minds, smaller park, all perspectives lost. The little girl looks at me. She has beautiful, round, green eyes. She is perhaps ten years old with hair not brown or blonde, clean or greasy, long or short, styled or lazy. Her hair falls off her head like uncooked spaghetti. The girl's face, like the face of all children, is too young to point to any definitive character. I can't tell if she'll grow up to be a lawyer, or an out of work actor.

I can't tell if she'll take life as it comes, or try to bend it to her will.

She's too young to read, like a book with no pages.

Everything is ahead of her, though right now, ahead of her is me.

Her pink coat is puffy, like a life jacket. She wears blue jeans and a thick cream jumper. Her face is soft and squishy and not yet defined by the bumps, punches, emotional anguish, tears, laughter, sun, wind, alcohol, smoke and work that come to define an adult's face. This girl doesn't have a hair style. She doesn't look like she's going to look, and she can't put her own socks on.

A little girl with power greatly disproportionate to her life status.

The big man asks her softly, one last time, if I'm the man.

She's a baby, yet as she nods and says yes, tiny butterfly wings blow a tornado through my life.

I want to hit Little Big Head for being ignorant. I want to bash his head into the tree until he stops breathing. I don't know what I'm being accused of. I control myself. I control my thoughts. Maybe this will all blow over and I'll get a chance to explain. The truth will out, and the truth is, I haven't done anything wrong.

Except kill a fox.

I look at Little Big Head's stupid grin, the worst kind: he thinks he's being clever, but I know categorically, he's being an idiot. The giant in the suit looks down at me like I took him out for his birthday meal but my card declined so he had to pay. The girl looks at me. She makes a face like a fish gasping for air. As she does, her eyes bulge and she pokes out her tongue. Not the appropriate face for the moment. She is too young to have an accurate expression, but familiar enough with having a face to know this is the right time to express a different one.

I see a police car coming from behind the girl with the gasping-for-air fish face.

This is a bad joke. This is, *why did the chicken cross the road?* Only without the chicken, or the road.

Little Big Head nods in the police car's direction. The blue lights on the car flash once followed by one short burst of police siren. A policeman gets out of the car. He walks over to me. He joins the crowd of people surrounding the homeless man. I'm sat looking up at a policeman, a midget who hates me, a businessman who thinks he's doing the right thing by his daughter, and a little girl at the centre of it all, too young to know her words carry weight.

I have to go to the station.

They won't tell me why, but we're all going.

I'm not to worry about anything, everything is just super, it will all be okay.

But it won't be okay for me.

For the little girl, life will work out. For the upstanding citizen and for the hard-working, disabled park keeper, everything will be fine. But not for the homeless guy with a missing tooth, wearing the same jumper he's been in all week, sitting with a Chinese Shar Pei dog strapped to each leg.

I ask if I'm being arrested. I'm told no, not yet, just questioned. I tell them all to wait, to slow down, and let me think for a moment. I ask for a minute to take things in. Hold up, I say, just everybody STOP! They all look at me, like *I'm* the crazy one for shouting. All these people want to take me somewhere without hearing my side of whatever story this is, without finding out the truth. And *I'm* crazy?

The policeman takes a step back. I think, this is it, this is what life is all about: rumours picking up pace, explanations on cardboard, intelligence used for stupid things, arrogance dictating policies, the greedy need to pocket dictating banks, those in power led by morons, idiots revelling in their own fears. Leave me here, leave me by my tree, I think.

JUTHT FUCK OFF AND LEAVE ME HERE!

I say.

My lisp nibbles part of the first word of the only statement I'll make today. The girl is moved behind the guy. The police officer steps forward and tells me to calm down. Little Big Head is laughing, enjoying the process of pouring all of the worst things that live inside him, inside me.

The police officer tells me to listen. I tell him I haven't done anything wrong, but I'll talk to him, if he wants. Take *Edward* away, just take *Edward* away and we can talk.

Maybe for an easier life, he asks *Edward* if he has anything better to do. He tells *Edward* if he needs him he knows where to find him. As *Edward* walks away I imagine him stepping on a land mine.

And everyone runs toward the explosion, but they don't really run toward *Edward*.

The police officer isn't fat but I can tell he will be. He is in his forties. He has completed his time on the beat. He has chased muggers and shoplifters into dead ends that never led to new beginnings. He has a pointed nose and an impartial face. His expressions are open to interpretation. He has short, greying hair, and a white shirt buttoned all the way to the top, which to me, says he's tightly wound and prone to long periods of disengagement separated by sporadic bursts of uncontrollable rage. He thinks his top button fastened means he's serious about presentation, and because he's serious about presentation, he's very serious about bigger issues like the law and its details.

Perhaps the police officer is not aware life's more comfortable with the top button undone.

He's married. His wife takes him for granted.

The officer tells the little girl and parent they can leave. He thanks them for all of their help. He tells the girl the park is safe, she has nothing to worry about. He tells me he doesn't have a pen, I'm not being arrested, so this is off the record, but if nothing changes, there will be no future warnings. (So it's not off the record then.)

I still don't know what this is about, what I'm meant to have done.

I glance at the officer's top button, fastened tightly, accurate, specific, then note he forgot a pen: a curious conflict.

I tap the top of my leg with my fingers, then think maybe that's what guilty people do so I move my hands into my pockets, but then think maybe guilty people put their hands in their pockets, so I move them under my armpits and think I look like I'm trying to not look suspicious.

I return my hands to the top of my leg.

Being in the presence of a police officer is making me feel guilty of a crime I haven't committed. I'm aware of everything my body is doing. Every part of my body is independently doing *things* that make me look guilty. He tells me he just wants to talk, and that he's here more as a community worker than to bust skulls and arrest people, but I'm pretty sure that's what people say when they want you to relax, in the moment before they get you to confess to something terrible. His true intentions lurk menacingly behind his luxurious position of hierarchical anonymity, a horrifying child-eating monster in a closed book written for the young, waiting to spring to life in the imagination as soon as the first page is turned by unsuspecting children.

Me and him, under my tree. He is a guest in my house, but I have no tea to serve him, just cold North London wind, that bites all over his skin.

He tells me he is Police Constable Whirled, the community support officer for Willesden Green. There is a roughness in the back of his throat, continuous radio static, a smoky voice, a monkey with his head stuck in a biscuit tin. Occasionally his voice is high pitched and squeaky, but with a background groan of discomfort. We share a similar pain when it comes to names. I resist asking him if he knows anywhere I can buy a new wireless adapter for my computer.

When you have a silly name you have to take names seriously, no matter how silly they are.

He tells me yesterday the little girl saw me kill a fox. She was looking through one of the slats, and witness me bash the animals skull into concrete. He calls me *mate*, and tells me that might not be the biggest problem I have. I know, I think, my biggest problem is Dickface, or then again it could be not having gloves, because I can't feel my hands. I tell the officer I killed the fox to put it out of its misery. I tell PC Whirled I found the fox wounded, dying, and if he thinks about it, I took the fox to a place far away. The intention was to not be seen. I tell him the reason I moved the fox from where I found it was to move it away from children.

He nods in agreement, but his nod says he's yet to discuss the real problem.

I wait to be told what my biggest problem is. I don't like the way he calls me *mate*.

He knows something I don't, and he's enjoying the gap in knowledge.

How everyone sounds to someone.

"*Edward* tells me you're killing animals in his park."

I tell him that's as ridiculous as it sounds. The policeman nods and smiles, but I can't tell if he's agreeing, or mocking me because I've just called killing animals in a park ridiculous, ten seconds after confessing to killing an animal in a park.

"*Edward* tells me he caught you performing a sex act in the toilet, now, if I wanted to, if *Edward* complained about this, I could arrest you for that alone."

Fuck Edward. Stupid *Edward*, too hell bent on getting me arrested for murder when he should be watering plants. I hold my hands up. I tell the officer I'm sorry about the fox and being caught masturbating. I'm embarrassed for the latter and traumatised about the first.

thorry mathterbating embarraththed traumatithed

I tell the officer what about me, what about my missing tooth? I tell the officer I've been bullied and harassed since I arrived.

haraththed miththing

He tells me people have heard me talking to the trees. I tell him that's a lie, I do no such thing. He says this morning people heard me shouting *turnip* at bins. I laugh, and tell him not to be silly.

treeth

I've got to watch my step. Admit to nothing and he'll go away.

He says yesterday I was seen walking a badger on a string. I tell him the fox I found, had been strangled in wire.

thring thrangled

He asks me how long I've lived here, what date it is, who is in charge of the country, what do I think when I imagine the colour red, what do I think about war, do I think children are attractive, how often do I shower, what food do I eat, what's my favourite book, have I ever been the victim of a crime, or of domestic or any kind of violence? And I realise, the community support officer doesn't care about me, or *Edward,* or the fox, or the park. He isn't here to decipher my guilt. All of this, to the police force, is small potatoes. He's here to decide if I'm crazy. He is here to decide if I need to be taken away from the park, and committed to a mental home for tests. He asks me how come I'm in the park, and I lie. I lie because he's the definition of the system, and if I tell him I left a good job and my own flat, if I told him I chose this life because I think there's something we're all missing while sitting in our comfortable sofas at night watching *Eastenders,* if I told him *that,* he would think I was crazy.

And if he thinks that's how I think, I'm going to be taken away.

My will would become irrelevant, because the state would be able to say I don't know what I'm saying. As soon as I'm committed, everything and nothing I say will be taken with a pinch of crazy. Life would be stripped away from me. I would be kicked out and avoided, entirely legally. I'm walking on the top of eggshells. He calls me *mate* again, and it pains my heart. Pains my heart this man thinks he's doing good, thinks I'm stupid enough to not see his plan. His vernacular, his soft voice, his repetition of the word mate, the way he cocks his head to one side sympathetically as he listens: it's all designed to get me comfortable, so he can lock me away. So he can finish his shift early, and the machine views him as a positive influence on society.

Little Big Head, Blobfish, the old woman from the toilet, the man in the business suit, all of them, everyone I've spoken to, and possibly Grace. Even my old landlord, most likely, and he was the craziest fucking bastard I've ever met. All of them might have signed a piece of paper, or agreed on an email, that someone from the law should to enter the park and ask me these questions: because they all think I've lost it.

They need to prove I'm mental, to make them sane.

Well fuck them all, I'm not playing. I see this game.

PC Whirled tells me other people have reported I'm living in a park and losing my mind. Some think I should be detained for public safety. I thank him for the job he's doing. I tell him to thank everyone for their concern. His serious nature and robotic demeanour indicate he's having a hard time separating a dead fox and being caught pleasuring myself in a regretfully accessible toilet, from an actual crime.

If I am losing my mind, the person in front of me right now has to be the last person to find out. He tells me it's odd someone else could be in this park and not be seen by anyone other than me.

Blobfish, the spineless non-polyp, has told everyone I've said there's a creature with claws and a pale face eating the animals in the park. Nobody else has seen the monster, so they have all concluded that I'm suffering from some sort of multi-personality disorder. The greatest acts of evil in human history have all been committed by those convinced they were acting out of moral righteousness.

PC Whirled asks me if I've ever taken medication, if I've ever seen people before who aren't there, if I ever had an imaginary friend as a kid, do I sometimes feel sad, alone, depressed? Every single person in this world could answer yes to those questions. I've taken paracetamol for headaches, thought I'd seen someone only to realise I'm being an idiot, had an imaginary friend as a kid, and I've felt sad, who hasn't? And that's the danger, every question, could be a yes, from anyone. What if I needed to be liked, as much as this idiot needs approval? I'd give him the answers he wants to hear, and he'd tick the boxes that would make him a good person. He'd go home and kiss his children's heads and tell his wife he saved someone today, I would go to hospital, be locked up in a cell, and nobody would hear my screams. The walls in mental facilities aren't really padded to stop people hurting themselves; they are padded so the people outside of the rooms can go about their lives without hearing the screams of their victims.

I don't want to put a single tick in any of the yes boxes. That's all he's going through. He's going down his long list of crazy, a crude black and white government form in his head, all boxes looking for ticks. If you really feel he's your friend, buy in to his vernacular, and open up too much, then that's it. You are done for, life over. Forever labelled crazy, kept in a safe box away from society. And he thinks he's good. He thinks he's helping. With every *tick* placed in a box about other people's mental frailties, he crosses a box in the mental assessment of himself. Like all *experts*.

He's exactly the type of person who needs to live a bit, because in order to tick boxes on behalf of someone else, you first need a few ticks in some of the boxes yourself.

I tell the guy one night I *thought* I was being watched by someone, but it turned out to be a tree. Terribly stupid, I say, terribly embarrassing.

thtupid embarraththing

He nods. I can see through his eyes he ticks a few boxes in my favour.

He says he's spoken to my old landlord, and was told I quit my job, quit my life.

Here it is, the hook. Forget the dead animals, forget the sexual acts, I've stopped going to work. I've walked out on my house.

I must be crazy.

There is no way I can explain in words the insanity of my ex-landlord.

His big crayon is poised over a form. All the little questions have burnt down to this one. In large letters, ARE YOU CRAZY? And beneath the question, there are only two boxes. YES and NO. How I respond, will dictate what box he ticks, and my life from here on. He's almost ticked the YES box, before I've explained. My old landlord: a bloody bastard.

I tell the officer his facts are wrong. My old landlord is so old he probably thought he was talking about someone else.

thomeone elthe

I tell him I was forced out of my home because my landlord put my rent up, and because my job failed to give me a pay rise. I couldn't afford my life. It happens all the time. The problem, is on the rise.

He nods.

"So you had a breakdown?"

No, I tell him, no, I'm fine. A break-*up* maybe, with my life, which suddenly sounds positive.

He doesn't know how to listen to my words with those ears.

I don't know myself anymore, how I got here, why I'm here: my intentions of changing the world have been lost somewhere in the changing of me. If I'm going crazy and losing my mind, I'll do it on my own thanks, in peace. He tells me not to get worked up, but he has some paperwork in the car. If I signed it now, he could take me somewhere I could be helped, somewhere I might be more comfortable. Which we all know means I'm making people uncomfortable. I tell him no. I thank him for his concern, I'm polite, but I tell him I won't be going anywhere today. I tell him I'm fine, if I need help I'll ask.

A silence falls between us I sense I'm not meant to fill.

This is his pause, his moment of drama, not mine to interrupt.

He stares at me. His eyes are small and hardly visible: brown and yellow teapots in autumn.

Leaves blow around us. They whip up and circle around his trousers.

All this looking up is making my neck hurt. I know he's cold, but he can't show it. Or maybe he's forgotten how to feel anything at all. I hold his look. I don't know what he thinks about my eyes. Maybe he sees the cold, dead eyes of a killer. We continue staring.

He sighs.

He pulls a photograph out from his inside pocket and looks at it. I can't see the image, only the back.

I expect an ink splodge: his last attempt to incarcerate me for my own good.

The atmosphere is tense.

The officer thanks me for my honesty, and for giving him my time. He tells me he has one more thing he wants to discuss. Like Colombo, I think.

He tells me he needs to ask me if I've seen the missing girl in the photograph he's holding.

I'm disorientated. I ask him if this is some kind of joke, or test.

tetht

He tells me he isn't joking. The girl is only six years old. He tells me the girl went missing from a house near to the park. She's not been seen since. She went missing once before and was found here. Her family love her, he says. Her family want her back, and they won't stop until they find her. She went missing about the same time I turned up, and the timing is odd.

My mouth is dry, I'm confused. I speak. My words feel like dumbbells and taste like lies.

I ask him if this is a witch hunt, pin everything on the homeless. He tells me he's just doing his job, *the members of the Nazi party said the same.* He tells me the girl they're looking for is part of the family I met earlier. The sister of the little girl, I think, the daughter of the large man with crisp-packet hands. He tells me he's been asked by them to press me on the matter, and after ascertaining my sanity, he has decided I can indeed by pushed on the matter.

I tell him, go on then. Show me the photograph. He turns the photograph around. The white background becomes an image I want no part of. Her eyes are a pale grey and surrounded by white. They are expressionless. Her head is smaller than most six-year-olds. Her smile and mouth are hidden. In the picture she grips a mirror tightly, her only possession. She balances on a wooden beam. Her chest and shoulders are broad and her legs too thin. Overall she looks healthy. Her skin shines, her eyes are lucid. She is facing the camera proudly, but the bell above her head is out of place. I imagine she rings the bell when she wants food. Seeing her in a cage doesn't feel right.

The officer tells me her name is Madness.

He is looking for madness, I knew that already.

He explains the story of Madness the parrot. The little girl called Chloe, the father called Oleg. He lost his wife, and the girl lost her mum, Bridgette, to cancer. The ashes they put into their parrot, at the request of the will. The parrot has escaped. They are certain the parrot is in the park. That's why Chloe saw me murder the fox: she was looking through the gaps for her parrot.

I tell him if I see any parrot, I'll let someone know.

The grey day of the park behind us looks a little brighter from where I'm sitting now. I wish I could walk away from this guy, this officer, this community supporter.

PC Whirled sighs like a computer fan powering down for the night. His performance is over.

He warns me, of course. I need to be careful and stop talking to trees. I tell him I will. He tells me there are no more chances. He tells me to tell him that I understand.

"I underthtand."

"What?"

I give him two thumbs up, which works better. He stands, rubs his hands together, and leaves me sitting at the base of my favourite tree, my only friend in the world. I watch him get in his car, search for a pen in his top pocket, which he doesn't find, shake his head and then drive away. He is off to find the next person mentally insecure enough for him to open up, pull apart, and define his brilliance with.

The man who can't remember a pen.

Even though he knows my truth, nobody else does. In the mind of everyone in this park I'm the park animal murderer, and labels stick, but worse, I'm the main suspect in the dead mum inside a missing parrot escapade.

I wrap my hands under armpits, trying to warm them somehow. I visualise being a penguin in the middle of other penguins, like a penguin Russian doll. I mentally waddle around in a circle to avoid the cold.

The little girl, bless her. She saw me kill a fox, and now thinks I'm going to kill her mum.

Day Ten

A fist in the fat face

I wake up. I know it's early because it's still dark. This is the time of day only seen by the cleaners and the homeless. The only light is a streetlamp twenty feet away from where I am sleeping, down by the path. The light shines up into a tree, making it glow.

The tree looks sinister, and the darkness is eerie.

I wish I was dreaming. My life is the moment you wake up from a nightmare, and struggle against hope not to fall back in. My 450GSM sleeping bag is failing to stop the wind peeling back my skull and breathing ice into my brain. I try and fall back to sleep but I can't. I roll over in my sleeping bag. I stare into the darkness of the park. I stare at the streetlamp and the tree. Underneath the streetlamp is one of the park benches and a bin. The streetlamp flickers. Making the branches on the tree look animated. There's nothing else to see, light, bin, dark, nothing, light, bin, dark, nothing, light, bin, dark, monster.

The light from the streetlamp hits the path and spills in a circle on the ground beneath.

On the edge of the circle, just about in the dark, is the fine silver outline of Death.

Death is watching me sleep. Its knives for fingers hang down by its sides.

How long has it been there watching me?

I don't know what to do.

Death sways gently, a broken pendulum on a windy day. The outline of fingers moves left and right: a small and terrifying silver line of lighter darkness, gently bobbing in and out of my vision like an empty ship on calm waters. The weakest slither of light splashes faintly over its front.

Death's face is so pale, but always covered in darkness.

The creature closes its hands, making fists. Its nails move, they curl like sharp snakes gripped by their throats. It takes a step into the light and looks up. The light hits its face. The creature is not wearing its hood.

Negative thoughts, paranoia, jealousy and controlling impulses are all thrown into the same expression. Too many lines, too many voices spiral through its dark holes for eyes. Its jaw hangs at an unnatural angle, flapping loosely to the right like a pigeon with a mutilated foot. Death's teeth are black and dead. Death is long beyond the help of root canal surgery. Its teeth have wilted away like the health of its brain.

Death has no hair. Two lumps rise from the top of its skull. They are horns. Death opens its mouth. Its jaw flaps to one side. It moves a tongue out from its throat. Its tongue is black.

My throat closes. I can't catch my breath. I'm drowning in the sea of my experience. I sweat. I am having a panic attack. I need to breathe. I need to calm my thoughts down.

What am I doing? Remember: think of Death as a squirrel. Imagine.

I look out from my dark tree and gaze into the light. I do the only thing I can think of. I imagine Death as an eight-foot squirrel, instead of an eight-foot monster. I move my eyes down from the light, and focus on my new vision. The squirrel is eight feet tall. The squirrel's head twists and bobs in movements. It's unsure of the light. The squirrel knows it's an easier target in the light, but it's also afraid of the dark. Its face is chubby and brown.

Its eyes are large and moist, and ever so friendly. The squirrel has two front teeth that poke out from its whiskered face.

My breathing slows. This is working.

The chubby squirrel looks away from the light and in my direction. The squirrel is holding a plastic bag. The cute squirrel rummages through the bag.

My breathing is back to normal. I love squirrels.

The cute, chubby, wet-eyed squirrel brings a large nut from its bag and holds it in my direction.

Fox's head.

The cute eight-foot squirrel is overjoyed. He shakes his nut and bits of nut fall all over the floor.

Blood.

The squirrel's eyes grow even larger, until its face is all chubby cheeks and eyes staring gleefully into the night.

I can't ignore what the monster is doing. My imagination is broken by the horror of reality. The pale-faced creature has removed the head of the fox from the bag. The monster is holding the skull of the fox up to me and shaking it. This is a message. A warning I'm not sure I understand.

The sun is rising, but needs to rise faster.

I'm frozen in the moment: a moth anywhere but the flame.

A moment of falling, while on the ground.

A skinhead asking the time, when he's already wearing a watch.

The creature is looking in the tree above me. *Something* is in the tree above me.

I don't want to know what's in my tree. I don't want to know what's been waiting in the tree above me as I slept, but I need to know. I need to find out how close I am to death. I need to look my last moments in the face, so I can remember I lived as I died, and died not how I lived.

I roll over, slowly, breathing shallow. I look up into the tree. I search between dark branches for whatever has excited Death.

I'm angry, but not surprised. I'm scared, but not shocked. In the branches, hanging high in the tree is Dickface: an obsessive personality disorder, obsessing orderly. His brain told him he can't live without me.

Come on sun. Rise, please.

Killing me would be easy, there are no people around, and nobody misses the missing.

My eyes dart from the creature plotting to kill me, back to Dickface, also plotting to kill me.

Dickface is one of those people you can immediately tell is completely unaware of their own strength. I imagine him hugging me, breaking my ribs and popping my head off. I see him clearly putting my head back on, saying sorry, but somehow losing my head. I imagine him going to the bins, finding a replacement head, returning with a shoebox, fastening the shoe box to my neck with a stick, walking through the park with my corpse with a shoebox for a head, like we're best friends.

He's got that look about him.

He could leap down from the tree and swipe my face from my skull. To him, removing my face would be as simple as pulling the skin off a rice pudding.

He smiles the blank smile of a man who doesn't know what amusement is, but smiles because he's experiencing an emotion he doesn't connect with.

The smile of Dickface doesn't mean he's happy, quite the opposite. I find it menacing.

Dickface hasn't jumped on me because he's seen the pale-faced creature. Dickface knows being violent in front of others results in punishment.

Death stands in the darkness. He places the fox's head back in the bag with the body. Death does not advance. Death does not come for me, I believe, because it's seen Dickface above. They both wait in silence. All three of us are contributing; all three of us are paying into the bank of my death. They both wait for the other to leave, so they can brutally murder me in peace. I need Death and Dickface to both stay, even though I desperately want them both to leave: a peculiar quandary. If one leaves first, the other will drink away my life, like soup.

My eyes move from Dickface to Death. I watch Death take slow steps backwards, an old Victorian horse and cart. It moves out of my line of sight, out of the line of light.

I stare up at Dickface in the tree. I wait to be attacked.

At least if Dickface kills me, I won't be put in a bag and eaten later as hors d'oeuvres.

The creature has left, leaving the kill to Dickface. Death's disappearance back into darkness has given the green light to madness. From the black above, I can see red eyes and hear heavy breathing. Somewhere in the twisted branches he sits, contemplating when to drop down and break my neck.

Each second is a lifeline. Each second is a shortening of my lifetime.

A whisper falls from the branches above, like leaves falling gracefully onto a crime scene.

"*Where is my clock?*"

The last pictures my memory collects: a yellow smile under red eyes.

Dickface doesn't jump. He doesn't leap onto me from above. Instead, his hand moves over the bulge in his trousers, his other obsession. He shouts *trains*. His voice is like someone letting go of a balloon at a funeral: manic, high pitched and out of place in the dark silence of the park.

I move fast, recalling how excited he becomes. I'm quickly out of my sleeping bag. I grab my bags. I move my life away from the landing zone. The rumbling noise from behind me tumbles relief into my body. My fear subsides; a moment to catch my breath that almost entirely left me. I buckle and wobble. I place my hands on the ground so that I don't fall. The rumbling of the vehicle that isn't a lawnmower gets closer. I'm about to black out.

I feel a hand on my shoulder. A friendly voice tells me I'm up early. I'm groggy. My heart palpitates.

Blobfish wipes a pool of sweat from his forehead and face. He asks me if I'm okay. He tells me he thought I looked crazy yesterday, but my eyes are something else today. All I can tell him is it's too cold to sleep.

I'm in shock, I think. A human grunt from the branch comes from above Blobfish.

Blobfish doesn't move. He should have.

The semen from Dickface lands on Blobfish's forehead and runs down the side of his face. The stuff is in his ear, and sticks to the back of his head.

I'm dizzy, delusional, light-headed, brain-split, civility parted, a lead chandelier, a dead swan at a wedding.

I laugh, the first genuine laugh I've had in ages: a complete release from thinking I'm going to die.

Fuck, it's good to be alive. We can forget that sometimes, as people. But every single second is a blessing. Every single moment is an experience unique to us.

My laugh is long, hard and tearful.

Blobfish doesn't respond.

I pull some wet wipes from my bag. While laughing and wiping tears from my eyes I tell Blobfish in the land of the man with the semen on his face, the homeless man with the wet wipe is king.

Blobfish doesn't smile.

Blobfish isn't saying anything.

Blobfish isn't there.

Blobfish has gone to his safe place: a cupboard stored in the hull of a pirate's ship at the bottom of the ocean guarded by mermaids with machine guns.

I wipe Blobfish's forehead clean. I use a separate wipe to clean his ears, the top of his head, his nose, his cheek, his chin and the side of his neck. On the fifth shout of Blobfish's name he blinks. He turns his head. He says nothing about where he went and offers no explanation. He's back to normal, like nothing happened at all. Quite disturbing to witness. I begin to wonder if the only normal person in this park is me.

Blobfish tells me he heard I was arrested yesterday. He sounds normal but mermaids still patrol his eyes. I tell him he heard wrong, I had a conversation with a community support officer, nothing else. He smiles and tells me I don't have to worry about *Richard* coming after me with a hammer.

I wish he would call him Dickface, just once, but telling him my name for the man in the tree might not go down well. Blobfish tells me *Richard* doesn't want to hurt me. He tells me *Richard* thinks I'm a train. He tells me *Richard* told him yesterday that he loves me, and wants to have my children.

"I no longer have to have to worry about being attacked by a mental patient who thinkth I have his clock?"

Blobfish's eyes widen. He nods gently, encouraging me to continue my thought.

"Inthtead I have a mental patient who wantth to have thex with me becauthe he thinkth I'm a train?"

"Exactly."

I try to weigh up what's worse, but it's impossible.

One is a quick bludgeoning to death which I won't know much about.

The other a repetitive, lighter, bludgeoning that I'm alive afterwards to recall for the rest of my troubled life.

Blobfish tells me everyone thinks I've eaten the parrot. I tell him to tell me something I don't already know. He says Oleg and Chloe are walking around the park with shovels, looking for shallow graves. The girl is in tears, Oleg is squeezing an onion, and appears broken by sorrow.

"Preparing for another funeral, that family," says Blobfish. He tells me it's a shame. He tells me like he's trying to get me to tell him where I buried the body. I realise that's why he's here.

My only friend, a complete bastard. No different from my ex-landlord.

I tell him I know what the parrot means to the family. Blobfish explains the missing parrot gives Little Big Head a chance to do something beyond his disability, he loves the idea of being a hero. And the police are looking for an opportunity to justify bringing in and pushing forward new powers to police public parks, as they feel they are powerless when it comes to dealing with the homeless. Blobfish explains the police want to smash the pattern of the homeless cycle:

Go to a park, get arrested for a minor crime; go back to a holding cell, get fed. Get a bed. Get released on a minor charge. Go back to the park. Repeat.

I tell Blobfish he's preaching to the converted. The parrot is a wife to a man, a mum to a little girl, a symbol of transcendence to a midget, a chance for the police to get rid of the likes of me from public spaces, a chance for Blobfish to do the right thing for a little girl, and for me, I tell him, the parrot is a chance to clear my name and prove to everyone I'm not insane.

Madness is my one chance to stop people seeing me through the eyes of all their worst fears come true. Finding Madness is my one chance to be seen as who I am, and not who people think I am.

tranthcendence liketh piththfearth

Blobfish nods his head. He says he understands my reasons, even if there is something in his voice that says he doesn't believe in them. I tell Blobfish I'm going to hide my bags. Blobfish asks me to give Richard a chance, now I'm not in any danger. I'm still in danger, just a different kind, so politely decline. Blobfish has semen on his shoulder. I don't tell him. My little jab into the belly of mankind. My little way of saying I know you think I killed the parrot.

I walk along the black fence, to the corner of the park before the world wakes up and the day begins. I hide my bags behind the black fence, in the wilderness. Funny how my bags used to be the biggest problem I had, my only concern, but as soon as I hid them where they can never be found, all the problems in the world found me.

A thought gently bats away at my mind until I open myself up to it, like a fly bumping over and over against a window until it opens.

What if the pale creature wasn't looking at me or Dickface this morning, what if it was looking at the parrot? Everyone is enraptured by this parrot. Everyone has a reason to get their hands on Madness, myself included. Maybe the monster does too.

The fly escapes into the world.

I know the pale creature has been the eating animals in the park, it's not such a stretch to think it might have seen the parrot and, tired of the standard park cuisine, decided to pursue the bird until its wings are curled up inside its belly, never to fly again.

I walk back up the hill to Roald Dahl. I look into his branches, hoping to get some sign of parrot.

Blobfish has gone, but Dickface hasn't moved. Dickface may have been up the tree for the same reason as Death: Madness the parrot. Perhaps this morning's entire episode had nothing to do with me at all. I call Dickface down from the tree and he comes, a crazy mix between a horny pet that any second might start humping my leg, and a strawberry faced art teacher who doesn't know when his eyes leak. I ask Dickface if he's seen a parrot. He points to the railway tracks. I flap my wings like a bird to indicate parrot, but he gets so scared, he runs away screaming. He runs across the path and toward the duck pond.

A moment later I hear ducks quacking, splashing water and a woman screaming.

Dickface will return when he's ready.

The sun is up. Time flies when you're having fun, or fearing for your life.

I decide to do a little investigating.

I climb the tree. I grab and move through the branches of Roald Dahl, until I'm sitting on the same branch Dickface had been perched on. Dickface has his clock on one branch, and a blue metallic box on another. Dickface is neck high in ducks and screaming women, so I open up the box. I look inside. What I see, is a curious snapshot into the mind of the lost. There's a blue police siren. I imagine Dickface putting it on his head and running around making a noise like a police car. I lift up the police siren, and underneath, the type of black rubber brick used to teach children how to swim. Next to the brick is a piece of paper with a picture of a grey snake on it. Next to the bit of paper is a long grey feather. Underneath the feather is a box of Fox biscuits. The foxes on the packet have eyes that judge me.

I wonder if the feather is from the African Grey Parrot.

Was Death following Dickface because Dickface knows where Madness is?

Dickface was scared when I flapped my arms. The idea of a bird, freaked him out.

Has Dickface eaten Madness?

My grey matter slowly stretches. Inside my brain an exhausted Egyptian slave wearily turns an important cog. As the Egyptian successfully completes the turn of his cog a large penny falls from the darkness above him, passes him, and drops into the darkness below.

He never knows where the coin lands, or if it ever does.

As the penny drops I have another idea.

What if I've been giving the intelligence of Dickface a disservice? What if he's acting crazier than he is? What if Dickface was in the tree this morning, not because he wants my children, but because he was hiding from Death because he knows the pale creature wants to know what he knows?

I need to know what Death thinks it knows Dickface knows. Is this why Blobfish told me earlier to give Dickface a chance?

Does Blobfish know something about Dickface or the parrot that I don't?

Thinking it over, over thinking it.

Maybe it's not a parrot feather; it could just be a pigeon feather. Maybe Dickface is a lunatic in a tree, who likes taking his clothes off and masturbating in public.

There's one way to find out, I need to befriend Dickface.

I put the feather in my pocket, and close the box. I climb down out of Roald Dahl, leaving the box where it was. I hurry to the duck pond. Time is of the essence. If Little Big Head reaches Madness first I believe his hate for me is so strong, it's possible he might decide he wants to be a hero less than he wants to frame me for its murder, and kill the parrot himself. And if Death or Dickface eat Madness, and her body turns up in the park, I'll be blamed.

I need the parrot to live. I need it unharmed.

I hurry up the path, grey feather in my inside pocket. I turn the corner to the duck pond.

Sitting in the middle of a circle of pensive ducks is Dickface. He sits in the middle of the pond, water up to his waist. The brown water from the fountain cascades down his head and over his face. His ginger wig covers his eyes, and crawls over his ears. A large green leaf rests on his shoulder, a flattened frog that never made it across the road.

I call his name, not *Richard*, but Dickface. His fat, sad head looks up. He smiles. He says *Dickface* back to me. His voice is now less like a balloon at a funeral, and more like two balloons in a toy store. He seems to prefer the name Dickface to *Richard*. I tell Dickface we'll see the trains if he gets out of the pond, but rather than rush at me smiling like a football on a five-minute break, he stays sitting in the pond, waist high in water, like he's decided trains aren't his thing anymore.

thee trainth

He cocks his head to the side like he's had an idea.

"Trains!"

I know he doesn't mean trains. He means me, because, according to Blobfish, I am his train. According to Blobfish, Dickface finds me sexually attractive, but I simply draw the line at prostituting myself to a mental patient for information about a parrot.

I don't have many lines I'm not prepared to cross, but this is one of them.

At least, I think it is. I consider the consequences of not getting any information out of Dickface.

Nobody will ever know. Take him into a bush.

I promise Dickface if he gets out of the pond and comes back to Roald Dahl with me, I'll put my finger in his mouth. I try all sorts of alternative low-key physical scenarios, like taking my top off and giving him a hug first, but it's the finger in the mouth that gets him out of the pond and back to the tree.

I don't know why and I don't want to.

Underneath Roald Dahl, I ask Dickface if he's seen the parrot. He responds by saying train. I ask him again. He defiantly shakes his head. He shakes his head so hard I'm certain he's hiding something. As he shakes his head, I rub his saliva from my finger and into my trousers.

A prostate examination without the glove.

Wet ginger wig flicks across his face, and sticks to his forehead. The green leaf hangs off his knee. Other pond life clings to his elbows. If I tipped him upside down newts and toads would fall from his pockets. His lower half is soaked, and he doesn't care. I like him for that. Most adults run from raindrops like they're bullets, Dickface didn't want to get out of the pond.

The equivalent of jumping on a grenade and laughing.

I show Dickface the feather to let him know I know he knows what I want to know. He responds by saying train. He wants more of me, I think. I have a dilemma, because if I put more fingers in his mouth, this might end with me living in trees with a family of fat headed, red-faced children.

I tell Dickface if he takes me to the parrot I'll put two fingers in his mouth. I waggle two fingers under his nose, and he smells them like he's smelling an open bottle of 1997 Domaine de la Romanée-Conti.

Dickface smiles and nods his head. He stares at my two fingers. Drool falls from his fat chubby mouth and crawls down his face like a drunk in a bowling lane. He makes no gesture to wipe his chin. He opens his fat mouth. His jowls wibble. I move my fingers from under his nose and leave the tips of my fingers on the edge of his sloppy lips. Dickface grins. He opens his mouth, and I push my fingers into his wet mouth. His dry eyes brighten.

The weather looks better today. Not so many clouds.

A lady walks along the path and doesn't look up. She peeks at the scene out of the corner of her eye. Seeing a homeless man with two fingers in a fat, disabled man's mouth is probably unsettling. This woman is so intent on not looking up she falls into a bush. Her legs flummox about and kick the air as she recovers in embarrassed silence.

When we're children, before we stare into television screens and films showing us dismembered limbs and cannons firing, when we see something out the corner of our eyes, we bring back rainbows and teddy bears. And then someone explains to us what ghosts are, and our heads are filled with things to fear that don't exist. War takes the rainbow out of our mind, and pours in money, greed and consequential human suffering.

The woman hobbles away. Dickface sucks hard on my fingers, bringing my attention and thoughts back to him. After fifteen seconds his eyes bulge. I give him a look telling him I need my hand back. He's not happy, but slowly lets my two fingers slide out of his mouth.

He runs again. I run to keep up.

Dickface stops in no particular area of the park. He says trains.

We're in the middle of the park. Too central to pick any specific tree or direction from, but I get the game now, I know why he's stopped. I know how to get him going again.

I pop *three* fingers into his fat, gregarious, ginger head. And wait.

Old people kissing with tongues outside a Wetherspoon's pub.

A cat swallowing a flapping goldfish.

Milking a cow with no hands or modern machinery.

His eyes bulge. He spits my fingers out. They are covered in slobber. He's happy with this, I can tell by his face. He likes this better than trains, he likes this more than having my children and living in the trees together like Ewoks.

He's off again, running away from me at decent speed for a big man with deformed ankles and crippled feet. There is a chance, the thought tumbling into my brain as we run, that Dickface has no idea what a parrot is. He runs toward the tennis courts. He turns to face me. The running has done strange doings to his face. He is now a tomato.

The sun is in the sky. The day is not bitterly cold.

The storm that looked like it might be coming, has gone somewhere else.

A good day to run around the park. A good day to find a parrot.

I shove four fingers into his mouth. He sucks hard on my hand.

Punching a plunger.

My hand down a toilet.

An experience you never figure out if you enjoyed.

An accessory to my own hand assault. His eyes bulge. He spits out my hand and he's off, running toward a collection of trees beyond the tennis courts. Dickface better be running toward the parrot, because I'm running out of fingers. He stops running at the base of a cluster of tall green trees, nine trees in total. He turns and says *trains*. I shake my head. I tell him no more trains. He screams TRAINS louder than needed.

Dickface is greedy for man hand. Dickface somehow holds all of the cards. He can tell I'm not sure. He says *trains* again, not in a demanding way, but reassuringly, calmly, as if he's saying *don't worry, I do this all the time.*

Dickface opens his mouth as wide as he can.

I think of the African Grey Parrot and how the entire world thinks I'm a killer.

He wants me to put my whole fist in his mouth.

Information, for a fist in his face.

I ball my hand. I move it to the edge of his mouth. The knuckles of my hand rest against the lips of a man. It won't fit. I feel his teeth against the end of my knuckles. My thumb pushes against his tongue. I'm thankful it's not possible. Dickface makes a noise like an eighteenth-century baker walking along a street hit with a bucket of urine from a window above. He wails. His mouth opens further. His teeth move from the end of my knuckles to above them. His tongue dips inside his mouth. He moves underneath my thumb. He takes my entire first. He somehow has the ability to dislocate his own jaw. The act is both disgusting and impressive in equal measure.

I stand in the park with my entire fist in his mouth, or his entire face over my fist.

A new low. And I've had a few.

"Now if this was a film, it would *have* to be called *Dude, Where's My Carpal Ligament?*"

Blobfish smiles like he's overseeing a child's first crayon picture of a house. I tell Blobfish I'm trying to get information. He smiles and tells me to look up. I never looked up when I should have. I should have checked the tree above me before fisting Dickface. I guess part of me needs my fist in Dickface, and I think Dickface needs my fist in him. We are sharing a moment.

Blobfish says don't mind him, he was just grabbing some stationary.

Dickface's eyes bulge. The sign he's had enough. I pull my arm back, but my fist doesn't move. I try again. There's still no give. There's no room to manoeuvre. My fist is in the smallest ball I can make.

"I can't get my fitht out."

Blobfish laughs. I tell Blobfish I'm serious.

therious

He says I can't be. I tell him I am.

Dickface bulges his eyes again and again. He moves them up and down. He darts them around. His eyes reflect a herd of petrified antelope escaping Godzilla on a hangover. I tell Blobfish Dickface is panicking. I panic too, I don't want to be dragged around the park by Dickface's face.

His teeth break my skin, both of us are losing it.

I imagine my fist popping his teeth out: a fountain of red.

Help me Blobfish, for fuck's sake, do something.

fucth thake thomething

Blobfish stands behind Dickface. Sweat drowns his face. He puts his hands either side of the waist of Dickface. He counts to three. On three I pull my fist back and Blobfish pulls Dickface away. Dickface's powerful jaws snap down on my wrist. Dickface could chomp through my wrist and swallow my hand. I scream in pain. I tell Blobfish if Dickface bites down any harder he's going to open a vein. I'll bleed out right here, underneath the tree, underneath the parrot that might have saved me. Blobfish screams to open my fist, I'm confused. He tells me again: open my fist, reach my fingers out, stretch them, stretch them out into Dickface's mouth as hard as I can, flick the back of his throat. Rattle his tonsils, he screams, give them a thrashing. Hold nothing back, it's you or him. Make him gag, make him throw his guts up. Make him throw up your fist with his stomach lining.

The consequences of the idea are not ideal, but Blobfish is right.

I stretch my fingers out inside his wet mouth, walls stretching during baby producing. My finger brushes against something dangly. I flick it hard, and then tickle it soft. Dickface knows I'm on to him. He knows deep down there's only one way this is ending. He retches once, but not enough. I brush every side of his dangling tonsil with all four of my fingers, giant snakes giving a baby maggot a coochie coochie coo. His jaw flicks wider. His stomach tenses, and as it does I pull back as hard as I can, a reverse punch. My fist comes free. I tumble back onto the grass.

Dickface throws up his stomach contents.

His sick is bright yellow. I don't want to know why. I look at his sick. I give his sick that quick glance people can't explain, a throwback to cavemen days, like looking back into the toilet after it's been used: the same impulse at play. I watch a spider, still alive, spring to its feet and attempt to escape the sick. It scurries, broken-legged across treacherous land, but the escape attempt is hopeless. Dickface sees the spider. His attention is immediately drawn to the movement. He picks the yellow covered spider out from his own sick and puts it back into his mouth.

A treat, something sweet to eat after the dentist.

Even Blobfish stops laughing at the sight.

I wipe my fist on my beige trousers. Trying to be clean is pointless, trying to feel clean, knowing where my fist has been, worse. Blobfish wipes his forehead, removing the ocean of sweat that has appeared and submerged his sad flat facial features.

Dickface stands on his feet, I stand too, Blobfish joins us.

A circle of three, a triangle of almost good people.

We don't speak. At the same time all of us look up into the tree. Right at the very top, sitting in the highest branch, is the parrot. Alive and well, most definitely not eaten. Completely unaware of the fuss it's making, not aware it's a wife or a mother. A status symbol, proof I'm not a murderer.

A tasty meal to the monster nobody else has seen but me.

Dickface wipes his sick from his face with his hand. He looks at his hands, and then wipes them on his top. His upper half is full of sick, his lower half is full of ducks.

We talk, all eyes on the parrot.

I ask Blobfish how long he's known Dickface knew where the parrot was. He tells me since yesterday. I sarcastically say thanks for letting me know, and he thanks me for letting him know Dickface's semen was on his shoulder. He makes a fair point, I think.

Not taking our eyes from Madness, the bizarreness of the situation strikes me for a moment. I ask to no one in particular if life is ever ours to control, or if we're all the inevitable consequence of other events, of someone else's story? Blobfish says he doesn't know, but if I want to bore him, I can do it later. Dickface farts.

The good news is that Madness is alive.

The bad news is that she's sat at the top of the tallest tree in the park.

Blobfish says nothing, because he doesn't need the parrot like I need the parrot.

I need to save Madness to save myself from being labelled mad.

Blobfish has helpfully prepared a ladder, which will take me a third of the way up the tree.

He holds a cage with grass in.

Blobfish has never tried to catch a parrot before, but then neither have I, or Dickface. We both doubt Dickface even knows what a parrot is, so as a group, our parrot-capturing skills are against us. Blobfish tells us he once took home the school hamster for half term. He took the hamster out of her cage to put her in the exercise ball. When Blobfish put the hamster back into her cage, he caught her head in the bars and pulled with the wrong strength the wrong way, accidentally snapping the little hamster's neck. The story of Blobfish snapping his hamster's neck in a cage makes him the most cage and animal experienced of all three of us, so we make him the brains behind our rescue attempt.

I have no stories about cages, and Dickface has no stories.

We look away from Madness, and face each other.

A triangle of almost good people, trying to save the day, but only to save ourselves.

Blobfish holds up his cage, like a man following a noise in a dark church with a lantern. He explains his plan.

"You climb the tree and open the cage. Make a noise parrots like, Madness walks into the cage and eats the grass. You shut the cage and we all go home. Well, except you two."

A weak plan. *The Titanic* with not enough lifeboats.

A winning lottery ticket thrown away by a husband who never checked the numbers.

Neither Blobfish nor I know if parrots eat grass, and Dickface knows nothing about grass or parrots. I ask Blobfish what sound he thinks will attract a parrot. He doesn't know, and I have no idea.

Dickface excels himself by making a clicking noise and saying:

"Light switch."

Blobfish can't think of a better sound, and neither can I. We stand at the bottom of the tree looking up at Madness, emulating the sound of a light switch. Dickface makes the best light switch noise, Blobfish and I suspect he's had practice. Blobfish tells me my light switch noise sounds like the gingerbread man reverse parking over an old lady eating toffee. I assure Blobfish if I didn't have my missing tooth my sound would be better. He says with a full set of teeth my click might, just about, qualify as the gingerbread man getting out of his car to call an ambulance after realising he's hit an old lady eating toffee while reversing his car.

I never seem to win with Blobfish. He always has the last word.

With the grass in the cage, and our light switch noises harmonised, I take the cage and climb the tallest tree in Gladstone Park.

I climb the ladder to the first branch, saying nothing, then reach up and pull myself through the tree.

Branch to branch I edge higher until I'm level with the world's most important parrot.

Madness is a fat parrot, ugly too, looks like a bastard, actually. We immediately don't get on. There's something about her, I think. A self-importance: she has the eyes of a celebrity. She expects people to assume she is amazing, before she's even said a word. I have a great urge to punch her in the face, but I don't. Something about *him*, she thinks back. Grey feathers cover most of her body apart from the tail, where a single white feather breaks up the grey.

I open the cage door, bring the grass nearer to the entrance, and make my light switch noise.

Madness looks over at me. She bobs her head up and down, and blinks. I make another light switch noise and imagine my dad telling me off for wasting energy. I make less clicking noises, but make them more intense, in the hope Madness is perhaps just fussy when it comes to the type of light switch she responds to. Madness stares into my eyes. She gives me a look like I'm being an idiot. I ruffle the grass in the cage, hoping to entice her portly belly to wobble toward food, dragging the rest of the parrot with it, but this elicits no response either.

"What's happening?"

Blobfish calls out in a whisper from below.

I shout back softly that nothing is happening. Nothing at all.

I'm clicking, I say, clicking all different kinds of clicks and clacks, but nothing, I'm not getting anything back.

clickth clackth

Ignorant, I tell Blobfish, this parrot is fucking ignorant.

Madness looks over at me, as if to say *that's no way to talk about the bird that might save your life.*

Blobfish tells me I'm getting my clicks and clacks backwards, and to try reversing the click and clack. Turn the sounds inside out. I think about this, and almost fall out of the tree. I practise this new sound, a reverse click, which ends with the tongue hitting the top of my mouth and begins with my tongue flapping down. A noise I've never heard before.

I try this at Madness. Madness makes the noise back. Not a click, I guess, but a kcilc.

I try a backwards clack, a kcalc.

Madness kcalcs back. I try a long, soft kcalc and Madness responds.

I've got her, got her on the run now. Any moment, she'll be ours, and I can get back to fucking up my life like everyone else.

I kcilc then kcalc and shake the cage and nod in the direction of the door. My facial expression resembles a member of staff working on reception at an expensive hotel. I tell Madness she should relax, put her feet up, eat grass and enjoy her stay. Her kcilc back, a deep broody kcilc, tells me she's stayed in better hotels and she's been met by better looking, and smarter dressed, hotel porters.

We hold eye contact. A silence falls between Madness and I, the type of silence that settles when conversation runs dry. The bastard on the branch, the bastard holding the cage trying to do the right thing, because the parrot will die outside of the cage, but only because we put her in one in the first place. Madness speaks with a series of kcilcs followed by a whistle. She bobs her head up and down at rapid speed, spreads her wings out, and moves from one foot to the other on the branch. This series of kcilcs, whistles, wing flapping and foot hopping has left me confused. Madness is lost on me. We speak different languages, a French hippy talking to a Chinese banker. She rocks back and forth, and bobs up and down. She turns her back to me. Her wings ruffle, like she's up to something. She turns back to face me again. Now she has two pencils stuck into her beak. She's acting crazy, her attempt to get out of being sent to war. I look her straight in the eye and tell her parrots don't go to war, war goes to parrots. Blobfish tells me to stop being mental. I tell Blobfish I'm connecting with Madness.

Madness jumps onto another branch and, in several motions, steps to the end of the tree. She looks up into the sky. She lowers her head, as if she is about to take flight.

Don't go. Don't fly away you self-righteous bastard, I think.

"I'm trying to help you. Please. Don't jump. Don't fly. Give me a break, please," I say.

Madness, as if deciding to cut me some slack, walks back along the branch toward me.

Finally, a break. This is all going to end up okay.

"Thank you. I bloody love parrots."

I open the door to the cage. I smile. Madness turns her back to me. She waddles back up the branch, and without looking back, she launches herself into the sky.

What a bastard.

For a second, she soars, a majestic creature all wings and grace. Then, she falls from the sky like a brick. She falls toward the ground. The ground is a long way down. I've killed the parrot. The parrot flaps her thin wings. She gets some control. She slows her descent a little before landing on the grass. She's alive. Thank goodness. She flaps her wings on the floor and runs away like a chicken. Blobfish gives chase. I watch from the tree as Blobfish chases the grey chicken in a figure of eight. He asks me to drop the cage so he can trap Madness. I shout I'm coming down, don't go anywhere. Blobfish shouts drop the cage again.

THE SQUIRREL THAT DREAMT OF MADNESS

I'm not sure I should. His history of putting animals back into cages is so far one dead, no filled cages.

Not a great track for putting an animal in a cage.

He shouts *what are you waiting for*. I drop the cage.

I watch the cage drop from my branch. I watch the two continue their figure of eight dance. I watch Blobfish run under the line of the falling cage. I hold my breath. I grit my teeth as he's about to get hit. But Blobfish keeps moving. The parrot cuts back, runs through his legs, and stands in the wrong part of the park. The cage lands on her at some speed, from some height.

I've killed Madness.

How am I EVER going to explain this?

Blobfish stops running. I look down from the tree, mouth agog.

This isn't happening.

Dickface steps out. His mood seems to change. He looks greatly affected by the death of the parrot, like the end of the bird is the end of his world. He is aware a great accident has occurred.

Blobfish shouts up I'm an idiot. I don't have anything to say back. I climb down.

P A N I C.

It takes me a few minutes, down branches, the day getting darker, trying to find my way out, dropping down slowly. It's harder to get out than in, as is the nature of ways. My leg searches for the top of the ladder, waggling about, searching nervously, the moment before you think you might be about to get hurt. I find the top of the ladder, lower myself down carefully until my feet are finally on sure ground. I run out from under the tree, shouting it was an accident, everyone saw it, I didn't mean it. I say over and over again I'm sorry, I'm sorry.

thorry thorry thorry tho thorry

Blobfish is doing that look again where he's disappeared. He is no longer in his head.

Mermaids swim in his eyes, I shake him. I ask him what's going on. He blinks, and he's back: the horrific moment you realise ego is transient. Blobfish is saying sorry to me. I tell I killed Madness, not him. I tell him I'll make a full confession. I tell him I'll go and see the community support officer. I say I'll hand myself in to the police and I mean it. There's enough evidence now. I can't ignore it, something must be wrong in my head.

madnethth

He shakes his head. He lifts up the cage from the ground, and points to the floor.

No dead parrot.

I ask where Madness is. I ask what happened in the few minutes it took to get out of the tree. He tells me he lifted up the cage and the bird was alive, a bent wing, but still light on its feet, still strong, still full of beans, not dead, certainly not dead. He grabbed the parrot and tried to stuff it into the cage. Oh God, I say, then ask him if he's broken the parrot's neck. We could take a squashed parrot back and say an animal did it, or it was a natural death, we could say the truth and say he fell out of a tree.

A broken neck we couldn't explain. Not on a parrot, not on anything.

Blobfish tells me no. He tells me he grabbed the parrot. He was putting the parrot back in the cage when everything went dark. He doesn't know what happened. He doesn't know where Madness is.

We both think for a moment. Eyebrows furrowed, lines being drilled into our faces.

Dickface is pulling his trousers down and pointing his bum ring into the grass. His reaction to the missing parrot seems extreme. Or, maybe and most likely he isn't reacting at all, just being his usual disconnected self.

We ignore him. We try to focus on the problem at hand. Water pours from underneath the arms of Blobfish. A wave of salty moisture patters across his back, like pebble-dashing over pavement.

I tell Blobfish I think I know what happened. I tell him he had a hamster relapse. When he went to put the parrot in the cage he must have broken down because of the guilt over the last time he stood by a cage with an animal, switched off for a second. Retreated back to his safe place.

But I never think of it, he says.

We never do, I say back: our bad memories think of us.

Dickface is a tomato again. Green explodes out of his derrière all over the floor around him. A spider, once yellow, now green, this time stays still, hoping not to be seen. Dickface is not a well man, and he is clearly in need of a nutritionist.

Blobfish and I look around for Madness. We don't know how damaged she is, we don't know how far she could have got.

Dickface doesn't wipe himself. His top half is covered in sick, his lower half is pond water, and the rest of him is literally shit.

He joins us, the triangle of the world's worst heroes complete again.

No longer almost good guys, now the almost killers of Madness.

Dickface is looking at something. We follow his eyes. In a tree, opposite to where we are, sitting in the top branch, head bobbing up and down, is Madness. We have the perfect view to watch Madness hop off the top branch again, a brave or stupid parrot, and drop like a brick. Only this time, perhaps lessons learnt, she flaps harder and faster. She eventually takes to the sky.

Rocky, rickety, certainly a bad flyer.

A kid behind a wheel learning to drive.

A parent holding a Playstation control.

But she does, she flies, this time she flies. She flies as the sun sets. A beautiful dark silhouette against lushes of reds, yellows, pinks and blues. We share an odd moment of relief and pride. Although we need to get to Madness before she's killed by Death, and we've effectively hurt the parrot and almost killed her ourselves, Madness is still alive. She's a tough old bird.

She's flying; she's flying better than she flew before.

I feel Blobfish's arm on my shoulder, pulling me close in a hug. My first human contact in a long time. I don't look at him because I don't want him to see me cry. He tells me he doesn't think he's going to have a problem about the hamster anymore. He says something about watching Madness fly away makes him feel okay. I tell him I'm happy for him, and accidents happen, but maybe if we can rescue Madness, and do it right this time, maybe we can both make up for things we can't change.

acccidenth madnethth thith

I ask Blobfish if there's any way we could not take *Richard* with us, because he stinks, and Blobfish smiles and says sure, just tell him to stay here. He points to the dark shape of the parrot now in the distance. We both watch the parrot land on top of the abandoned house.

The parrot slips. She tumbles down the roof. She flaps her wings and disappears out of sight.

The parrot is a fucking idiot, I say.

Blobfish says *who in this world isn't.*

As we look at the roof of the old abandoned house, and the parrot tumbling down it to the ground. I imagine the pale creature sitting beneath. The pale creature doesn't know where it will find the parrot. It searched all last night, and slept all day. Now it sits in the grounds of the abandoned house, waiting for darkness to come. Waiting for the light it can walk out into, the only light people can't see its deranged face in. The pale creature sits on an upturned beer crate, leaning back, its hood covering its face. Death worries if it keeps eating the animals in the park, eventually the evidence will start to point at its presence on earth. Death is aware that its killings are being blamed on an innocent homeless human. Death would smile if it had a face. It couldn't have planned it better. Usually it would have already been chased away by townspeople and pitchforks. But now the pale creature has all the time in the world to eat the parrot, the last food it wants to eat.

I imagine Death putting its bony claws behind its lumpy head. I can see it clearly looking up, as a tumbling flapping sound it can't place comes from above. The tumble tumbles closer.

Madness the parrot falls into its lap. A present to Death, from God.

The pale creature picks the bird up by the throat. It holds the bird in front of its eyes. Madness is petrified. The bird remembers me on the branch and regrets not hopping into the cage. Death resists the temptation to rip the bird's head off with its teeth. This is an event. This is the event of the pale creature's life.

This feast will replace the horrible memories of the elephant it could never eat.

Death licks the beak of Madness. It smells the bird. It walks into the abandoned house, and starts planning its meal.

Dickface, Blobfish and I walk in the direction of the abandoned house. Blobfish radios Little Big Head. He picks us up in the vehicle that isn't a lawnmower. We all get in. I'm finally riding the vehicle I know isn't a lawnmower. At closer inspection I'm still completely baffled as to its purpose. We drive across the park. On the way Blobfish confirms my story to Little Big Head. He tells Little Big Head he thinks there's a creature in the park, eating animals and living in the abandoned house: a creature who isn't me. Little Big Head doesn't believe Blobfish. Little Big Head thinks I'm a liar. He believes time will prove him correct, and reveal me to be the psychotic killer he thinks that I am. We explain to Little Big Head the parrot has flown into the house, and the parrot's life is in imminent danger. Little Big Head puts his foot down on the accelerator that doesn't accelerate.

The warm day is turning into a cold night.

I ask Blobfish what we plan to do when confronted with the monster in the house. Blobfish says not to worry. I say I do, and question if we are planning on killing. Blobfish says of course not, but we might have to throw some punches, and scream loudly in a threatening manner.

I confess I've never hit anything. Blobfish concurs he's never thrown a punch.

Little Big Head asks what that smells is. We both nod toward Dickface.

Blobfish and I confess to being beaten up several times, often by people smaller than us. Dickface says nothing, he only speaks when he's about to do something anti-social. Little Big Head stops the vehicle that isn't a lawnmower. He stares at us both. He tells us we're lucky he's with us. He tells us he used to be a champion midget boxer. He says he expects nobody to be in the house, but if there is, he'll take care of them. Then he looks at me. He says he knows it will be me he fights tonight. An eye for an eye, says Little Big Head. He tells me I have killed animals in his park, and tonight he is going to hurt me for payback. I tell him if everyone took an eye for an eye the world would be blind. Blobfish chips in and says if everyone took an eye for an eye the world would be full of people walking around with only one eye. They would be pissed off and fall over a lot. But they wouldn't be blind. Just as I think we're getting on, he pushes me away.

Little Big Head starts the engine on the vehicle that isn't a lawnmower. We move again toward the house. Everyone is silent as it dawns on us we're going to fight a monster. Blobfish sweats. He is more wet skin, than dry. He glistens in the night.

I can't stand the ignorance of Little Big Head. Two people are telling him something is in the park eating animals, and still he refuses to listen. Little Big Head turns on the radio.

The park is now dark.

The radio is tuned to a cheesy love station. The host introducing the next song is a polished leather shoe with a sports sock background. The competitive voice with a leather tongue says the next song is Bonnie Tyler. He tells us Bonnie Tyler is totally eclipsing his radio station.

The voice of Bonnie Tyler fills the vehicle.

"Turn around, every now and then… "

My big toe spasms as I remember being eaten by a beautiful woman surrounded by Oompa Loompas.

Little Big Head says he loves the song. He turns up the volume. He sings. Blobfish joins in. Dickface waves his fingers but looks sad, in his head he conducts a starving orchestra with a baguette. We drive across the park in darkness. Blobfish and Little Big Head shout at the top of their voices:

"I get a little bit terrified and then I see the look in your eye. Turn around bright eyes."

And so I join in. Dickface wails *trains* over the top of all of our singing, and almost in time to the music. We are four men in an unidentified vehicle travelling to an abandoned house singing *I'm in a powder keg giving off sparks…*

The chorus hits. We all sing, this motley crew, this band of brothers. We all sing out to the night, and for a second in the darkness the stars look like flashing cameras. For a moment, before the blood, we are Take That performing a cover version in a slow-moving vehicle on stage at a packed-out concert. Dickface is Gary Barlow. Blobfish is Robbie Williams.

"Once upon a time TRAINS I was falling in love, TRAINS but now I'm only TRAINS falling apart. Nothing I can TRAINS do, a total eclipse TRAINS of the heart, TRAINS."

A moment shared.

Little Big Head cuts the engine outside the abandoned house. We sit in the dark, for a heartbeat, sharing silences.

I ask Little Big Head what the vehicle that isn't a lawnmower is.

He tells me it's a lawnmower.

His answer makes me feel like an idiot, and immediately breaks the bond built up through song.

Blobfish suggests nobody makes a noise. He says we should think of a plan of attack, to maximise our chances. Little Big Head ignores Blobfish and the advice. He grabs a shovel from the ridiculous looking lawnmower. He shouts NONSENSE before storming away. He marches up to the broken slat, and disappears into the grounds of the abandoned house.

"Give a man a fish and he'll eat a fish. Give him a fishing rod and if you haven't explained fishing to him, he'll eat the fishing rod and possibly drown."

I ask Blobfish what he means. He tells me Edward is about to eat a fishing rod and possibly drown. I look confused. He clarifies it's not a good thing.

"Thit."

Blobfish, the guy who snapped a hamster's neck, myself, the homeless guy who has never thrown a punch (but has killed a fox) and Dickface, the man obsessed with trees and touching himself in public, follow an arrogant midget into the home of a pale creature I am certain will kill us all, to save the life of an ungrateful bastard parrot called Madness.

The temperature drops further.

A cold night for heroes.

Chasing Madness

We are all inside the grounds of the abandoned house. I stifle a laugh as Little Big Head storms into the six-foot-high weeds and gets caught, flips and wriggles: awkward embarrassment, a fish photographed on a romantic date with a hook. He leans his full weight into the weeds and falls through them onto concrete.

To this guy, weeds are beanstalks.

My laugh leaves my mind, he's our muscle.

He's flattened the weeds for the rest of us.

I reach down to offer him a hand. He pushes my hand away with his forehead. He storms ahead again, determined to prove the monster I say lives here, only lives in my head.

The concrete is stained with fox blood, no sign of fox.

Stephen Fry sobs in my head.

Little Big Head marches around the corner. His little arms are by his side, like a child playing at war.

Me, Blobfish and Dickface reach the end of the concrete path. We turn just in time to see Little Big Head, shovel in hand, storm into the house. We follow. I enter the old abandoned house with Blobfish on my left and Dickface on my right.

The three amigos of Gladstone Park. The three donkeys of the apocalypse.

A tingle crosses the cold air, and nips at my ears. The sound is like someone dropping a large spoon into glass, but it's the sound of a shovel falling to concrete.

I face the sound and witness what I first think is a little girl asking for an autograph from a Rugby player, but what I'm actually seeing is the start of the battle between Little Big Head and Death.

Little Big Head is frozen to the spot. His bowels are slowly vacating the premises of himself.

I tried to warn him. I tried to explain. Death is four-foot taller than Little Big Head, its black holes for eyes and loose jaw are petrifying.

Little Big Head thought the creature didn't exist, now he knows it does. Death places a mighty claw on Little Big Head's head. I brace myself. Little Big Head drops to his knees. He cries like a dropped baby. He grabs Death's legs and begs not to be hurt. He cries that he really likes replica model aeroplanes and warships, and is only half-way through building his replica of Robert Fulton's Nautilus submarine.

Death looks over at us. This is embarrassing. For a moment I actually want Death to decapitate Little Big Head.

Our band of brothers, our tribe of men: we have been turned into a triangle of cowards.

Death knows we're out of our depth.

The midget boxing champion has exposed all of us.

To the sound of a tearful rant about submarine models, and never being loved at school, I scan the room: there are two mattresses in the corner, large burgers without the meat, and a black stain on the concrete where fires are lit. Litter sprawls across the concrete floor, along with broken glass from smashed windows never replaced. There is no love here. Not in this room. Nothing has been repaired; everything has been left to stagnate. Broken bottles lay shattered at the base of a staircase. The stairs, covered in weeds and missing steps, lead up to a floor going nowhere. Before the drop are two doors, both closed.

I can't see Madness, the parrot wasn't outside. The parrot is nowhere inside I can see. She must be in one of the rooms, possibly eaten, or tied up with her beak in a pot of boiling water, with onions and carrots and *turnips.*

I tell Blobfish to distract the hulking monster. Blobfish is silent. His sweat speaks for him: he has become more jellied eel than human. I move for the stairs to find the parrot. Madness is our leverage, our bargaining chip, our only way out of here alive.

Death watches me move. Blobfish stands looking frustrated, like he's waiting at a bus stop in the snow. His nose looks flatter than I've ever seen it. He stands, and does nothing.

A torch shone in the face of the sun.

Thanks, mate, nice one.

Death moves to match my run toward the stairs. I feel a force knock me sideways. My shoulder hits the wall. My head bounces off it.

My soft head is pressed fast into hard concrete, or wood, I'm not sure what way round I mean. Is my head wood or cement? Suddenly I'm not thinking straight. My vision is blurred. A new word for falling up something unintentionally: stumple. Now is an odd time to think of new words.

I'm falling to the floor. I feel my head. I move my hands in front of my face, they are covered in my blood. I'm bleeding.

This is bloody serious.

Death clutches my throat. The lack of air brings me out of my daze. *Its* knives for fingers claw at my neck. Death squeezes my throat; it moves its pale face close to mine. I can't scream. Its grip is too tight. I squeak. I lose vital air. The pale creatures jaw hangs to the side of its face, an unwanted drunk in a midnight choir. Its eyes are so dark, holes for vision. Its skin is tight and made from more bone than being. The creature's pale face is littered with rings and burns. They cover its forehead and face, one burn looks like a hot iron placed into skin. Its mouth is a battlefield, its face is a civil war against itself. Its teeth are soldiers left behind to die. The dark hood clings to its pale skull. There is no doubt, this is Death. It snaps at the space between us twice, a starving piranha wildly gnashing at flesh. Its top lip is the creature's to control, its bottom lip has mind of its own. The creature is horrifying. Sweat drops from its top lip, and falls down its face. I drop to the floor. I gasp for air. I can't see properly, I'm suddenly wearing horse blinkers. I place a dirty hand on my neck. There is blood. I hear movement and look up. The blinkers subside. I take breaths, thankful to be alive, a great pain throbs inside my head. I watch from the floor. Blobfish runs up the broken staircase and straight through the first door.

Find Madness, is all I think, *find the parrot, let's live.*

I can hear screaming. Blobfish is screaming. I see his hands on the door handle. He screams that he doesn't want to die. He doesn't want to fall. The door opens and closes. He's hanging above the floor from the door handle. If he lets go of the handle, the fall will break both of his legs.

There is no room, no floor on the other side of door number one, I realise.

Door number two, that's where we need to be.

Little Big Head is in the middle of the floor in the foetal position; his tiny hands hug his little knees, his head tucked under his chin. He's curled in a ball, talking about submarine models and glue. He sits in his own piss, rocking back and forth, completing the tale of the little boxing champion who never was.

Death, briefly distracted by the screaming Blobfish, turns its attention back to me. Its shadow swallows my own.

I sense I am going to die.

I'm blacking out. An idea hits me: a desperate cry from my subconscious. A thought designed to keep me alive, the last roll of the die. I yell for Dickface. I see behind Death, Dickface looks over, but he's too afraid. Death kneels down to the floor, it moves its pale face to within a few inches of mine. It's studying my fear, thriving off of it.

"DICKFACE! IT'S GOT YOUR CLOCK! IT JUST TOLD ME IT HAS YOUR CLOCK!"

Death pauses for a second. Behind it, the dark Dickface rises. The expression on Dickface turns from fear, to hate. This is the Dickface I need. It's time to turn the lunatic against the asylum. The mental, against the monster.

"IT TOLD ME IT'S NEVER GOING TO GIVE YOU YOUR CLOCK BACK!"

Dickface charges at Death. Death stands and turns, and I roll out of the way as Dickface slams Death into the wall, while howling like the devil the word *clocks*.

Someone hear Blobfish scream, please someone hear him screaming for help.

I pull myself up to one knee, and lean against the fallen cupboard for support. The world feels like it's moving too fast for me.

Thank God for Dickface. The reason I'm alive: beautiful lovely Dickface.

A mentally challenged Godzilla fighting Goth King Kong.

Two buildings falling into each other, people like ants falling from their eyes.

Perhaps we will be heroes after all.

I stand up. I spit blood from my mouth. I clench my fists. I don't feel like dying today.

As I stand and stare across at Dickface and Death, I feel Colossus: this is my moment. This is what I was born to do. This is why I was named Colossus by my parents. This is my destiny. My name for the first time in my life isn't a stupid hindrance, it is prophetic. I am now fulfilling my own prophecy.

I am a colossus versus a giant.

Dickface lands a punch to Death's head, Death reels back, hurt. The bringer of the end to humanity has pain receptors.

The moment Rocky cuts Ivan Drago.

I imagine Death as an eight-foot squirrel: it's the only way

I can move. We need to take Death now, the creature won't be surprised for long.

I circle the two fighting goliaths and get on all fours behind the giant squirrel. Dickface pins the furry animal back with clubbing left and right fists. Dickface hits the giant squirrel again. The squirrel topples back and falls over me, sprawling to the floor. An old classic, but it bloody worked. I scream at Dickface to sit on the creature with all his weight, while I search for a scaffolding pole to bash the giant squirrel over the head with.

bathh thquirrel

Dickface doesn't know what I'm talking about. Dickface doesn't take instruction. I should have stayed quiet, not said anything. He stares at me and doesn't understand. He makes a high-pitched squeal, five kettles reaching boiling point two seconds apart.

Dickface squeals two words: *severe delays*.

He falls to his knees. The giant squirrel takes his furry paw from the genitals of Dickface.

I look over at Little Big Head. Little Big Head looks at me and shouts *move*, but he shouts it too late.

The giant paw of the big fluffy squirrel crashes against my cheek, and I crumple to the floor, face different, softer and squishier. Shock leaves my brain and pumps around my body, a boost to deal with the pain, to keep me alert so I can find help and not die.

Madness the parrot must be upstairs wondering what the quickest and most pain-free way of killing herself is, because if this is her rescue, she's as good as dead.

I didn't enter the house wanting to die, but as I fish around in a daze on a casino floor looking for coins never dropped, the giant squirrel scurries over to its mattress and searches for something. The squirrel stands upright with a sickle in its paws. It turns and faces me. The image is too much. I can't hold on to the squirrel. Death is back before me. Fear ripples through my blood cells and floods my atoms. The thin-faced, deformed monster stands in its black hood holding a sickle.

The Grim Reaper. A little bit of hell on earth.

I've never thrown a punch, Blobfish hasn't, and Little Big Head's champion boxer story is clearly a lie. We should've discussed a plan. We should've raised bullet points to discuss at our common sense approach to rescue attempts meeting we never had.

But we didn't. I close my eyes. I wait to die.

Blobfish is by my side, his hands are underneath my armpits. I'm pulled to my feet.

Little Big Head is upstairs. He's rescued Blobfish while I swished about in a daze with a squishy face. The little bastard, I love him. Upstairs I see him moving into the second room, feverishly making clicking and whistling sounds to attract Madness. Blobfish looks at me. He tells me help is not coming. He tells me our only hope is if we attack Death together. He tells me if we both go at the same time, maybe one of us lives. Maybe we both die. But we don't die alone, and we die making a fist of it.

Stand our ground: speak our minds.

I'm not sure what Blobfish means. I don't think Blobfish knows either. I know he's never thrown a punch in his life and he knows neither have I. He doesn't look scared. He tells me to trust him. He tells me half the journey to becoming Colossus is pretending I am.

Death lunges toward us, sickle in claws, needing to take life to breathe.

I make myself small and close my eyes. I can't see what Blobfish is doing, but I don't hear him running toward Death.

A great speech, but words alone do not make men of mice.

Little Big Heads shouts from upstairs. His annoying voice has never been more relaxing.

I open my eyes. Blobfish does too. The Grim Reaper stops.

Little Big Head has Madness the parrot in an old potato sack. He shouts to Death that he has the parrot. He holds the bag up for Death to see, an extremely brave move, for a small man standing in his own bowel movements.

Death floats up the staircase, after the midget and Madness.

Little Big Head screams like a girl. The Grim Reaper floats toward him. Little Big Head looks down at me. He calls for my help. He looks at Blobfish. He shouts for us to not just stand there, he screams at us to help him, to do *something*.

But there's nothing Blobfish or I can do. There is no time to save him. No time to think.

I scream NO and Blobfish screams EDWARD, but we're helpless. Goodnight Edward, so long, we'll say nice things about you. Tell tales of your bravery, not mention the bowel movement or until your last moments you were mostly a dick.

Little Big Head backs up as far as he can. Behind him is a one-way drop to the ground, in front of him the Grim Reaper stands. Death raises its sickle in the air, and the old floor beneath it gives way. Death falls through the floor, down into the concrete below. It hits the ground beneath with a slapped thump. There is a moment of stillness. Death moves. The monster starts to get back onto his feet. A slab of concrete breaks free from the staircase, and falls.

The slab hits the creature with a sickening thud.

We look away with faces like pigs chewing onions. We look back again, our eyes watering. Death is buried under rubble: its claws stick out from under the concrete, like the witch from Oz, only more evil and flattened.

I make a wincing face at Blobfish, like I've just nipped myself with a sharp knife cutting carrots.

Crushed bones, no groans. Perhaps Death does not fear itself.

Blobfish makes a face like he's sucking on a strong mint. Another slab of concrete falls. The second slab of concrete lands on top of the first.

We hear multiple bones snap. A large pop blossoms, as something inside Death explodes.

Blobfish stops making a face. I stop making a face too.

We both look up at the staircase. The largest slab wobbles. We don't want to kill the Grim Reaper, but before we can move, the largest slab falls from the ceiling.

The slab lands.

We hear heavy concrete slab pummel bone, pushing a rib cage through heart and liver. We all stand still, not sure where to look.

I hear a sniffle. Death is under the slab, trying to cry in silence.

I look at Blobfish and make a *how do we stop this* face. He responds by holding his hands up and turning into Robert De Niro trying to understand his grandson's iPad2. We look to the staircase. Another slab wobbles. We look to Edward, who turns his palms to the ceiling. He hunches his shoulders.

The sobs of the monster fill the room.

The last slab falls and lands with a loud slap. The slab lands directly over the area where the head of the pale-faced creature had been.

The sobs, which were blurting out at random and sounded uncontrollable, immediately silence.

Nobody knows where to look, or what to do. This doesn't feel heroic.

We look to Little Big Head. He shakes his head and looks down. He makes a cross sign with his hands. He agrees, this has nothing to do with being heroes.

This is how soldiers feel, after they've shot someone for real.

Dickface runs over and stands on top of the rubble, he has a big grin on his face, and he's naked. He whirls his underpants above his head like a helicopter. He repeatedly whoops like he's just scored the winning goal in the 1966 World Cup final. He jumps up and down. His massive penis flaps against his belly.

I tell Dickface to get down, but he isn't listening. This is his wedding day, the birth of his first child, this is all of the moments he never got to have because of how he was born.

He's living them now. And who are any of us to stop him.

Blobfish says he thinks we've killed Death. I say he might be right: we've killed Death with a building.

We look up at Little Big Head. We look at the man standing in his own expulsions. The little man who saved all of our lives, holding a potato sack with a parrot in.

He asks how to get back down.

Nobody knows.

Oleg and Chloe arrive on the scene, having been out looking for their parrot, they followed the screams. Oleg holds a cage, and inside the cage is Madness.

The stupid grey bastard, looking happy.

Oleg says he's sorry for thinking I was someone I wasn't. I tell him don't worry, it's an easy mistake to make. Something we are all, always doing.

We ask Edward what he has in the potato sack, if it's not the parrot. He smiles and throws the bag down to us. The bag opens when it hits the floor, and the fox I killed spills out. The head rolls along the floor until it stops at the feet of the young girl. The girl screams and automatically hugs the cage with her parrot in. Oleg stares at us all. He asks us what the hell is wrong with us.

He turns and leaves, taking his crying daughter with him.

What's wrong with us? Us band of brothers, us tribe of men, absolutely nothing.

I'm homeless and talk to trees, Dickface is mentally ill, Little Big Head is a midget and a compulsive liar and Blobfish has to supplement his income by making small jellies for children's parties and he never stops sweating, but there is nothing wrong with any of us. I know that now. If I'd never killed the fox, Edward's potato sack would have been useless, and we'd all be dead. Life, is a funny thing. Maybe the right thing for the right reasons is the right thing, and the greatness of the act exonerates the reason.

Blobfish asks me what I'm thinking about. I tell him I'm thinking of leaving the park. He says if I ever need a job, there are worse places to work than in Gladstone Park. And I agree. Working in a park would be great, it's the living in one that's not ideal.

He asks if I need any medical attention. I tell him all bruises and cuts, nothing that won't heal. My cheekbones are sore, and ache, and tomorrow will be a long day, but they're not broken or anything.

Dickface is made to put his clothes on. We all go home. Blobfish to wherever he goes and Edward back to his wife. Dickface runs off alone, peeling his clothes off again as he goes.

All I know is, tonight, he doesn't follow me. Nobody does.

I walk from the house. I walk back to my tree.

A familiar chill hits my face: I've had enough.

I've had enough of this life, this struggle, of living in the wishing well.

As I lay down under Roald Dahl, I know tomorrow I'll leave the park.

I'll leave and I'll never look back, or leave and always look back.

A wind whips up the park. Trees bend in the wind. Branches snap and bushes blur against the night. A sad squirrel is caught in the middle of the grounds. The squirrel is aware it needs to find cover from the incoming storm. The squirrel is nibbling the edges of a drying pool of yellow sick, which had been left earlier beneath the tallest tree in Gladstone Park.

Now the sick has dried, it's possible to see the bones that have appeared: the small bones of a dog, and the small bones of the squirrel's wife who died from impalement.

The wind kicks the squirrel in the side of his face. He has to say goodbye to his wife. He knows by first light tomorrow, the bones will be gone, cleaned up by the suspiciously efficient park keepers.

Tears fall from the squirrel's eyes. He places his paw one last time in the paw of his wife. She is just decomposed bone now with a missing heart, but she was once full of energy and was the love of his life. Lightning cracks the sky. Rain pelts the side of his face. The squirrel puts a single nut, the biggest one he could find, in the middle of the bones of his wife.

The squirrel runs. He has to. He runs across the park as fast as he can. Tears run down his face. His thoughts are ablaze with the memories of him and his wife. He runs until there is nothing left in his lungs to give. He decides he would die. He would rather die than live without her.

He darts up the nearest tree to him. Exhausted.

The wind howls and spins. The leaves give sound to the wind, turning the invisible angry.

A blue box, sitting on one of the branches, wobbles.

The box falls from the tree.

The blue box hits the ground beneath and opens.

The contents of the box spill over black grass.

The image of a grey snake flutters in the wind.

It spins and twirls, and lands upside down.

On the other side of the piece of paper with the grey snake on, crudely etched in hand, are tear-stained words written years ago by a determined Dorangel Vargas.

~~Elera~~

Afrikan Gray Parrot ✓ ☺

After writing these words on the back of the piece of paper with the grey elephant trunk, Dorangel knew he had to keep them safe, so he found a blue box, and kept it with him for the rest of his life.

Dorangel had changed a lot since he was twenty-five. He had grown fatter. He had grown red. His head had grown a ginger wig. He grew a healthy fear of the planet and lived in trees. His broken jaw had become many chins.

When he saw the parrot fly into the park, it was the greatest day of his life.

The pale-faced man who was crushed under the weight of the falling house was never traced to any home or location. He was just another faceless homeless man, blamed for the crimes of another. He had obviously felt threatened when four wild men entered his makeshift home, but his sickle turned out to be just a broken branch from a tree. He was like me, in many ways. The entire time I was complaining about people wrongly accusing me, I was wrongly accusing him. I had even labelled him as an 'It' and as Death. All because of how he looked. I couldn't see the wood for the trees. My eyes had blinded me. In this world of judge and be judged, that's all our eyes ever do.

Day Eleven

I wake. I feel the cold in the bones of my face. The cold has found a new way of getting underneath my skin. The cold taps the surface of my bruises, and rubs salt into my wounds. I want to throw up. Morning sickness, but for no reason other than I'm alive. This cold makes me want to strip back to before I had bones.

I pack away everything in my life. I put it all back into my bags and stand. Me and three bags: everything about me. The measure of the man, or the man not measuring up to much. I don't know where I'm going to go. I'm not sure what I'm going to do. I don't think the answers are here anymore. I don't think there are answers in the system either, just more questions surrounded by shadows. I know answers aren't in the nine to five, but no answers are found sitting under a tree, hoping someone pulls up to me in a magical car, offering me the life I want for free.

I say thank you to Roald Dahl, my last words to him. I don't think I was ever crazy, not really, not crazy like getting up before you've properly slept crazy. Not coming home every night and wondering what life is all about crazy. Not going to a job you don't like, because you aren't sure if you can say no to what isn't making you happy crazy. Not waiting for something to change crazy. Not taking out my frustrations with life by getting drunk and convincing myself life is okay as long as I keep topping up my glass crazy. Not watching other people get to places crazy.

No, I was never *that* crazy.

Not crazy at all. Not crazy if you really stop to think about what crazy is and what crazy isn't. Not crazy if you stop to ponder the madness of the person behind the form who decides what madness is.

Carrying my bags, taking them out of the park, doesn't seem right. The act doesn't fit well with me. I walk with my bags along the black fence. I hop over the fence, and leave them in the wilderness.

I leave them in the bushes. Hide them one last time. This time they are hidden forever, my memories. I leave my bags in the bushes, in the wilderness, as a reminder there are alternative routes we can take in life that are not working in jobs we hate, for people we fear.

You don't have to be trapped by your fears. You don't have to fear losing what you have, when you don't really want what you do. You can give it all away. You can go into your job and tell your boss you think he's a prick and walk away. You can start living and working toward your dreams right now if you want to. Don't be afraid. If you don't like or love the life you have made, throw a hand grenade at it. The scariest thing is death, and you won't die from quitting the job that you can't stand, but if you don't, you will eventually die having never lived.

I quit my job and lived in a park. I'm still here, I'm still alive, and all I have is a different experience to draw from. There is nothing to be afraid of.

I walk down the hill, across the park one last time.

Bag free, no possessions. I turn at the gates. The gates are always open. I look one more time at Gladstone Park. I say thank you. I thank the entire park.

I'm not just leaving a park, but an event, a moment in time that I won't forget.

I hear my name, and turn around. Blobfish runs up to me, smiling. He is sweating, like always, only now he looks less troubled, less sorrowful. I say hello, and goodbye.

He says he understands I want to leave, but before I go he wants me to know something.

"I never told you my real name, did I?"

As a matter of fact, no, he never did.

"My name is Craig Stone."

He tells me I am he. I don't exist he tells me. He tells me I never walked into a park, he did. He tells me he quit his job and walked into a park, sat under a tree, and invented me to keep his sanity.

Craig puts his hand on my shoulder. He tells me it's possible he's lost his mind.

If he's gone crazy, then maybe it's possible I wrote the story and he doesn't exist. Or maybe we all exist in the mind of Dickface, or worse, Death or Little Big Head.

I consider telling Craig he should take a holiday, get away from the park: take a break from his work. He sounds like he's on the edge of some kind of breakdown. I consider telling him that spending all day every day at work, and not having any time for your life could drive you crazy and into an office. But something about his face tells me he already knows.

I reach out my hands and thank Blobfish, or Craig, or whoever he is. I tell him goodbye. He smiles, and pulls me in for a hug. He says goodbye, Colossus. I take my first step back into the real world. He tells me not to worry. I look back, for one last moment. He tells me the very same second he closes this book and puts me into darkness, is the very same second someone else opens me up and breathes new life back into me. That's how everything works, he says, how everything always has.

There are no endings, only beginnings. He tells me there is nothing to fear.

His words make a curtain fall over the window of my soul. I can't feel anything. I can't think.

The sun darkens in the sky.

Everything fades to white.

The Beginning